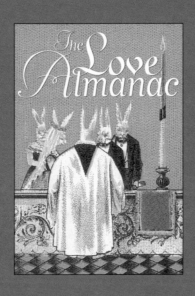

Edited by
Katrina Fried & Lena Tabori

Designed by
Timothy Shaner & Christopher Measom

The Love Almanac

Welcome
BOOKS

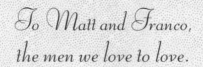

To Matt and Franco,
the men we love to love.

~K.F. and L.T.

Published in 2003 by Welcome Books®,
An imprint of Welcome Enterprises, Inc.
6 West 18th Street, New York, NY, 10011
(212) 989-3200; Fax (212) 989-3205
email: info@welcomebooks.biz
www.welcomebooks.biz

Publisher: Lena Tabori
Project Director: Katrina Fried
Designers: Timothy Shaner and Christopher Measom

Original text by: Kristen Behrens, Lawrence Chesler,
Megan J. Elias, Katrina Fried, Nicholas Liu, Peter Lubell,
Rona Mark, Karen Odyniec, Monique Peterson, Marta Sparago
Recipes by: Natasha Fried and Lena Tabori
Project Assistants: Amy Bradley, Nicholas Liu,
Jasmine Faustino, and Marta Sparago
Production Assistants: Naomi Irie and Kate Shaw

Distributed to the trade in the U.S. and Canada by
Andrews McMeel Distribution Services
Order Department and Customer Service: (800) 943-9839
Orders Only Fax: (800) 943-9831

Library of Congress Cataloging-in-Publication Data on file.

Printed in Hong Kong

FIRST EDITION

10 9 8 7 6 5 4 3 2 1

Contents

Contents

Chapter Three
Love and Marriage

Contents

Chapter One
Looking for Love

Divining Love

Predicting romantic destiny is a tradition as old as love itself. Here are just a few of the many ("highly") scientific) ways to determine what fate has in store for you:

💗 In a tradition that dates back to the 1600s, single wedding guests are sometimes sent home from the reception with a small sliver of cake to sleep with under their pillow. Superstition holds that this will make the guest dream of their future mate.

💗 Apples know everything. If you twist an apple stem while reciting the letters of the alphabet, you will be destined to marry someone whose first name starts with the letter you are saying when the stem breaks off. To discover their last name, poke at the skin of the apple with the stem, again saying the alphabet. When the skin breaks, you have found your true love's second initial. If you can cut your apple into four equal pieces without slicing through a seed, all your dreams of romance will come true.

💗 Eat a teaspoon of salt before bed, and your future mate should bring you water in a dream.

He Loves Me, He Loves Me Not

The practice of plucking the petals from a daisy (or dandelion in Australia) and alternating the phrases "He loves me" and "He loves me not" originated in Victorian England. The language of flowers was very popular during this period, and men and women sent each other carefully composed bouquets as messages of their romantic intentions. An unplucked daisy stood for innocence. In a variation on the tradition, once all the petals are plucked, the center of the flower is torn up and tossed into the air. The number of pieces that fall onto your outstretched hand represent how many children you will have.

💗 Place a four-leaf clover under your pillow to bring the image of your perfect love into your dreams.

💗 If you happen to see the first flower of spring on a Wednesday, there is marriage in your future.

💗 A love *wanga* is a cloth doll prepared by a voodoo priest or priestess. According to tradition, you tell the doll your wishes for love and it works its magic in your life.

💗 In a medieval British tradition, a woman could learn a lot from the birds on Valentine's Day. If she saw a robin flying over her, she would marry a sailor. If she saw a sparrow, she would end up married to a poor man, but they would be very happy. The rare sighting of a goldfinch meant a rich man.

💗 If you cannot decide between two lovers, place two chestnuts on a fire, giving each the name of one of your possible mates. The nut that cracks first is the one you will marry.

💗 It is a Chinese tradition for single women to toss mandarin oranges into a lake on the fifteenth day of the new year. The offering is intended to convince the god of love to send them husbands.

Love sought is
good, but given
unsought is
better.

—WILLIAM SHAKESPEARE

To Mr. Town:

Dear Sir,

You must know that I am in love with a very clever man, a Londoner; and as I want to know whether it is my fortune to have him, I have tried all the tricks I can hear of for that purpose. I have seen him several times in coffee-grounds with a sword by his side; and he was once at the bottom of a tea-cup in a coach and six and two footmen behind it. I got up last May morning, and went into the fields to hear the cuckoo: and when I pulled off my left shoe, I found a hair in it exactly the same colour with his. But I shall never forget what I did last Midsummer-eve. I and my two sisters tried the Dumb Cake together: you must know, two must make it, two bake it, two break it; and the third put it under each of their pillows, but you must not speak all the time, and then you will dream of the man you are to have. This we did; and to be sure I did nothing all night but dream of Mr. Blossom. Our maid Betty tells me, that if I go backwards, without speaking a word, into the garden upon Midsummer-eve, and gather a rose, and keep it in a clean sheet of paper, without looking at it till Christmas-day, it will be as fresh as in June; and if I then stick it in my bosom, he that is to be my husband will come and take it out. If I am not married before the time come about again, I will certainly do it; and only mind if Mr. Blossom is not the man.

I have tried a great many other fancies, and they have all turned out right. Whenever I go to lie in a strange bed, I always tie my garter nine times round the bed-post, and knit nine knots in it, and say to myself, "This knot I knit, this knot I tie, to see my love as he goes by, in his apparel and array, as he walks in every day." I did so last holidays at my uncle's, and to be sure I saw Mr. Blossom draw my curtains, and tuck up the clothes at my bed's feet. Cousin Debby was married a little while ago, and she sent me a piece of bride-cake to put under my pillow; and I had the sweetest dream—I thought we were going to be married together. I have, many is the time, taken great pains to pare an apple whole, and afterwards flung the peel over my head; and it always falls in the shape of the first letter of his surname or Christian name. I am sure Mr. Blossom loves me, because I stuck two of the kernels upon my forehead, while I thought upon him and the lubberly squire my papa wants me to have: Mr. Blossom's kernel stuck on, but the other dropped off directly.

Last Friday, Mr. Town, was Valentine's day; and I'll tell you what I did the night before. I got five bay-leaves, and pinned four of them to the four corners of my pillow, and the fifth to the middle; and then, if I dreamed of my sweetheart, Betty said we should be married before the year was out. But, to make it more sure, I boiled an egg hard, and took out the yolk, and filled it up with salt: and when I went to bed, eat it shell and all, without speaking or drinking after it, and this was to have the same effect with the bay-leaves. We also wrote our lovers' names upon bits of paper, and rolled them up in clay, and put them in water; and the first that rose up was to be our Valentine. Would you think it? Mr. Blossom was my man.

Dear Mr. Town, if you know any other ways to try our fortune by, do put them in your paper. My mama laughs at us, and says there is nothing in them; but I am sure there is, for several misses at our boarding-school have tried them, and they have all happened true.

Your humble servant,
Arabella Whimsey

Praying for Romance
The Gods and Goddesses of Love

In ancient times, there existed a plethora of deities—and in each culture's pantheon at least one love goddess or god—all of which required propitiation. The Norse tradition revered Freya as the powerful goddess of love, marriage, and motherhood. Freya's daughter Hnossa, however, was the goddess of infatuation, while the goddess Lofn was in charge of smoothing love's difficulties and reuniting estranged partners. Meanwhile, the goddess Var made sure that unmarried lovers kept the promises they made to one another, wreaking vengeance on those who broke their vows.

In ancient Sumeria, and later ancient Babylon, the goddess of love was also the goddess of war. Ishtar's passion was so powerful that it killed her lover, Tammuz, who was the god of the harvest. The world's first winter began upon his death, because nothing could grow while he was trapped in the underworld. To gain his release, Ishtar stripped herself bare and stood before the goddess Eriskegal, the underworld's ruler. Thus was born spring. Every year the endless cycle of death and rebirth, of love and renewal, is repeated.

Modern-day lovers are most familiar with Aphrodite and Venus. They, with their sons Eros and Cupid, ruled matters of the heart in Greek and Roman mythology. Cupid in his current incarnation is a chubby-faced cherub whose arrows inflict love on the unwary. Aphrodite's name, meanwhile, is the root of the word "aphrodisiac"—meaning those mythical substances said to induce the craving for love.

Some Deities of Love

Alalahe: Polynesian goddess of love

Arianrhod: Welsh goddess of fertility and "wanton" love

Astarte: Canaanite goddess of love, procreation, and war

Branwen: Irish goddess of love

Brigit: Irish goddess of fertility

Hathor: Egyptian goddess of marriage, fertility, love, beauty, and death

Isis: Egyptian goddess of magic, fertility, motherhood, and death

Kama: Hindu god of love

Kanikanihia: Hawaiian goddess of love

Oshun: Yoruban goddess of love

Voluptas: Roman goddess of sexual pleasure

Pride and Prejudice

JANE AUSTEN

When alone with Elizabeth afterwards, she spoke more on the subject. "It seems likely to have been a desirable match for Jane," said she. "I am sorry it went off. But these things happen so often! A young man, such as you describe Mr. Bingley so easily falls in love with a pretty girl for a few weeks, and when accident separates them, so easily forgets her that these sort of inconstancies are very frequent."

"An excellent consolation in its way," said Elizabeth, "but it will not do for us. We do not suffer by accident. It does not often happen that the interference of friends will persuade a young man of independent fortune to think no more of a girl, whom he was violently in love with only a few days before."

"But that expression of 'violently in love' is so hackneyed, so doubtful, so indefinite, that it gives me very little idea. It is as often applied to feelings which arise from an half-hour's acquaintance as to a real, strong attachment. Pray, how violent was Mr. Bingley's love?"

"I never saw a more promising inclination. He was growing quite inattentive to other people, and wholly engrossed by her. Every time they met, it was more decided and remarkable. At his own ball he offended two or three young ladies by not asking them to dance, and I spoke to him twice myself, without receiving an answer. Could there be finer symptoms? Is not general incivility the very essence of love?"

Catch me if you can:
Romantic Games

Games of love and flirtation have long been a favorite pastime of young and old alike. Such diversions can be a fun way to liven up a singles mixer party or for couples who want to indulge in romantic play. Kissing games have prevailed on the playground for several hundred years with the likes of Kiss in the Ring, in which a kiss is the reward for catching a partner, or Post Office, during which players temporarily pair off.

Here's a look at some old favorites along with a few new love games. When played by adults, they're just silly and sexy fun:

Spin the Bottle A group sits in a circle with an empty bottle in the center. Players take turns spinning the bottle; whoever the bottle "points" to receives a kiss.

Seven Minutes in Heaven Participants draw names or roll dice to pair off in a dark closet for seven minutes.

Flashlight This game is best played outdoors on a pitch-black night or in a large, dark room. Players pair off and sit in the dark. One person with a flashlight is "it." When "it" shines the light on a couple, they must be kissing. If not, "it" trades places with a member of the couple.

Pass the Orange Players line up and attempt to pass an orange from player to player by cradling it under their chins. If players are caught using their hands, the orange returns to the beginning of the line.

Strip Poker This game follows the rules of the regular card game, but players must take off items of clothing each time they lose instead of giving up chips or cash.

Sardines Played in a darkened building or large apartment, it involves sending out a pair to find a cozy hiding place. Players then stumble through the dark looking for them (of course they're somewhere making out!) When someone discovers the couple, they have to quietly join them. The game ends when all the players are packed into the hiding place, or the "hiders" get tired of making out and start laughing so hard they give away their location.

Mad-Lib Confessions This fill-in-the-blank game can be played among two or more people. Participants write phrases, leaving key words out and replacing them with their parts of speech. For example, "It makes me (adverb) (adjective) when I (verb) my partner's (noun)." Other players offer appropriate words to fill in the blanks then the phrases are read aloud.

Word Games In these variations of Scrabble and Boggle, the object is to score with words related to love and romance.

Karaoke In this serenading contest, wooers "win" partners with the best romantic performance.

If you can't be with the one you love, love the one you're with.

—STEPHEN STILLS

Brown Penny
W. B. Yeats

I whispered, "I am too young,"
And then, "I am old enough";
Wherefore I threw a penny
To find out if I might love.
"Go and love, go and love, young man,
If the lady be young and fair."
Ah, penny, brown penny, brown penny,
I am looped in the loops of her hair.

O love is the crooked thing,
There is nobody wise enough
To find out all that is in it,
For he would be thinking of love
Till the stars had run away
And the shadows eaten the moon
Ah, penny, brown penny, brown penny.
One cannot begin it too soon.

Singles Cocktail Party

A singles-only mixer is a great way to meet new people and find romance. Invite a bunch of single pals and ask each of them to bring along at least two other unattached friends—just make sure the male-to-female ratio is roughly equal. This festive Mexican-themed menu for margaritas with chips and dips will add plenty of spice to the party's atmosphere. So let the tequila flow, and get out there and mingle!

Margaritas

A little tequila (made from fermented and distilled agave juice) mixed with a little something sweet and a little something sour makes a delicious classic cocktail. White or silver tequila is the most common, while gold tequila is aged in oak barrels. For a strawberry margarita, add 4 ounces strawberry juice; for an orange margarita, add 4 ounces orange juice. In both cases, reduce the lime juice to 1 ounce. (FYI: 4 ounces = $\frac{1}{2}$ cup; 1 ounce = 2 tablespoons)

> $1\frac{1}{2}$ oz. tequila
> $\frac{1}{2}$ oz. Triple Sec
> 2 oz. fresh lime juice
> 1 tablespoon superfine sugar
> heaping scoopful of chipped ice
> coarse salt
> slice of lime for garnish

1. In a cocktail shaker, combine and blend everything except the salt and the garnish.
2. Moisten the rim of the glass with water, and then dip in the salt to coat.
3. Toss in some ice, fill glass, and garnish with lime slice.

Makes 1 drink

Guacamole

Everyone's passion for this avocado dip is what's responsible for millions of new avocado growers. Be sure your avocados and tomatoes are ripe. Make as close to serving time as possible. You can prepare everything in advance except the avocado.

> 6 ripe avocados
> 1 $\frac{1}{2}$ cups diced white onion
> 6 cups diced tomatoes
> 6 tablespoons finely chopped chile serrano
> $\frac{3}{4}$ cup coarsely chopped cilantro
> 3 tablespoons fresh lime juice
> 4 teaspoons coarse salt, or to taste

1. Cut each avocado in half and remove the pit.
2. Score each half into lots of small cubes and scoop them into a bowl.
3. Mash them as little or as much as you like. Add the rest and mix.
4. Cover with plastic wrap until ready to serve.

Makes 9 cups, enough for 15

Tortilla Chips

Of course, you can buy your choice of tortilla chips, but these are the classic, brilliant crispy corn chips that are the perfect companion for salsa and guacamole. You can make them ahead of time and reheat them to serve warm.

> 24 fresh corn tortillas
> vegetable oil
> salt, to taste

1. Cut each tortilla into six wedges and spread on a baking sheet to dry at room temperature for several hours.

2. Heat 1 inch of oil in a skillet over high heat to 375°.
3. Fry tortillas in batches for about 1½ minutes, or until bubbling has nearly stopped and chips are crisp and golden.
4. Transfer to paper towels to drain.
5. Salt to taste and store in an airtight container.
6. Warm before serving in a 350° oven for 8 minutes.

Makes 12 dozen, enough for 15

Salsa Verde

Spicy, bold, pungent, and delicious, this salsa is the perfect companion for guacamole and margaritas. Buy your tomatillos bright green and hard to the touch. Pulse quickly when blending so you retain the coarse, chunky texture. Serve with tortilla chips.

3 lbs. tomatillos, husked and rinsed
2½ cups chopped white onions
2 cups chopped tomatoes
8 large garlic cloves, peeled
6 chiles jalapeños
6 tablespoons vegetable oil
2 teaspoons coarse salt
1 teaspoon freshly ground black pepper
1 cup coarsely chopped cilantro

1. Preheat the oven to 450° F.
2. In a bowl, toss together everything except the cilantro.
3. Bake for 45 minutes. Remove, cool, and pulse in a food processor until coarsely processed.
4. Add cilantro, and pulse to combine. Cover and chill.

Makes 9 cups, enough for 15

> *I don't want to live—*
> *I want to love first,*
> *and live incidentally.*
>
> —ZELDA FITZGERALD

"MATCHMAKER. MATCHMAKER, TAKE ME TO LISDOONVARNA!"

Set in the atmospheric spa town of Lisdoonvarna in the Burren Mountains of western Ireland, the annual Lisdoonvarna Matchmaking Festival has a long history of successfully pairing eligible bachelors with prospective brides. The festival has its roots deep in Irish history, in a time when matchmakers were in the business of knowing whom among the area's farmers, their sons and their daughters were available for marriage. In September, after the harvest was over, lonely farmers would descend upon the town looking for wives among the many holiday-goers. Because of its mineral wells, Lisdoonvarna was always a popular spot for vacationers looking to "take to the waters." There must have be something extra-special in those waters, because matchmaking soon overtook mineral cures as the town's main preoccupation.

Today the Lisdoonvarna Matchmaking Festival is the largest singles' event in Europe. Starting in late August and lasting until October, the festival offers nonstop *craic* ("fun") for single guys and girls with nightly live music, dances, horse races, and organized matchmaking events presided over by a bona fide Irish matchmaker. The activities culminate with the crowning of "Mr. Lisdoonvarna" and the "Queen of the Burren," the most eligible bachelor and bachelorette of the festival. If you're interested in finding Mr. or Ms. Right in misty green Lisdoonvarna, check out *matchmakerireland.com* for details about this year's festival.

I Love
Sappho

He is almost a god, a man beside you,
enthralled by your talk, by your laughter.
Watching makes my heart beat fast
because, seeing little, I imagine much.
You put a fire in my cheeks.
Speech won't come. My ears ring.
Blind to all others, I sweat and I stammer.
I am a trembling thing, like grass,
an inch from dying.

So poor I've nothing to lose, I must gamble . . .

Advice to the Lovelorn

Ovid wrote *Ars Amatoria* in 1 B.C.E. This semi-satirical guide advised men how to win—and keep—a woman's love, and how women could attract and satisfy a man. Among his tips: "Do not let the stink of goat invade your armpits."

Top Ten Pickup Lines

These days, men and women alike quake at the suggestion that they include pickup lines in their dating arsenal. "They're so passé, cheesy, obvious." Some are, others aren't. Often it's not what you say, but how you say it. As in many areas of *l'amour*, delivery and timing are everything.

1. I write for the Love Almanac. (It's OK. Go ahead, use it!)

2. Hi, I'm a masseuse, what do you do?

3. May I buy you a drink?...How about a car?

4. How'd you like to complicate your life a little?

5. Has anyone ever told you, you look just like [name of a gorgeous celebrity]?

6. Marriage and kids don't scare me at all. How about you?

7. You know, I used to be worth a lot of money.

8. And to think, I almost didn't come out tonight.

9. You look so familiar. Did you go to [name of your alma mater]?

10. Care to dance?

If you love something, set it free; if it comes back, it's yours, if it doesn't, it never was.

—RICHARD BACH

Breakfast at Tiffany's

TRUMAN CAPOTE

"Never love a wild thing, Mr. Bell," Holly advised him. 'That was Doc's mistake. He was always lugging home wild things. A hawk with a hurt wing. One time it was a full-grown bobcat with a broken leg. But you can't give your heart to a wild thing: the more you do, the stronger they get. Until they're strong enough to run into the woods. Or fly into a tree. Then a taller tree. Then the sky. That's how you'll end up, Mr. Bell. If you let yourself love a wild thing. You'll end up looking at the sky."

Benjamin Franklin Advising a Young Man
as to the Selection of a Mistress

[Philadelphia,] 25 June 1745.

My Dear Friend:

I know of no medicine fit to diminish the violent natural inclinations you mention; and if I did, I think I should not communicate it to you. Marriage is the proper remedy. It is the most natural state of man, and therefore the state in which you are most likely to find solid happiness. Your reasons against entering into it at present appear to me not well founded. The circumstantial advantages you have in view by postponing it, are not only uncertain, but they are small in comparison with that of the thing itself, the being married and settled. It is the man and woman united that make the complete human being. Separate, she wants his force of body and strength of reason; he, her softness, sensibility and acute discernment. Together they are more likely to succeed in the world. A single man has not nearly the value he would have in the state of union. He is an incomplete animal. He resembles the odd half of a pair of scissors. If you get a prudent, healthy wife, your industry in your profession, with her good economy, will be a fortune sufficient.

But if you will not take this counsel and persist in thinking a commerce with the sex inevitable, then I repeat my former advice, that in all your amours you should prefer old women to young ones.

You call this a paradox and demand my reasons. They are these:

1. Because they have more knowledge of the world, and their minds are better stored with observations, their conversation is more improving, and more lastingly agreeable.

2. Because when women cease to be handsome they study to be good. To maintain their influence over men, they supply the diminution of beauty by an augmentation of utility. They learn to do a thousand services small and great, and are the most tender and useful of friends when you are sick. Thus they continue amiable. And hence there is hardly such a thing to be found as an old woman who is not a good woman.

3. Because there is no hazard of children, which irregularly produced may be attended with much inconvenience.

4. Because through more experience they are more prudent and discreet in conducting an intrigue to prevent suspicion. The commerce with them is therefore safer with regard to your reputation. And with regard to theirs, if the affair should happen to be known, considerate people might be rather inclined to excuse an old woman, who would kindly take care of a young man, form his manners by her good counsels, and prevent his ruining his health and fortune among mercenary prostitutes.

5. Because in every animal that walks upright, the deficiency of the fluids that fill the muscles appears first in the highest part. The face first grows lank and wrinkled; then the neck; then the breast and arms; the lower parts continuing to the last as plump as ever; so that covering all above with a basket, and regarding only what is below the girdle, it is impossible of two women to know an old one from a young one. And as in the dark all cats are grey, the pleasure of corporal enjoyment with an old woman is at least equal, and frequently superior; every knack being, by practice, capable of improvement.

6. Because the sin is less. The debauching a virgin may be her ruin, and make her for life unhappy.

7. Because the compunction is less. The having made a young girl miserable may give you frequent bitter reflection; none of which can attend the making an old woman happy.

8thly & lastly. They are so grateful!!

Thus much for my paradox. But still I advise you to marry directly, being sincerely

Your affectionate Friend,
Benjamin Franklin

If you would be loved, love and be lovable.

—Benjamin Franklin

A Sacred Space
Lau Tzu

Your love requires space in which to grow.
This space must be safe enough
to allow your hearts to be revealed.
It must offer refreshment for your spirits
and renewal for your minds.
It must be a space made sacred
by the quality of your honesty,
attention, love, and compassion.
It may be anywhere,
inside or out,
but it must exist.

Feng Shui for Love

Feng shui is the ancient Chinese system of placement that strives to achieve harmony between human beings and their environment. Based on the tradition of perceiving nature as five elemental energies (*chi*), feng shui deals with the natural order of cause-and-effect—why things happen to us when they do, and by extension, what we can do to steer ourselves onto a different path. Reorganizing *chi* in your environment can affect every aspect of your life, even your chances for romance. Here are a few tips to help steer your love life in the right direction:

❀ According to feng shui the southwest corner of a room is the corner that affects issues of love. The love corner should be decorated with a representation of a pair of mandarin ducks, a symbol for double happiness.

❀ Red is a very auspicious color for romance. Eager practitioners may even want to paint their love corner scarlet.

❀ Other items you should consider placing in the love corner are red lanterns, red and yellow candles for yang energy, a clear quartz crystal, pictures of mountains to activate earth energy, the lover's mystic knot in your carpets, and narcissuses or peonies to symbolize openness. Water is thought to enhance the chances for lasting love.

❀ Double up when you decorate. For instance, instead of one bedside lamp, consider a pair.

❀ Whatever you do, don't keep a vase of red roses in the boudoir—they are considered very negative—particularly if they have thorns!

When the Heart Needs a Little Help
Great Advice Columns

Need relationship advice? Who doesn't? Luckily, when it comes to matters of the heart, there seems to be an infinite number of columnists out there, ready to console and instruct. Just remember the old joke, "Those who can't do, teach." (And, as Woody Allen added, "…those who can't teach, teach gym.") Below are a few suggestions of whom to seek out when your heart's all strung out.

Dear Abby and **Ann Landers**: The Grand Dames of all lonely hearts columnists. Ann herself may be gone, but her byline lives on in newspapers around the country, dispensing the kind of straightforward, no-nonsense advice that made her and sister Abby classics. They give the kind of counsel you'd want to hear from your mom, except that you wouldn't want to hear it from your mom, you know?

The *Village Voice*'s **Savage Love**: As the name implies, columnist Dan Savage can be tough and blunt with his replies. No coddling here—but his heart and mind are definitely in the right place. (Available on line, too.)

Cosmopolitan: There's something so charming—and in this day and age, simply remarkable—about the fact that the Cosmo girl, essentially unchanged since her inception, is not only still around but going strong. No doubt this is due in part to the sincere yet sassy guidance provided by its sages, both in print and on line. (The names alone of *Cosmo's* advice givers are without rival. On line, under "Agony Advice," Irma Kurtz handles the tough, serious questions on everything from sex to self-image. For the steamier queries, there's the "Bedroom Baroness," written by Baroness Sheri de Borchgrave. C'mon, you can't beat advice from a baroness!)

Speaking of sex advice, one can instantly hook up with hundreds of thousands of columnists on the Web. Hmm. Who knew sex was so popular? Here are just a few good ones (mind you, as with lovers, an advisor hailed as a guru by some will leave others cold). There's Sasha at *Eye.com*, who's pretty racy and writes in what seems to be a British tone. Hot *and* genteel—what a combo! At *Nerve.com*, Em & Lo are astute and funny—they don't pull punches, but they're gentle, too. They also have the humility to dub themselves "Near Experts." At *Time Out New York*, Jaime Bufalino works bad puns and a lot of alliteration into his "Get Naked" column. But he's clear, concise, sensitive, and funny. All of the above field letters from all over—Europe, even.

High Fidelity

NICK HORNBY

A while back, when Dick and Barry and I agreed that what really matters is what you like, not what you *are* like, Barry proposed the idea of a questionnaire for prospective partners, a two- or three-page multiple-choice document that covered all the music/film/TV/book bases. It was intended: a) to dispense with awkward conversation, and b) to prevent a chap from leaping into bed with someone who might, at a later date, turn out to have every Julio Iglesias record ever made. It amused us at the time, although Barry, being Barry, went one stage further: he compiled the questionnaire and presented it to some poor woman he was interested in, and she hit him with it. But there was an important and essential truth contained in the idea, and the truth was that these things matter, and it's no good pretending that any relationship has a future if your record collections disagree violently, or if your favorite films wouldn't even speak to each other if they met at a party.

A man falls in love
through his eyes,
a woman through
her ears.

—WOODROW WYATT

When I Was One-and-Twenty
A. E. Housman

When I was one-and-twenty
I heard a wise man say,
"Give crowns and pounds and guineas
But not your heart away:
Give pearls away and rubies
But keep your fancy free."
But I was one-and-twenty,
No use to talk to me.

When I was one-and-twenty
I heard him say again,
"The heart out of the bosom
Was never given in vain;
'Tis paid with sighs a-plenty
And sold for endless rue."
And I am two-and-twenty,
And oh, 'tis true, 'tis true!

Honky Tonk

Starring Lana Turner and Clark Gable, 1941

CANDY
Have you any idea what a gal like you can do to a gent like me?

ELIZABETH
I'd like to know. Tell me.

CANDY
Well, I've seen women I'd look at quicker but never one I'd look at longer.

ELIZABETH
Well, that's a good start. Go on.

CANDY
I could put you in my vest pocket and lose you in the small change. And me—now I've always gone for women with something to 'em. The kind that could stand up and slug it out with me toe to toe. You slug me just by looking at me.

Tell me about yourself—
your struggles,
your dreams, your
telephone number.

—PETER ARNO

Getting to Know You...
Top Ten First Dates

After your eyes meet, after smiles are exchanged, after you somehow get her number, after you trade messages five times and then at last get a chance to talk, you will suddenly realize that asking her out means *asking her out!* Don't panic—just peruse this list for an idea that appeals to you.

1. **An outdoor movie.** Many cities show movies outdoors in the summer. This combines the classic dinner-and-a-movie date with a romantic evening under the stars. Or if you have a laptop with a DVD player, you can have a private screening.

2. **A restaurant.** Pick one that neither of you has ever been to before. This can be the first of many things you discover together.

3. **A planetarium.** Very high school, perhaps, but consider how the enormity of the universe can bring you closer together...

4. **An obscure foreign film.** You may end up being the only two people you know who've seen it—a shared experience to build on.

5. **A day at the racetrack.** There is something very bonding about pooling your resources to win on a long shot.

6. **Karaoke.** You have to be brave for this one, but it's a great way to let loose, get a little silly, and possibly reveal hidden talents.

7. **A museum or art gallery.** Going to a museum or gallery can give you tons of new things to talk about (and you can learn a lot about a person by how they respond to art.)

8. **A hike in the country.** Lots of time to talk, and the beauty of nature to enjoy together. *Tip: Agree on the distance before you start.*

9. **An amusement park.** Roller coasters and haunted houses tend to bring out the fun side in people. And you will have the perfect excuse to hold on tight.

10. **A picnic.** Like dinner but less formal. A friendly game of Frisbee will loosen up even the shyest date.

Let's Get Personal:
Great Places to Take Out a Personal Ad

Once, many of us looked at personal ads, either in a magazine, newspaper, or on line, and thought, with more than a little self-satisfaction, "There, but for the grace of God, go I." It didn't matter that we also may have been outrageously single and love-starved at the time. Thankfully, much of the shame and desperation that used to be associated with this activity has vanished. Why? Because personal ads work! Here are some of the best places to go looking—and to be found.

New York magazine and the *Village Voice*—Both can lay reasonable claim to helping to kick off the "Personals" phenomenon. They were there at the start, and are still the gold standard for personals in print. Among the first to make the personals "required reading," *New York* is known for its cosmopolitan clientele, while the *Voice* is more funky and free-spirited. Check 'em out. The best thing is, although they're both based in New York, they're read everywhere. You can get them on line, too: *newyorkmetro.com* and *villagevoice.com.*

Of course, due to its ease of use, anonymity, and speed, the web gets the most credit for taking personals to a whole new level. The irony is, now that they've gone mainstream, there are so many sites with so many people, finding that special someone may take more work than ever! Huge sites like *match.com* and *lavalife.com* post all who'll pony up the fee. Which is not to say there aren't oodles of worthy connections to be made there—just that it's like entering a school auditorium the size of an airport hangar! Another option is *craigslist.com*, available in many cities, which does not post pics, but is free. It feels like a trendy club—a tad exclusive—but once you're in, perhaps there's a greater chance that you'll meet more like-minded types.

CHECK OUT THESE:
REAL PERSONALS

WANTED: your emotional baggage

SEEKING: Relationship baggage and bulls**t*

Must have excellent command of academic, patronizing vocabulary, particularly when used in passive aggression, and must perform other advanced sadistic psychological maneuvers.

*(actual relationship optional)

What's not to like? (Besides the basics.)

OK—so I'm a train wreck. We all stop to look, don't we? Attractive (that's debatable) professional (also a stretch) in great shape (10 years ago) guy, available (for this weekend, anyway) to spoil you (if you like Thai food and a movie—if you want to shop, we might stop at Filene's basement). You waited in the traffic jam for an hour—why not stop and look around at the accident?

Classic Pre-1955 Wanted

SWM, 30s, tall, slim, smart wants to borrow low-maintenance, Manhattan SWF classic-built before 1955. Will change oil, buff paint, exercise engine. No expensive luxury models. Uncomplicated leasing terms only.

Red Eye Equals Red Eyes!

Just flew in from lala land and I need help staying awake today. Tell me a joke, tell me something I don't know. It is always such a TREAT when a parent lets there child run laps around a plane at 3 am, argh! Perhaps if you're witty (most important) enough and hot enough (between 25 and 40) a friendship, and/ or friendship (see I told you I am tired!) could evolve. Email me a pix because I must see the eyes with whom I speak. Even Manson would look approachable with shades. I don't have a boy-friend and am not looking (usually he finds me).

Let's Get Married

Dating takes too damn long. It is just horrible and disappointing. I'm getting impatient. I want someone spontaneous, funny, confident, interesting, intelligent, independent, HONEST, trustworthy, between the ages of 28–34, decent looking, at least 5'10".

Lets meet, fall in love, get engaged, and have a big wedding with a kick ass crazy fun reception. Then we will go to Rio, Montmartre or maybe Disneyworld for our honeymoon. Maybe all three. We will go snorkeling and get golden tans, catch a Moulin Rouge show, and we will go on every single ride, (with our honeymoon pass) and get our picture taken with Mickey.

Then we will come home and buy a house. We will cook dinners together, listen to each other's stories about our good/bad days, snuggle on the couch and watch our favorite shows. We will have great sex and go to bed. Or maybe we will go out to dinner, meet up with some friends, have a few drinks, go dancing together, then come home, have great sex and fall asleep.

In the morning, we will sleep in, and take long hot showers together. We will…Well, I could go on forever but maybe you get the idea. It doesn't take years of dating a person to know if they are right for you. Why wait? I'm going to go to bed now and have dreams that this insane, incredibly farfetched scenario could actually happen.

Simple Math

x + y = Happiness! x: SWM, 35 6'4", 275 lbs, construction worker, nice guy. y: Truly nice girl, 25–40 Let's hook up.

Sadie Hawkins' Day

Al Capp, who penned the cartoon *Li'l Abner*, started an American tradition. In the cartoon, homely Sadie Hawkins was without a single suitor. So her father, the town mayor, decided to hold a race in which unmarried girls would pursue the town's unwed men. If a girl caught her man, the couple was married. The cartoon was published on November 13, 1937. A year later, on November 9, the first Sadie Hawkins Day dance was held. In 1938, more than 200 such dances took place.

The Geography of Love

Playing the Odds

According to the 2000 U.S. Census, your best chances of meeting a single man are in Crowley County, Colorado, where there are 205 men for every hundred gals. Runners up were West Felician Parish, Louisiana (191 men: 100 women), and Aleutians-East Borough, Alaska (184 men: 100 women).

For guys, try Clifton Forge, Virginia, where there are 78 men for every 100 women—that's the lowest male–female ratio of any county in the nation.

Living in Love

There are nine towns or cities across the United States with love in their names: **Loveland**, Colorado; **Lovejoy**, Georgia; **Loves Park**, Illinois; **Lovelock**, Nevada; **Love Valley**, North Carolina; **Loveland**, Ohio; **Loveland Park**, Ohio; **Loveland**, Oklahoma; **Lovelady**, Texas.

From the Heart

There are four places in the United States with heart in their names: **Heart Butte**, Montana; **Sacred Heart**, Minnesota; **South Heart**, North Dakota; **Heartwell**, Nebraska.

Location, Location, Location
Top Ten Places to Meet your Mate

At the risk of undermining the importance of the following list before even beginning, we feel it's important to remind you that you can never know where or when you're going to meet The One. It could happen anywhere, anytime. The person who'll be your soul mate or next fabulous fling—or both! Why, they might be sitting behind you at this very moment! Go ahead, look over your shoulder...

If you were just greeted with a look of alarm by your dream date, or with one of chastisement by your boss for reading this at work, try one or more of the following:

1. **Speed Dating** Yes, the round robin has finally come to the art of hooking up. This last one combines many aspects of the above suggestions—it's a sort of ultimate shop-around for love. These are planned social meets where you sign up and then have seven or eight minutes to chat with a potential match. Then, after both writing down privately whether you want to see each other again, you move on to the next table and repeat the process with the next person. At the end of the night, all the men have met all the women. A day or so later, the organizers gather the results and give you the contact info of everybody you said "yes" to—and who said "yes" to you.

2. **Back to School** Could be a yoga class, "The Secrets of Pasta Perfection," Conversational French, etc. The point is, it's an opportunity to stumble through a group activity that is sure to yield cute anecdotes. You may find love over linguine, or with the person who laughs uncontrollably at the way you butcher the pronunciation of *pamplemousse* (French for "grapefruit"). At the very least, you'll learn something new.

3. **Supermarket** Depending on where you live, there may be a market near you known as the new, hot place to meet babes. This trend has become so popular that people get all decked out to buy groceries. ("Hmm. I need broccoli. Should I wear the skirt, or the leather pants?") So, slap on some hair gel and go shopping for produce! The only decision left is which aisle to scope out first . . .

4. **Bookstore** Now that so many bookstores offer coffee as well as Camus, it's only natural that folks go looking for love among the shelves. Go to a reading by a visiting author, grab a latte, brush up on your eighteenth-century Romantic poets, and you're all set.

5. **The Beach** Maybe its the soothing sound of the surf (or the fact that we're practically naked!) but the combination of sea, sand, and sun tends to leave us all a little more mellow and relaxed—a.k.a. "approachable." Invite him or her on a waterside stroll and let those ocean breezes do the rest.

6. **The Net** People were skeptical at first. Objections ranged from "Only nerds would use that" to "Where's the romance?" But there's no denying its results. What was once strictly the domain of an intrepid few has become almost commonplace. There's no longer a stigma. And while it may seem impersonal at first, the comfort of being able to say exactly

---

Women want men with "swerve." A man's version of "swerve" is a woman who's "fine." That's what we want. That's always Plan A. But men are practical. If we can't get the fine ones, we'll move quickly to Plan B. Can't be with a woman who's a ten? You go for two fives. Or five twos. Adds up to the same thing. Personally, I draw the line at ten ones. We're talking self-respect here.

ROCK THIS!

CHRIS ROCK

what you want, when you want to, actually enables many to get intimate much quicker than they would in person. So come on in, the water's fine! Post an accurate picture, be straight about what you've got to offer and what you're looking for, and you may type your way to relationship bliss in no time. One tip: Make sure your spelling and grammar are correct—mistakes can be as damning in the world of online dating as they are on a resumé!

7. **The Park** Always a good bet, particularly in spring, when people start shedding layers and are so happy to be out from under the doldrums of winter that they want to embrace the sun—and hopefully you. And if you have a dog, bring it. If you don't, get one! Men or women will approach you and start talking about Rex before you can even open your mouth. They don't call the dog "man's best friend" for nothing! Come to think of it, bring your dog with you to as many other places on this list as possible. It can't hurt.

8. **Dinner Party** A dinner party is a great way to meet new people in a relaxed and comfortable atmosphere. You're among friends, and potentially making new ones. You're a friend of the host, not just any shmo off the street, so you've got instant credibility—pre-

> *I know that somewhere in the universe exists my perfect soul mate—but looking for her is much more difficult than just staying at home and ordering another pizza.*
>
> —ALF WHIT

sumably! There's also less pressure and fewer distractions than when you go out to hit the town. And there's food. Not to mention drink...

9. **The Gym** Staying healthy and in shape is a great reason for going to a gym. It isn't the only reason, however. People are scantily clad, drenched in sweat, and hopped-up on endorphins. Need we say more?

10. **The Bar** Yeah, the meat-market scene is crowded, noisy, and smoky, and everyone tends to be on their guard, bracing for yet another pickup line and wary of guys on the prowl. Why do we go back? Because every once in a while, you really do meet someone! We've all got that one friend who went to a watering hole to drown his sorrows over the one who got away, only to meet the love of his life over stale pork rinds.

So get out there. And let the games begin!

Essential Terminology

■ **Essential oils** can be found at apothecaries or health food stores. You can also try extracting oils from certain plants yourself, as by squeezing oils from the peels of citrus fruit.

■ **Fixatives** are ingredients that keep a fragrance from fading too quickly. Animal fixatives such as musk, civet, or ambergris last longer than plant fixatives, like oak moss, sandalwood, myrrh, and benzoin.

Selecting the Right Scent

■ For **romantic** notes, choose floral scents, such as iris, gardenia, heliotrope, hibiscus, hyacinth, lilac, peach, rose, rose geranium, tuberose, violet, ambergris, wallflower, wisteria, and ylang-ylang.

■ For an **energetic** pick-me-up, use crisp and spicy scents. These can literally make your heart beat faster: cinnamon, cloves, coffee, allspice, star anise, cardamom, cumin, ginger, grapefruit, lemon, lime, nutmeg, pepper, tangerine, and verbena.

■ For a **comforting** fragrance, consider beach notes such as seawater, driftwood, or coconut oil, or try the soothing scents of lavender, chamomile, fennel, vanilla, and sweet pea.

■ When feeling flirtatious, try **exotic** scents such as mandarin, red citrus, ambrosia, patchouli, saffron, jasmine, civet, and vetiver.

■ Woodsy notes and lush nature scents are often **seductive**. Try oak moss, sandalwood, cedar, birch, rosewood, amber, musk, and bamboo.

Love is in the Air

What is it about a particular fragrance that can drive us wild with romance, make us nostalgic, or bring us a sense of bliss? Our olfactory system is inextricably linked to the part of the brain that controls memory and emotion. A mere whiff of cinnamon, jasmine, or citrus can evoke associations with a place, event, or person in a way that mere words cannot.

Perfumes and scented oils are a powerful way to attract the attention of a suitor by communicating nonverbal, emotional messages or heightening a particular state of mind. With a few dabs of scent on your body, you can create a sense of romance, femininity, tranquility, vigor, erotic sensuality…You decide.

To make your own custom blend of perfume, all you need are a few ingredients and a willing nose. Experiment with different scents and see what kinds of results you get!

Materials: Assorted essential oils, eyedroppers, small vials or bottles, fixatives (see box for definition), toothpicks, small strips of filter paper, grain alcohol (such as vodka; do not use wood alcohol or rubbing alcohol)

1. To begin, choose an essential oil as a primary scent that will be your "top note." With an eyedropper, measure about twenty drops into a clean vial.
2. Add 4 drops of a fixative for your "middle note."
3. Add 2 drops of a "base note," which can be either a fixative or an essential oil.
4. Seal the vial and gently shake the mixture. Allow the blend to stand for a day or two.
5. To test your scent, dip a clean toothpick into the vial and transfer a drop onto filter paper. Allow the paper to stand for a few minutes before deciding if you like the aroma. If it's not quite to your liking, add additional essential oils or fixatives, one drop at a time. Allow the scent to "rest" for a bit before each new modification or "test sniff."
6. Once you are pleased with your blend, add four times as much alcohol by volume to the mixture to make perfume.

That Come-Hither Smell

Pheromones, found in human sweat, are chemically-secreted molecules which, when released into the air, carry messages about our genetic makeup. When a group of women were asked to sniff and rate men's sweaty T-shirts, each woman gave high ratings to the man who had an immune system most dissimilar to her own. If sniffer and sniffee were to have children, this dissimilarity would boost their offsprings' chance at healthy immune systems. No need to go straight for the armpits on your next blind date, though; scientists think that kissing may also be a way to "read" pheromones.

Bridget Jones's Diary

HELEN FIELDING

Sunday 15 January

126 lbs. (excellent), alcohol units 0, cigarettes 29 (v.v. bad, esp. in 2 hours), calories 3879 (repulsive), negative thoughts 942 (approx. based on av. per minute), minutes spent counting negative thoughts 127 (approx.).

6 p.m. Completely exhausted by entire day of date-preparation. Being a woman is worse than being a farmer—there is so much harvesting and crop spraying to be done: legs to be waxed, underarms shaved, eyebrows plucked, feet pumiced, skin exfoliated and moisturized, spots cleansed, roots dyed, eyelashes tinted, nails filed, cellulite massaged, stomach muscles exercised. The whole performance is so highly tuned you only need to neglect it for a few days for the whole thing to go to seed. Sometimes I wonder what I would be like if left to revert to nature—with a full beard and handlebar moustache on each shin, Dennis Healey eyebrows, face a graveyard of dead skin cells, spots erupting, long curly fingernails like Struwwelpeter, blind as bat and stupid runt of species as no contact lenses, flabby body flobbering around. Ugh, ugh. Is it any wonder girls have no confidence?

7 p.m. Cannot believe this has happened. On the way to the bathroom, to complete final farming touches, I noticed the answerphone light was flashing: Daniel.

"Look, Jones. I'm really sorry. I think I'm going to have to give tonight a miss. I've got a presentation at ten in the morning and a pile of forty-five spreadsheets to get through."

Cannot believe it. Am stood up. Entire waste of whole day's bloody effort and hydro-electric body-generated power. However, one must not live one's life through men but must be complete in oneself as a woman of substance.

9 p.m. Still, he is in top-level job. Maybe he didn't want to ruin first date with underlying work-panic.

11 p.m. Humph. He might have bloody well rung again, though. Is probably out with someone thinner.

5 a.m. What's wrong with me? I'm completely alone. Hate Daniel Cleaver. Am going to have nothing more to do with him. Am going to get weighed.

Monday 16 January

128 lbs. (from where? why? why?), alcohol units 0, cigarettes 20, calories 1500, positive thoughts 0.

10:30 a.m. Office. Daniel is still locked in his meeting. Maybe it was a genuine excuse.

1 p.m. Just saw Daniel leaving for lunch. He has not messaged me or anything. V. depressed. Going shopping.

11:50 p.m. Just had dinner with Tom in Harvey Nichols Fifth Floor, who was obsessing about a pretentious-sounding "freelance film maker" called Jerome. Moaned to him about Daniel, who was in meetings all afternoon and only managed to say, "Hi, Jones, how's the skirt?" at 4:30. Tom said not to be paranoid, give it time, but I could tell he was not concentrating and only wanted to talk about Jerome as suffused with sex-lust.

Tuesday 24 January

Heaven-sent day. At 5:30, like a gift from God, Daniel appeared, sat himself on the edge of my desk, with his back to Perpetua, took out his diary and murmured, "How are you fixed for Friday?"

Yessssss! Yessssss!

Friday 27 January

129 lbs. (but stuffed with Genoan food), alcohol units 8, cigarettes 400 (feels like), calories 875.

Huh. Had dream date at an intimate little Genoan restaurant near Daniel's flat.

"Um . . . right. I'll get a taxi," I blurted awkwardly as we stood in the street afterwards. Then he lightly brushed a hair from my forehead, took my cheek in his hand and kissed me, urgently, desperately. After a while he held me hard against him and whispered throatily, "I don't think you'll be needing that taxi, Jones."

The second we were inside his flat we fell upon each other like beasts: shoes, jackets, strewn in a trail across the room.

"I don't think this skirt's looking at all well," he murmured. "I think it should lie down on the floor." As he started to undo the zip he whispered, "This is just a bit of fun, OK? I don't think we should start getting involved." then, caveat in place, he carried on with the zip. Had it not been for Sharon and the f**kwittage and the fact I'd just drunk the best part of a bottle of wine, I think I would have sunk powerless into his arms. As it was, I leaped to my feet, pulling up my skirt.

"That is just such crap," I slurred. "How dare you be so fraudulently flirtatious, cowardly and dysfunctional? I am not interested in emotional f**kwittage. Good-bye."

It was great. You should have seen his face. But now I am home I am sunk into gloom. I may have been right, but my reward, I know, will be to end up all alone, half-eaten by an Alsatian.

Someday my
prince will come.
—FRANK CHURCHILL AND
LEIGH HARLINE

Chinese Matchmaking

According to Chinese astrology, each year is represented by one of twelve animals: rat, ox, tiger, rabbit, dragon, snake, horse, goat, monkey, rooster, dog, or pig. Persons born under a particular sign are thought to take on characteristics of that animal. Certain pairs of animals are believed to make the best romantic matches. To find your ideal match, first figure out which animal you are by consulting this simple chart:

OX: 1901, 13, 25, 37, 49, 61, 73, 85, 97, 2009	DRAGON: 1904, 16, 28, 40, 52, 64, 76, 88, 2000
GOAT: 1907, 19, 31, 43, 55, 67, 79, 91, 2003	DOG: 1910, 22, 34, 46, 58, 70, 82, 94, 2006
TIGER: 1902, 14, 26, 38, 50, 62, 74, 86, 98, 1010	SNAKE: 1905, 17, 29, 41, 53, 65, 77, 89, 2001
MONKEY: 1908, 20, 32, 44, 56, 68, 80, 92, 2004	PIG: 1911, 23, 35, 47, 59, 71, 83, 95, 2007
HARE: 1903, 15, 27, 39, 51, 63, 75, 87, 99, 2011	HORSE: 1906, 18, 30, 42, 54, 66, 78, 90, 2002
ROOSTER: 1909, 21, 33, 45, 57, 69, 81, 93, 2005	RAT: 1912, 24, 36, 48, 60, 72, 84, 96, 2008

Chinese matchmakers take many variables into consideration, but these animal pairs are sure bets for everlasting love:

Rat & Monkey	Ox & Rooster
Tiger & Horse	Rabbit & Goat
Dragon & Rat	Snake & Rooster
Horse & Dog	Goat & Goat
Monkey & Dragon	Rooster & Dragon
Dog & Tiger	Pig & Rabbit

Looking for Your Face
Rumi

*From the beginning of my life
I have been looking for your face
But today I have seen it*

*Today I have seen
the charm, the beauty,
the unfathomable grace
of the face
that I was looking for*

*Today I have found you
and those who laughed
and scorned me yesterday
are sorry that they were not looking
as I did*

*I am bewildered by the magnificence
of your beauty
and wish to see you
with a hundred eyes*

*My heart has burned with passion
and has searched forever
for this wondrous beauty
that I now behold*

*I am ashamed to
call this love human
and afraid of God
to call it divine*

*Your fragrant breath
like the morning breeze
has come to the stillness of the garden
you have breathed new life into me
I have become your sunshine
and also your shadow*

*My soul is screaming in ecstasy
Every fiber of my being
is in love with you*

*Your effulgence
has lit a fire in my heart
and you have made radiant for me
the earth and sky*

*My arrow of love
has arrived at the target
I am in the house of mercy
and my heart
is a place of prayer*

Now, the search for this person starts early. From the minute we're born, boys and girls stare at each other, trying to figure out if they like what they see. Like parade lines, passing each other for mutual inspection. You march, you look. You march, you look. If you're interested, you stop and talk, and if it doesn't work out, you just get back in the parade. You keep marching, and you keep looking.

I was lucky. When I met the woman of my dreams, I knew. I saw her, and I was immediately unable to speak. My throat locked up, my stomach was in knots, I was sweaty, clammy, and nauseous often means you're in love. (Other times, it simply means you had bad clams, and you want to learn to distinguish between the two.)

But I knew this was it. And the more time we spent together, the more convinced I became—we fit. ♥

"THE SEARCH"

PAUL REISER

Among those who I like, I can find no common denominator, but among those who I love, I can; all of them make me laugh.

—W. H. AUDEN

Prince Charming

Among the *Wodaabe* of south-Saharan Africa, men compete for women by participating in a "charm dance." The men wear makeup and dance before female judges, who judge their charisma, as well as their physical attributes.

	ARIES	TAURUS	GEMINI	CANCER	LEO	VIRGO
ARIES	When two fiery Aries collide, sparks will fly.	Feisty Aries and stubborn Taurus often do not see eye to eye.	When Gemini meets Aries, there's double the energy, double the fun!	Watch Out! Sensitive Cancer may not appreciate hot-tempered Aries.	1 fire sign + 1 fire sign = 1 hot couple Enjoy!	Contemplative Virgo may want to silence the "talk first—think later" Aries.
TAURUS		Both stubborn and passionate, this pairing can either lead to great love or friction!	Caution! The adventurous Gemini may find Taurus too grounded.	A match made for marriage! Both these signs are sensitive, loving, and crave security.	Not a love match. Taurus can be too structured for spontaneous Leo.	A solid pairing. Taurus and Virgo are both known for their practical natures.
GEMINI			A good match. Geminis are big talkers, so prepare for some all-night chats.	Not the perfect couple. Emotional Cancer always wants to connect with the distant-minded Gemini.	If they can learn to share the spotlight, there's potential for lifelong love.	Instant chemistry, but needs work to last. Both like to talk, but can easily annoy each other.
CANCER				Known for their neediness, when two Cancers collide they may finally find their match.	Glamour-loving Leo and homebody Cancer will have to make a lot of compromises to live in harmony.	Clingy Cancer may clash with more practical Virgo.
LEO					Leo + Leo = Laughter & Love. Just avoid competition for the spotlight.	Abandon ship! Reserved Virgo is not usually impressed with the lively lion.
VIRGO						A good match. Keep that OCD in check though!

Hey, what's your sign?

Is your love written in the stars? Consult our astrological compatibility chart and discover the sign of your ideal mate.

Courteous Reader,
Astrology is one of the most ancient Sciences, held in high esteem of old, by the Wise and the Great. Formerly, no Prince would make War or Peace, nor any General fight in the Battle, in short, no important affair was undertaken without first consulting the Astrologer.

—BENJAMIN FRANKLIN

	LIBRA	SCORPIO	SAGITTARIUS	CAPRICORN	AQUARIUS	PISCES
	Though thoughtful Libra and spontaneous Aries have many differences, this is a clear case of how opposites can attract.	Though a very passionate pairing, Scorpio's jealousy can get in the way.	It's getting hot in here! The pairing of Sagittarius and Aries is full of fire and fun.	Capricorn is usually too mature and serious for Aries, the perpetual kid.	Aquarius looks ahead, while Aries lives in the moment, making this pairing tough for the long term.	A tough match. Sensitive Pisces needs more nurturing than the action-oriented Aries can provide.
	Proceed with caution. Sophisticated Libra longs for romance, while tough-talking Taurus likes to skip to the chase.	There's potential in this combo. Taurus enjoys sexy Scorpio, but honesty is key.	Beware. Homebody Taurus may have problems with jet-setting Sagittarius.	Both are hard workers in their careers and relationships. A fine match.	There may be some problems here. Taurus is too grounded for this sign.	A good couple. Practical Taurus will balance out dreamy Pisces.
	A great match. These two are easygoing and comfortable together right off the bat.	Scorpio is too jealous for the flirty Gemini. May start out hot but tends to cool off quickly.	Both these signs love their independence as well as their time together. A good fit.	Capricorn may be too serious for fun-loving Gemini. Not an ideal match.	A fun and daring duo. Both these signs are the life of the party, but may not last when it's time to get serious.	Spiritual Pisces may be a little too laid back for go-getter Gemini. But there's potential if both are willing to compromise.
	Libra will work hard to keep the relationship going, but Cancer's neediness may prove too strong.	Both are highly emotional, but constant Scorpio may not put up with Cancer's mood swings.	Polar opposites. Sagittarius loves to be free while Cancer just wants to cuddle.	Cancer relies on intuition, Capricorn on the rules. Though opposites these two might just balance each other out.	A tough fit. Aquarius is too aloof for maternal Cancer.	Both these signs are very emotional and sensitive, and have great potential for long term love.
	A great couple. Flirting and game playing come naturally to both.	A smoldering combination. Prepare for some turbulence, but it's well worth it.	Time together is filled with passion and laughter. But for this combo to work, Leo must be willing to give.	Both share a taste for luxury. But Leo's flare for drama may not mesh with Capricorn's conservative nature.	If romantic Leo can live with Aquarius's need for freedom, this match can ignite.	Not a love match. Pisces is untamable for the controlling Lion.
	Perfectionist Virgo may be frustrated with laid-back Libra.	Virgo meets an intellectual match with Scorpio. A very "heady" couple.	A strong sexual connection may not overcome the fact that Virgo is too much of a realist for big-dreaming Sagittarius.	Birds of a feather, these two earth sign are both practical and successful.	Neither sign is much for emotions, which makes a deep connection hard to come by.	Overly organized Virgo will be a mystery to laid-back Pisces. Not a strong match.
LIBRA	Double the creativity, but also double the indecision. This pair can work out well if one takes charge.	Intense Scorpio may overwhelm tranquil Libra in the long run.	Charming Libra can usually reign in wayward Sagittarius, making them a complimentary pair.	Commitment is no problem for these two, but expressing feelings might be. This obstacle can be overcome..	This match shares an intellectual connection, but passion is lacking, making longevity a challenge.	Pisces wear their hearts on their sleeves while Libras keep their emotions in check. Not an ideal pair.
SCORPIO		When Scorpios find love together, they are not just a couple, but a force to be reckoned with.	Passionate yet volatile, these two signs are polar opposites. Finding common ground might just bring happiness.	A good match, despite some emotional differences. Scorpio helps bring Capricorn's hidden depths to the surface.	Aquarius seeks distance from Scorpio's emotional intensity. Not a favorable match.	Sexy Scorpio and sensual Pisces are ruled by emotion and share a passion for love and life. A great, magnetic pair.
SAGITTARIUS			When two dreamers come together the result can be marvelous, so long as they both keep their feet on the ground.	Silly Sagittarius and serious Capricorn are an unlikely match. Though sometimes, opposites attract…	Off-beat and slightly bohemian, this pair shares great energy and a lack of rigidity.	You may share the same dreams, but Sagittarius can overwhelm sensitive Pisces.
CAPRICORN				Both are too driven and focused to enjoy each other. Not a love match.	When pessimistic Capricorn meets eternally optimistic Aquarius, the two simply clash.	Realistic Capricorn will keep Pisces down to earth, while Pisces will elevate Capricorn's moods. A good match.
AQUARIUS					Creativity, originality and energy abound. However, the intellectual connection outweighs the romantic.	Pisces is too emotional for aloof Aquarius. The odds for this match aren't favorable.
PISCES						A Pisces pairing can be intense. But a total lack of practicality can make this match a challenge for the long term.

Tell me whom you love and I will tell you who you are.

—HOUSSAYE

Love Potions & Spells

Concocting love potions and casting love spells are among the oldest ways of attracting a mate. Romance-seekers have gone to great measures to divine their future loves or to land the perfect partner. See if some of these age-old methods work for you.

Peel a lemon and cut a heart shape out of the rind. Let it dry and carry it in your pocket or purse until you meet your mate.

On the night of a full moon, peel an entire lemon in a single strip of rind, without a break. You will attract a new love within a month.

If you find a four-leaf clover, carry it with you. The first person you meet will be your intended.

Walk through a garden while scattering rose petals before your feet. The petals create a "path" by which your new love will find you.

Arrange fresh or dried lovage around a candle. Light the candle and read several verses of love poetry aloud. Do this three consecutive nights to attract romance.

Create an infusion of special ingredients for the bath. Choose from the list on this page. Repeat for three consecutive days.

You come to love not by finding the perfect person, but by seeing an imperfect person perfectly.

—SAM KEEN

Age-Old Love Potion Ingredients

Lemon balm—to pursue romance

Basil—to ensure lasting love

Bay—to attract love and good wishes

Almond—to capture essence of love that will survive all trouble

Cinnamon—to capture love

Coriander—to attract love magic

Iris—to bring love, romance, companionship

Lemon—to increase sexual activity

Lovage—to enhance inner and outer beauty

Marjoram—to bring romantic fulfillment

Patchouli—to attract sexual love

Primrose—to increase ability to attract love

Verbena—to attract mates, love, and sexual fulfillment

Cloves—to arouse sexual passion

Rose geranium—to attain sexual fulfillment

Marigolds—to divine one's love

Love Spell Bottle

If you're on the lookout for love, this love spell bottle might just do the trick. Spell bottles have been in use in America and Great Britain as part of the Wicca tradition since the 1600s. Often created for protection, they are sometimes hidden in the walls of homes or placed on open windowsills. Whatever the case may be, these magically empowered charms are always kept close to their creators. Good luck!

Materials: Dried rose petals, bottle, dried lavender, rose water

1. Take a handful of dried rose petals, and concentrate on all the things that remind you of love. When you are done, place them in the bottle.
2. Hold two pinches of lavender in your palms, and recall the times you felt you were strongly loved. Place these in the bottle.
3. Fill the bottle up with rose water and screw the cap on tight. While holding the bottle tightly against your chest, say the following words aloud:

    "Flowers drenched with love,
    Drench me with love."

4. Place the spell bottle somewhere in your bedroom, close to where you sleep.

www.truelove.com
The Best Online Dating Services

Love is just a click away! The Internet age has brought a whole new crop of online dating services that promise to find you a soul mate. Here is a sampling of some of the more popular ones:

The mother of online dating services, *match.com*, offers thousands of member profiles and pictures with an extensive list of criteria search options. Also has listings of social events in major cities.

Lavalife.com and *dreammates.com* have specific relationship community options. Whether you are looking to walk down the aisle, go on dates, or keep it a little less intimate, these sites have thousands of singles looking for the same thing: a companion.

Need advice? Want to chat? Along with the many profiles that *friendfinder.com* offers there's an online magazine and chat room to get the ball rolling.

The U.K.-based *datingdirect.com* is for serious people looking for serious partners. In an attempt to avoid most of the typical online dating gimmicks, this site caters to international singles looking for love.

Indianmatches.com, *blacksingles.com*, and *asiansinglesconnection.com*, great sites to help you find that special someone.

Love is not finding someone to live with, it's finding someone you can't live without.

—RAFAEL ORTIZ

Date.com, *matchclick.com*, and *kiss.com* all offer singles from around the globe the chance to get in touch and stay connected. Search by state or country for that special someone.

Try *jdate.com*, one of the biggest online Jewish dating services on the Net.

Adammeeteve.com, perfect for Christian singles seeking the same.

Muslimmarriagejunction.com, with thousands of listings and a chat room for Sunni, Sufi, and Shia singles.

One good thing about Internet dating: you're guaranteed to click with whomever you meet.

—MONGO

PRINCE EDWARD VIII & WALLIS SIMPSON

Next time you're feeling too lazy to get off the couch on a Saturday night and go to yet another mixer in the hopes of meeting The One, take inspiration from the fairytale romance of Prince Edward and Wallis Simpson. After all, they never would have met if they hadn't both attended the same party one fateful night...

Widely considered one of the greatest romances of the twentieth century, the marriage of Prince Edward VIII and Wallis Simpson proved to the world that few things are more important than love. When the couple first met at a party, in 1931, Simpson was married to her second husband and the prince was an internationally renowned playboy. Following an instant attraction, the two quickly fell head-over-heels, much to the displeasure of the royal family, who did not approve of the American divorcée. In 1936, the king of England died and Prince Edward took the throne. Although Simpson had returned to the States, her influence on Edward was still apparent. His royal duties were neglected, while his feelings for Simpson consumed him. Faced with choosing his country or his love, King Edward VIII abdicated the throne less than a year after his ascension. In 1937, he and Wallis were married in France after her divorce was finalized. The new king bestowed on Edward and Wallis the titles of Duke and Duchess of Windsor.

Following their marriage, the couple was completely ostracized by the royal family and spent the rest of their lives together abroad. After the death of Edward in 1972, Wallis spent her remaining days in virtual seclusion. She passed away in 1986. In keeping with her husband's request, she is buried by his side at Windsor Castle. ♥

Chapter Two
Love & Courtship

Camille

ALEXANDRE DUMAS

"Marguerite, let me say to you something which you have no doubt often heard, so often that the habit of hearing it has made you believe it no longer, but which is none the less real, and which I will never repeat."

"And that is . . . ?" she said, with the smile of a young mother listening to some foolish notion of her child.

"It is this, that ever since I have seen you, I know not why, you have taken a place in my life; that, if I drive the thought of you out of my mind, it always comes back; that when I met you to-day, after not having seen you for two years, you made a deeper impression on my heart and mind than ever; that, now that you have let me come to see you, now that I know you, now that I know all that is strange in you, you have become a necessity of my life, and you will drive me mad, not only if you will not love me, but if you will not let me love you."

"But, foolish creature that you are, I shall say to you, like Mme. D., 'You must be very rich, then!' Why, you don't know that I spend six or seven thousand francs a month, and that I could not live without it; you don't know, my poor friend, that I should ruin you in no time, and that your family would cast you off if you were to live with a woman like me. Let us be friends, good friends, but no more. Come and see me, we will laugh and talk, but don't exaggerate what I am worth, for I am worth very little. You have a good heart, you want some one to love you, you are too young and too sensitive to live in a world like mine. Take a married woman. You see, I speak to you frankly, like a friend."

"But what the devil are you doing there?" cried Prudence, who had come in without our hearing her, and who now stood just inside the door with her hair half coming down and her dress undone. I recognized the hand of Gaston.

"We are talking sense," said Marguerite; "leave us alone; we will be back soon."

"Good, good! Talk, my children," said Prudence, going out and closing the door behind her, as if to further emphasize the tone in which she had said these words.

"Well, it is agreed," continued Marguerite, when we were alone, "you won't fall in love with me?"

"I will go away."

"So much as that?"

I had gone too far to draw back; and I was really carried away. This mingling of gaiety, sadness, candor, prostitution, her very malady, which no doubt developed in her a sensitiveness to impressions, as well as an irritability of nerves, all this made it clear to me that if from the very beginning I did not completely dominate her light and forgetful nature, she was lost to me.

"Come, now, do you seriously mean what you say?" she said.

"Seriously."

"But why didn't you say it to me sooner?"

"When could I have said it?"

"The day after you had been introduced to me at the Opéra Comique."

"I thought you would have received me very badly if I had come to see you."

"Why?"

"Because I had behaved so stupidly."

"That's true. And yet you were already in love with me."

"Yes."

"And that didn't hinder you from going to bed and sleeping quite comfortably. One knows what that sort of love means."

"There you are mistaken. Do you know what I did that evening, after the Opéra Comique?"

"No."

"I waited for you at the door of the Café Anglais. I followed the carriage in which you and your three friends were, and when I saw you were the only one to get down, and that you

went in alone, I was vary happy."

Marguerite began to laugh.

"What are you laughing at?"

"Nothing."

"Tell me, I beg of you, or I shall think you are still laughing at me."

"You won't be cross?"

"What right have I to be cross?"

"Well, there was a sufficient reason why I went in alone."

"What?"

"Some one was waiting for me here."

If she had thrust a knife into me she would not have hurt me more. I rose, and holding out my hand, "Good-bye," said I.

"I knew you would be cross," she said; "men are frantic to know what is certain to give them pain."

"But I assure you," I added coldly, as if wishing to prove how completely I was cured of my passion, "I assure you that I am not cross. It was quite natural that some one should be waiting for you, just as it is quite natural that I should go from here at three in the morning."

"Have you, too, some one waiting for you?"

"No, but I must go."

"Good-bye, then."

"You send me away?"

"Not the least in the world."

"Why are you so unkind to me?"

"How have I been unkind to you?"

"In telling me that some one was waiting for you."

"I could not help laughing at the idea that you had been so happy to see me come in alone when there was such a good reason for it."

"One finds pleasure in childish enough things, and it is too bad to destroy such a pleasure when, by simply leaving it alone, one can make somebody so happy."

Be of love (a little) more careful than of anything.

—E. E. CUMMINGS

"But what do you think I am? I am neither maid nor duchess. I didn't know you till to-day, and I am not responsible to you for my actions. Supposing one day I should become your mistress, you are bound to know that I have had other lovers besides you. If you make scenes of jealousy like this before, what will it be like after, if that after should ever exist? I never met any one like you."

"That is because no one has ever loved you as I love you."

"Frankly, then, you really love me?"

"As much as it is possible to love, I think."

"And that has lasted since—?"

"Since the day I saw you go into Susse's, three years ago."

"Do you know, that is tremendously fine? Well, what am I to do in return?"

"Love me a little," I said, my heart beating so that I could hardly speak; for, in spite of the half-mocking smiles with which she had accompanied the whole conversation, it seemed to me that Marguerite began to share my agitation, and that the hour so long awaited was drawing near.

"Well, but the duke?"

"What duke?"

"My jealous old duke."

"He will know nothing."

"And if he should?"

"He would forgive you."

"Ah, no, he would leave me, and what would become of me?"

"You risk that for some one else."

"How do you know?"

"By the order you gave not to admit any one tonight."

"It is true; but that is a serious friend."

"For whom you care nothing, as you have shut your door against him at such an hour."

"It is not for you to reproach me, since it was in order to receive you, you and your friend."

Little by little I had drawn nearer to Marguerite. I had put my arms about her waist, and I felt her supple body weigh lightly on my clasped hands.

"If you knew how much I love you!" I said in a low voice.

"Really true?"

"I swear it."

"Well, if you will promise to do everything I tell you, without a word, without an opinion, without a question, perhaps I will say yes."

"I will do everything that you wish!"

"But I forewarn you I must be free to do as I please, without giving you the slightest details what I do. I have long wished for a young lover, who should be young and not self-willed, loving without distrust, loved without claiming the right to it. I have never found one. Men, instead of being satisfied in obtaining for a long time what they scarcely hoped to obtain once, exact from their mistresses a full account of the present, the past, and even the future. As they get accustomed to her, they want to rule her, and the more one gives them the more exacting they become. If I decide now on taking a new lover, he must have three very rare qualities: he must be confiding, submissive, and discreet."

"Well, I will be all that you wish."

"We shall see."

"When shall we see?"

"Later on."

"Why?"

"Because," said Marguerite, releasing herself from my arms, and taking from a great bunch of red camellias a single camellia, she placed it in my buttonhole, "because one can not always carry out agreements the day they are signed."

"And when shall I see you again?" I said, clasping her in my arms.

"When this camellia changes colour."

"When will it change colour?"

"To-morrow night between eleven and twelve. Are you satisfied?"

"Need you ask me?"

"Not a word of this either to your friend or to Prudence, or to anybody whatever."

"I promise."

"Now, kiss me, and we will go back to the dining-room."

She held up her lips to me, smoothed her hair again, and we went out of the room, she singing, and I almost beside myself. ♥

Picnic in the Park

Maybe it's the chirping of birds or the soft feeling of grass under your toes, but there's something about an outdoor picnic that lends itself to romance. A great picnic spread need not be complicated. With the list of ingredients below, you don't even need eating utensils—just a cheese knife and a bottle opener. You can slice the bread ahead of time and store it in a plastic bag for more delicate dining, or just tear it apart on the spot, the old-fashioned way. Here are the perfect picnic basket essentials:

loaf of French bread
$\frac{1}{2}$ lb. of brie cheese
$\frac{1}{4}$ lb. of fresh ham
$\frac{1}{2}$ lb. of pitted olives
1 lb. grapes, rinsed
1 lb. strawberries, rinsed
bottle of white wine, chilled
cheese knife
bottle opener
napkins
plates
glasses
blanket

Top Ten Romantic Dates

You've got a date. Good for you! Now what?! The pressure of planning a date is often as anxiety-provoking as getting the date in the first place. When the stakes are raised and the event calls for romance, the stress can be almost too much. Help has arrived. Our favorite romantic dates:

1. **Tickets for Two** Surprise your date with tickets to his or her favorite sporting event, concert, or play.

2. **Double Feature** Each pick a movie you want to see. Enjoy a candlelit dinner in between shows.

3. **Dining In** Show off your kitchen skills with a homemade meal for two.

4. **A Night of Opera** Pick her up in a limo with champagne on ice and dressed to the nines à la *Moonstruck*.

5. **Miniature Golf or Bowling** May be a little high school, but its fun to revisit our youth every now and then. Where's the romance? In letting your date win, of course.

6. **All-Day Treasure Hunt** Give your date a bunch of sealed, numbered notes. Instruct him/her to read each one in order and

> Dating is pressure and tension. What is a date really, but a job interview that lasts all night? The only difference between a date and a job interview is that in not many job interviews is there a chance you'll wind up naked at the end of it.
>
> —JERRY SEINFELD

do what they say. For example, a man can send his honey for a massage and then shopping for a dress—and so on—winding up with having her meet him at their favorite restaurant....

7. **Drive Time** Pick a great restaurant for lunch or brunch an hour or two away and hop in the car. You'll be sharing a new experience together, and the drive time will give you a great opportunity to talk. Don't forget to bring good car tunes.

8. **A Dance Class** Find out what kind of dancing your date likes and take her to a couples class. There's nothing more romantic than waltzing the night away.

9. **Sky Ride** There's nothing more romantic than taking a trip through the clouds together. Charter a balloon or helicopter and share the view from above.

10. **Any meal, on any rooftop, anywhere.**

Meeting at Night
Robert Browning

The grey sea and the long black land;
And the yellow half-moon large and low;
And the startled little waves that leap
In fiery ringlets from their sleep,
As I gain the cove with pushing prow,
And quench its speed i' the slushy sand.

Then a mile of warm sea-scented beach;
Three fields to cross till a farm appears;
A tap at the pane, the quick sharp scratch
And blue spurt of a lighted match,
And a voice less loud, through its joys and fears,
Than the two hearts beating each to each!

Get A Clue
Romantic Scavenger Hunt

Have some fun the next time you give a gift or go on a special date: Start off with a romantic scavenger hunt. Begin by presenting your loved one with a single clue that will lead to him or her to others around the house, or even around the neighborhood. With a little forethought and imagination, you'll bring smiles of surprise to your sweetheart's lips as he or she unravels each clue. Here are some ideas to get you started:

 Write riddles or clues that allude to special memories or romantic moments around the house. For example, "a favorite spot to cuddle on a cold winter's night" might lead to a clue by the fireplace. Or, "a view from last summer" might lead to a clue hidden in the pages of a photo album. Tuck a small piece of paper with a letter of the alphabet written on it into each hiding place along with the clue. Once your beloved finds all the letters, he or she attempts to unscramble them to spell a prize, such as name of a restaurant for a candlelit dinner or the title of a romantic movie.

You gotta learn to laugh, it's the way to true love.

—JOHN TRAVOLTA, *MICHAEL*

With each clue, hide a small gift such as scented soap, a chocolate truffle, or a CD. After your sweetheart unravels a trail of little gifts, let the last clue lead to a big gift.

Surprise your love at work with a bouquet of flowers and a note containing the first clue. Arrange to leave clues with various merchants around town. For example, "The best ice-cream parlor," "Our favorite place to shop together," or "Where we rent movies." The last clue can lead to a surprise event, such as a concert or a play.

Send your sweetheart into the outdoors to places that have had special meaning in your relationship. For example: "The first place we kissed," "Our favorite spot in the park," or "Where we met." End your hunt with a romantic outdoor activity such as canoeing, a walk along the beach, or a hot-air balloon ride.

Animal Attraction

Mating and Courtship Rituals in the Animal Kingdom

Falling for love

In early spring, the male woodcock, a small, round, brown bird, puts on a dizzying display to win mates. Normally quite shy, the woodcock-on-the-make begins his work at dawn by uttering a nasal cry for up to five minutes. He then flies high into the sky, only to dive-bomb back to earth in a zigzag pattern. He repeats the performance for up to an hour or until a female woodcock expresses interest.

Whole lotta shakin' going on

In order to attract females of their species, red-eyed tree frogs compete by singing and shaking. As soon as one male begins to croak, others join in, and they begin to compete for female attention—not only by vocalizing, but also by quivering violently, standing on all fours, and leaping wildly from leaf to leaf in order to establish their territory. Once they manage to attract a female, several males will attach themselves to her back and stay with her—sometimes for several days—while she looks for a suitable place to lay her eggs.

Plucking at the heartstrings

Male desert spiders attract their mates by performing an elaborate dance. The dance consists of waving their legs, swaying their bellies, and plucking at the strings of a female's web. It is essential to get each step right, because if a female spider turns out not to be in the mood for love, she will simply eat the male for lunch.

Come here often?

Grouper fish observe a peculiar mating ritual that scientists still find a mystery. Each year the fish swim hundreds of miles from their homes in coral reefs to mate in one particular spot. When they reach that spot, the whole crowd swims around in an inverted cone formation. The following year, the next generation will return to the exact same spot to mate.

Diets are for losers!

In the world of the elephant seal, bigger is definitely better. Only the largest males will be able to attract females and fight off opponents, so they spend a great deal of time bulking up to win the hearts of the little ladies. At one ton, females are only one third to one tenth the size of their men! While about 90 percent of all the male elephant seals won't mate at all in a season, one huge, successful male may make as many as 150 love connections.

Getting to know you

In late spring, female grizzly bears leave scent trails to alert males that they are ready to mate. A male who tracks a female may actually herd her to a spot where he can ward off any other potential suitors. The new couple will then take a few days to get to know each other. Dates include friendly chases, mock battles, nuzzling, and perhaps, if things go well, a little licking. If the couple decides to mate, their relationship will be brief, lasting only from a few days to a few weeks. Then it's back to the solitary lifestyle that grizzlies seem to enjoy.

I Love You, Pet

About 3 percent of pets in the United States will receive a Valentine's Day gift from their owners this year.

The torch of love is lit in the kitchen.

—FRENCH PROVERB

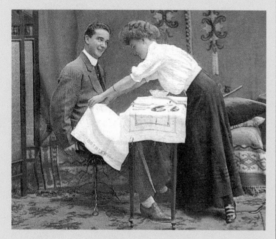

Dining In

When you're ready to impress your sweetie with a homemade meal, this delicious recipe is both elegant and easy to make, even if you're a novice in the kitchen. The key to home entertaining is to prepare as much as possible in advance so that you can spend time with your date, not with the stove! In this case, you can make both the rice and the dipping sauce ahead of time, and reheat them while you fix the salmon and asparagus. The Cake Roll with Conversation Hearts can be baked the day before. Make sure you serve hors d'oeuvres for your date to nibble on while you put the finishing touches on dinner. And don't forget to set the scene for romance with the right choice of background music and plenty of candles. This meal pairs nicely with a crisp, dry white wine.

Entrée
Broiled salmon with sesame-soy dipping sauce, Steamed asparagus, Coconut rice

> ½ cup sesame oil
> ¼ cup low-sodium soy sauce
> 1 tablespoon rice vinegar
> 3 scallions, finely sliced
> 2 tablespoons sesame seeds
> 1 cup jasmine rice
> 1 cup water
> 1 cup coconut milk
> 2 pieces salmon fillet, ½ lb. each
> 1 tablespoon kosher salt
> 1 bunch fresh asparagus, with ends removed
> 1 tablespoon butter
> salt and pepper to taste

1. In a small dish, combine sesame oil, soy sauce, rice vinegar, scallions, and sesame seeds to make dipping sauce. Mix well and then set aside.
2. In a medium-size pot, combine rice, water, and coconut milk and place over medium heat. When mixture begins to boil, turn heat down to low and cover. Let simmer for 25 minutes, stirring occasionally, until all the liquid has been absorbed and rice is soft and fluffy.
3. Preheat broiler. Place salmon fillets in a Pyrex baking dish skin-side up and sprinkle with ½ tablespoon kosher salt. Broil for 7 minutes. Remove from oven and turn fillets skin-side down. Sprinkle again with ½ tablespoon kosher salt. Broil for another 4 minutes.
4. Place asparagus in top of double boiler and cover. Steam for approximately 10 minutes, until tender. Toss with butter, salt, and pepper.
5. Arrange fish, rice, and asparagus attractively on serving plates. Pour dipping sauce over fish or serve on the side.

Dessert
Chocolate Cake Roll with Candy Hearts

Delicious and quick, this cake is always a hit. If you scatter it with those little Conversation Heart candies, you will be declaring your love over and over. If you're dinner date is not a chocoholic, use strawberry or raspberry jam as your filling.

> 4 eggs
> ¾ cup and 2 tablespoons granulated sugar
> ¾ cup sifted cake flour
> 1 teaspoon baking powder

1 teaspoon vanilla extract
2 tablespoons melted butter
granulated sugar
chocolate filling (recipe below)

1. Preheat oven to 425° F.
2. Beat eggs with ¾ cup sugar on high speed until very thick and foamy (10–15 minutes).
3. Sift flour with baking powder; fold into egg mixture.
4. Add vanilla and butter, and mix carefully.
5. Generously butter a jellyroll pan (15½" x 10½" x 1"). Pour batter into pan; bake for 8–10 minutes. When a toothpick or knife inserted in center of cake comes out clean, cake is done.
6. Remove cake from oven and loosen it from pan. Turn out on a piece of wax paper, sprinkle with 2 tablespoons granulated sugar, and place the pan on top of the cake to keep it moist. Let cool 20–30 minutes.
7. Remove pan and spread cake with Chocolate Filling. To roll cake lengthwise, lift up two corners of the waxed paper and fold over about two inches of the cake onto itself. Continue to roll by lifting the waxed paper. The last flip should deposit the cake roll on a long platter. Dust top with confectioners' sugar and scatter with heart candies.

CHOCOLATE FILLING:

¼ cup butter (4 tablespoons)
¾ cup confectioners' sugar
1 egg yolk
1 teaspoon vanilla extract
¼ cup cocoa

1. Simply cream butter; add remaining ingredients and mix well.

Serves 15

Gourmet Meals by Mail

Want to treat your lover to a romantic gourmet meal by one of the world's top chefs in the privacy of your own home? It's just a double click away with **FiveLeaf**. Seven of the world's finest chefs have teamed up with the **A La Zing** website to offer delectable appetizers and entrées. Try Daniel Boulud's Salmon Escabeche as a starter, followed by Braised Veal Shank with Creamy Polenta or Chicken Breast with Fondue of Leeks & Chive Coulis from the French Laundry's Thomas Keller. Or Charlie Trotter's Beef Tenderloin with Gnocchi and Root Vegetables. The meals come frozen and can ship overnight. They arrive complete with wine suggestions, preparation instructions, and serving tips: *alazing.com* (and then click on FiveLeaf) or (888) 959-9464.

He was a baked potato—solid and you can have them with or without salt or pepper or butter. I was a fancy dessert—mocha chip ice cream.

—KATHERINE HEPBURN
ON SPENCER TRACY.

Courtship Customs Around the World

CUP OF JOE? Young people in the isolated region of Lapland often meet at winter gatherings and festivals. If a man is interested in courting a young lady, he will go to her house and offer to make coffee for her and her family. If his offer is accepted, the couple may court.

A ROSE IS A ROSE: When a man is dating a woman in Brazil, he will bring her an odd number of roses to suggest that she is the "rose" that completes the bouquet.

ROOM FOR DESSERT: In Angola, when a male admirer eats with the family of the woman he's wooing, he will always leave some food on his plate. This expresses that he is more interested in the object of his affection than in his meal.

DESIGNING WOMEN: The Surma of southwestern Ethiopia court in the quiet period after the harvest time. Both men and women paint beautiful designs on their skin. Then the young girls sit in the shade by the river and play tunes on thumb pianos.

BUNDLES OF JOY? The unique practice of "bundling" during courtship was found in both Europe and colonial America. A bed was divided down the middle by a plank, and one half of the courting couple slept on either side.

SAY IT WITH A SONG: Serenading remains a popular courtship custom in Spain. A man will sing to a woman outside her window in the hopes that she will indicate her interest by throwing him a flower.

PEBBLE TALK: One Apache courtship custom calls for a young man to place a pattern of stones along the walking path of the young woman he's pursuing. If she walks among the stones, she reciprocates his affection. If she passes by the stones, she is expressing her disinterest.

MIDNIGHT CALLER: An Amish suitor will pay a visit to his girlfriend during the midnight hour on Sunday nights. This ensures that the young couple will have time to spend alone while her parents sleep.

Love Coupons

The next time you feel inspired to treat your sweetie to something spontaneous, give a book of "love coupons" that can be redeemed whenever! You can make a book out of small pieces of note paper the size of business or index cards, decorate them yourself, and dream up all your favorite ways to spoil the one you love.

Materials: Hole punch, medium-grade colored notepaper, decorative adhesive borders or small stickers, colored pens or calligraphy pen, heavy-grade parchment paper, ribbon

1. Cut notepaper down to index-card size. Make as many note cards as you like.
2. Punch two holes along the left side of each note card. Decorate each coupon with fancy border script, calligraphy, adhesive borders, or small stickers.
3. Inscribe each card with a redeemable treat. A sample coupon might read, "The bearer of this card is entitled to . . ."
a candlelit dinner; a walk along the beach; a hike in the woods; a night on the town; a kiss; breakfast in bed; a play; win one argument; a bubble bath; be king/queen for a day; a tennis match; a boat ride; a horseback ride; a bed & breakfast weekend; a concert; a sensual massage; a sporting event; a picnic; a love-in
4. To make a cover, trim a strip of parchment paper about two and a half times the length of a coupon. Fold the parchment paper over the stack of coupons and punch holes to match the openings in the cards.
5. Thread two 6– to 8–inch ribbons through the holes to bind the coupon book. Tie each in a pretty bow.

> *Falling in love consists merely in uncorking the imagination and bottling the common sense.*
>
> —HELEN ROWLAND

Love's Archer
A Brief History of Cupid

In Greek mythology, Eros, god of love, was the son of Aphrodite, goddess of love, and Ares, god of war. In some myths, Eros had a brother, Anteros, who was the avenger of unrequited love. In Roman mythology he was called Cupid (from the Latin word for *desire*). He is generally represented as a mischievous boy who carries a bow and a quiver of arrows. Whoever he strikes with one of his arrows will fall in love with the next person they see. Cupid became such a popular figure in European painting after the Renaissance that the Victorians appropriated the image to use in the ornate valentines that came into fashion during the nineteenth century.

Anne Frank: The Diary of a Young Girl

Darlingest Kitty,

Remember yesterday's date for it is a very important day in my life. Surely it is an important day for any girl when she receives her first kiss. Then it is just as important for me too. How did I suddenly come by this kiss? Well, I will tell you. Yesterday evening at eight o'clock I was sitting with Peter on his divan. It wasn't long before his arms went around me. "Let's move up a bit," I said. "Then I don't bump my head against the cupboard." He moved up, almost into the corner. I laid my arm under his and across his back, and he just about buried me, because his arm was hanging on my shoulder. Now we've sat like this on other occasions, but never so close as yesterday. He held me firmly against him, my left shoulder was against his chest, and already my heart began to beat faster, but we had not finished yet. He didn't rest until my head was on his shoulder and his against it. When I sat upright and, after about five minutes, he took my head in his hands and laid it against him once more. Oh, it was so lovely. I couldn't talk much the joy was too great. He stroked my cheek and arm a bit awkwardly, played with my curls, and our heads lay touching most of the time. I can't describe the feeling that ran through me all the while. I was too happy for words and I believe he was as well. We got up about half-past eight. Peter took off his gym shoes, so that he wouldn't make noise when he went through the house and I stood beside him. How it came about so suddenly, I don't know, but before we went downstairs, he kissed me. Through my hair, half on my left cheek, half on my ear. I tore downstairs without looking around, and am simply longing for tonight.

Yours,
Anne Frank

> A kiss is a lovely trick designed by nature to stop speech when words become superfluous.
>
> —Ingrid Bergman

Sweets for your Sweet
The Best Candy

Believe it or not, not every sweet tooth is satisfied by chocolate alone. It's a good thing there are hundreds of other candies and sweets to choose from. Here are some of the best, along with ordering information:

♥

See's Old Time Candies A source of old-style candies, chocolates, and more. A classic: *sees.com* or (800) 347-7337.

♥

Jones Bee Company Honey for your honey! All-natural honey and honey-nut candies: *jonesbee.com* or (801) 973-8281.

♥

Kama Sutra Now A variety of sensual tasty gifts for lovers, including "honeydust" and edible body paints: *kamasutranow.com*.

♥

Pieces of Vermont Is your sweetie more maple than honey? Try giving her maple-sugar candy—a North American favorite: *piecesofvermont.com* or (800) 507-7721.

♥

Harry and David While best known for their amazing fruit, the company also offers a delicious selection of bite-size petit fours: *harryanddavid.com* or (877) 322-1200.

♥

Sally Williams Nougat Available through a limited number of merchants, including Chef Shop, this nutty nougat has won rave reviews: *chefshop.com* or (877) 337-2491.

♥

Candy Creek Lollipops The sweet treat of childhood at its best: *candycreek.com* or (800) 636-1299.

♥

Fat Witch Brownies Their website promises "New York style baked into a brownie," and their fans agree. Fat Witch offers eight varieties of decadent brownie goodness in an assortment of attractive gift boxes and tins. Find out for yourself why many swear this is the best brownie they've ever had: *fatwitch.com* or (888) 41-WITCH.

A ROMANTIC MOVIE MOMENT

Ball Of Fire

Starring Barbara Stanwyck, 1941

SUGARPUSS

Yes, I love him. I love the hick shirts he wears and the boiled cuffs and the way he always has his vest buttoned wrong. He looks like a giraffe, and I love him. I love him because he's the kind of guy who gets drunk on a glass of buttermilk, and I love the way he blushes right up over his ears. I love him because he doesn't know how to kiss—the jerk! I love him, Joe. That's what I'm trying to tell ya."

The Hundred Secret Senses

AMY TAN

"Miss Banner," I asked her, "you feel something for Yiban Johnson, ah?"

"Feel? Yes, perhaps. But just as a friend, though not as good a friend as you. Oh! And not with the feeling between a man and woman— no, no no! After all, he's Chinese, well, not completely, but half, which is almost worse. . . . Well, in our country, an American woman can't possibly . . . What I mean is, such romantic friendships would never be allowed."

I smiled, all my worries put to rest.

Then, for no reason, she began to criticize Yiban Johnson. "I must tell you, though, he's awfully serious! No sense of humor! So gloomy about the future. China is in trouble, he says, soon even Changmian will not be safe. And when I try to cheer him up, tease him a little, he won't laugh. . . ." For the rest of the afternoon, she criticized him, mentioning all his tiny faults and the ways she could change them. She had so many complaints about him that I knew she liked him better than she said. Not just a friend.

The next week, I watched them sitting in the courtyard. I saw how he learned to laugh. I heard the excited voices of boy-girl teasing. I knew something was growing in Miss Banner's heart, because I had to ask many questions to find out what it was.

I'll tell you something, Libby-ah. What Miss Banner and Yiban had between them was love as great and constant as the sky. She told me this. She said, "I have known many kinds of love before, never this. With my mother and brothers, it was tragic love, the kind that leaves you aching with wonder over what you might have received but did not. With my father, I had uncertain love. I loved him, but I don't know if he loved me. With my former sweethearts, I had selfish love. They gave me only enough to take back what they wanted from me.

"Now I am content," Miss Banner said. "With Yiban, I love and am loved, fully and freely, nothing expected, more than enough received. I am like a falling star who has finally found her place next to another in a lovely constellation, where we will sparkle in the heavens forever."

I was happy for Miss Banner, sad for myself. Here she was, speaking of her greatest joy, and I did not understand what her words meant. I wondered if this kind of love came from her American sense of importance and had led to conclusions that were different from mine. Or maybe this love was like an illness— many foreigners became sick at the slightest heat or cold. Her skin was now often flushed, her eyes shiny and big. She was forgetful of time passing. "Oh, is it that late already?" she often said. She was also clumsy and needed Yiban to steady her as she walked. Her voice changed too, became high and childlike. And at night she moaned. Many long hours she moaned. I worried that she had caught malaria fever. But in the morning, she was always fine.

Don't laugh, Libby-ah. I had never seen this kind of love in the open before. Pastor and Mrs. Amen were not like this. The boys and girls of my old village never acted like this, not in front of other people, at least. That would have been shameful—showing you care more for your sweetheart than for all your family, living and dead.

I thought that her love was another one of

Are You Still Longing
Yosano Akiko

Are you still longing,
seeking what is beautiful,
what is decent and true?
Here in my hand, this flower,
my love, is shockingly red.

her American luxuries, something Chinese people could not afford. For many hours each day, she and Yiban talked, their heads bent together like two flowers reaching for the same sun. Even though they spoke in English, I could see that she would start a thought and he would finish it. Then he would speak, stare at her, and misplace his mind, and she would find the words that he had lost. At times, their voices became low and soft, then lower and softer, and they would touch hands. They needed the heat

Boy, Do I Have a Girdle for You!

Among the Dai people of China, women wear wide silk sashes, like girdles, that are passed down through generations. If a girl gives her girdle to a young man, it means that she has fallen in love with him.

Taking the Hands
Robert Bly

Taking the hands of someone you love,
You see they are delicate cages . . .
Tiny birds are singing
In the secluded prairies
And in the deep valleys of the hand.

of their skin to match the warmth of their hearts. They looked at the world in the court-yard—the holy bush, a leaf on the bush, a moth as though it were a new creature on earth, an immortal sage in disguise. And I could see that this life she carefully held was like the love she would always protect, never let come to harm.

By watching all these things, I learned about romance. And soon, I too had my own little courtship—you remember Zeng, the one-eared peddler? He was a nice man, not bad-looking, even with one ear. Not too old. But I ask you: How much exciting romance can you have talking about cracked jars and duck eggs?

Well, one day Zeng came to me as usual with another jar. I told him, "No more jars. I have no eggs to cure, none to give you."

"Take the jar anyway," he said. "Give me an egg next week."

"Next week I still won't have any to give you. That fake American general stole the Jesus Worshippers' money. We have only enough food to last until the next boat from Canton comes with Western money."

The next week Zeng returned and brought me the same jar. Only this time, it was filled with rice. So heavy with feelings! Was this love? Is love rice in a jar, no need to give back an egg?

I took the jar. I didn't say, Thank you, what a kind man you are, someday I'll pay you back. I was like—how do you say it?—a diplomat. "Zeng-ah," I called as he started to leave. "Why are your clothes always so dirty? Look at all those grease spots on your elbows! Tomorrow you bring your clothes here, I'll wash them for you. If you're going to court me, at least you should look clean."

You see? I knew how to do romance too. ♥

I've Got You
Under My Skin

Cole Porter

I've got you under my skin,
I've got you deep in the heart of me,
So deep in my heart, you're really a part of me.
I've got you under my skin.

I tried so not to give in,
I said to myself, "This affair never will
    go so well?"
But why should I try to resist when, darling,
    I know so well
I've got you under my skin.
I'd sacrifice anything, come what might,
For the sake of having you near,
In spite of a warning voice that comes
    in the night,
And repeats and repeats in my ear;
    "Don't you know, little fool,
        you never can win,
    Use your mentality,
    Wake up to reality."
    But each time I do, just the
        thought of you
Makes me stop, before I begin,
'Cause I've got you under my skin.

Love Bites

These scrumptious heart-shaped finger sandwiches turn a regular meal into a romantic and thoughtful expression of your love. Serve with a refreshing glass of home-made lemonade garnished with a cherry and a sprig of mint.

3 tablespoons cream cheese
¾ cup watercress, chopped
2 tablespoons honey
3 tablespoons good Dijon mustard
¼ lb. turkey, sliced very thin
¼ lb. ham, sliced very thin
¼ lb. herbed Boursin cheese
½ cucumber, peeled and thinly sliced
1 loaf of bread, sliced very thin
heart-shaped cookie cutter

1. Combine cream cheese and watercress; set aside. Combine honey and mustard; set aside.
2. Make an assortment of sandwiches. Try any combinations that appeal to you. Options include: Herbed Boursin and turkey; watercress cream cheese and cucumber; ham, cucumber and honey mustard; herbed Boirson and ham.
3. Using the heart-shaped cookie cutter, turn your everyday tea sandwiches into little bites of love!

Serves 2

> *The perfect love affair is one which is conducted entirely by post.*
>
> —GEORGE BERNARD SHAW

Letters of Love

Elizabeth Barrett to Robert Browning

Elizabeth Barrett and Robert Browning were both established poets in their own rights when they struck up a courtship through correspondence that led to their marriage in 1846.

January 10, 1846

It seems to me, to myself, that no man was ever before to any woman what you are to me—the fullness must be in proportion, you know, to the vacancy. . . and only I know what was behind—the long wilderness without the blossoming rose. . . and the capacity for happiness, like a black gaping hole, before this silver flooding. Is it wonderful that I should stand as in a dream, and disbelieve—not you—but my own fate? Was ever any one taken suddenly from a lampless dungeon and placed upon the pinnacle of a mountain, without the head turning round and the heart turning faint, as mine do?

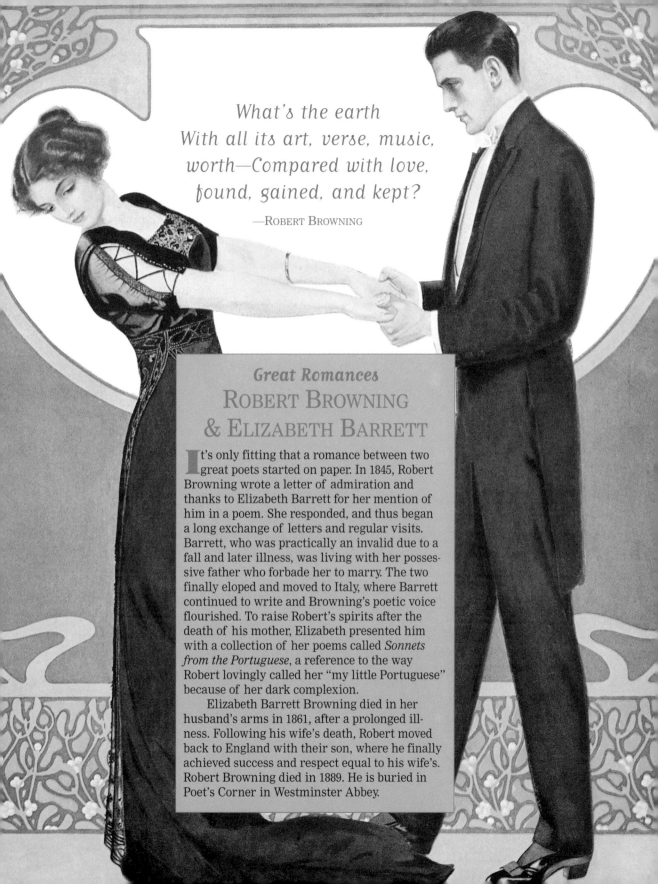

What's the earth
With all its art, verse, music,
worth—Compared with love,
found, gained, and kept?

—ROBERT BROWNING

Great Romances
ROBERT BROWNING
& ELIZABETH BARRETT

It's only fitting that a romance between two great poets started on paper. In 1845, Robert Browning wrote a letter of admiration and thanks to Elizabeth Barrett for her mention of him in a poem. She responded, and thus began a long exchange of letters and regular visits. Barrett, who was practically an invalid due to a fall and later illness, was living with her possessive father who forbade her to marry. The two finally eloped and moved to Italy, where Barrett continued to write and Browning's poetic voice flourished. To raise Robert's spirits after the death of his mother, Elizabeth presented him with a collection of her poems called *Sonnets from the Portuguese*, a reference to the way Robert lovingly called her "my little Portuguese" because of her dark complexion.

Elizabeth Barrett Browning died in her husband's arms in 1861, after a prolonged illness. Following his wife's death, Robert moved back to England with their son, where he finally achieved success and respect equal to his wife's. Robert Browning died in 1889. He is buried in Poet's Corner in Westminster Abbey.

Top Ten Date Video Rentals

The hardest thing about picking the perfect date rental is finding one movie that has enough romance to inspire further dates and enough action or humor to keep him from dozing off. We've gone more modern than retro with our top picks, but there's a pantheon of classic b&w films to choose from if that's your cup of tea. Pretty much anything starring Bogart and Bacall is a good place to start. To encourage cuddling, we couldn't resist throwing in one truly great horror flick...

1. *Annie Hall* Supposedly based on Woody Allen's real-life relationship with Diane Keaton, *Annie Hall* is the director-actor at his finest. Rapid-fire jokes and ceaseless neurotic rants make this one of the funniest and smartest comedies of all time.

2. *About A Boy* Hugh Grant plays an adult slacker whose life is changed when a weird kid forces friendship upon him. Hugh Grant has never been funnier as he helps the boy out of a social quagmire at school, falls in love with a single mother (Rachel Weisz), and finally grows up.

3. *Say Anything* This teen romance is one of the best the 1980s has to offer. Kick-boxing wannabe John Cusack falls for straight-A student Ione Skye in this touching and entertaining coming-of-age story. You'll cheer when Skye's father asks Cusack what his plans are for the future, and Cusack responds, "I just want to hang with your daughter." Ahh, young love…

4. *Swingers* A comedy about starting over, *Swingers* follows a group of buddies, led by super-cool Vince Vaughn, out on the prowl in L.A.'s trendy Swing scene. The brilliant cast, exciting dance sequences, and truly quotable dialogue make this cult hit appealing to all types.

5. *Moonstruck* An Italian-American widow (Cher) going on 40 is shocked when she discovers that she can love again, after falling for her fiancé's estranged younger brother, played by a hopelessly bitter Nicolas Cage. A tale of passion, adultery, and frequent hilarity, this perfect romantic comedy will hit you in the eye like a big pizza pie.

Summer Night
Alfred, Lord Tennyson

Now sleeps the crimson petal, now the white;
Nor waves the cypress in the palace walk;
Nor winks the gold fin in the porphyry font:
The firefly wakens: waken thou with me.

Now droops the milk-white peacock like a ghost,
And like a ghost she glimmers on to me.

Now lies the Earth all Danaë to the stars,
And all thy heart lies open unto me.

Now slides the silent meteor on, and leaves
A shining furrow, as thy thoughts in me.

Now folds the lily all her sweetness up,
And slips into the bosom of the lake:
So fold thyself, my dearest, thou, and slip
Into my bosom and be lost in me.

Relationships are like Rome. Difficult to start out, incredible during the prosperity of the "Golden Age," and unbearable during the fall. Then, a new kingdom will come along and the whole process will repeat itself until you come across a kingdom like Egypt... that thrives, and continues to flourish. This kingdom will become your best friend, your soul mate, and your love.

—HELEN KELLER

6. *Top Gun* In this high-octane, action love story, Tom Cruise plays a reckless Navy pilot who has it all—an F-14 Tomcat, the skill and talent to fly it, and a gorgeous flight school instructor turned lover (Kelly McGillis). When an accident forces him to reassess his life, "Maverick" has to prove that he's made of the right stuff. Guaranteed to "take your breath away."

7. *Out of Sight* Watch the sparks fly as a bank robber, (George Clooney) and a federal marshal (Jennifer Lopez) get together on screen for this stylish and sexy thriller. This film has it all: comedy, suspense, and some serious sexual tension.

8. *Jerry Maguire* A sweet romance set in the macho realm of a sports agency. Tom Cruise finds redemption in the arms of Renée Zellweger. Cuba Gooding Jr. also jumps off the screen with his Oscar-winning performance as Jerry Maguire's last hope.

9. *Bridget Jones's Diary* It may seem like just another "chick flick," but Bridget Jones isn't your average chick. The humor is sophisticated, sassy, and bound to leave the both of you wishing you had more.

10. *Halloween* OK, so there's no romance here. But this classic slasher film will have her diving for the comfort of your big, sheltering arms. Full of Freudian subtext and spine-tingling shocks, Halloween may be just the flick to bring the two of you closer together.

Star Magic

Here's a bright idea for a romantic gift: Name a star after your sweetheart. There are several companies that provide such a service. For about fifty dollars, they'll select a star that is currently only known as a number and give it any name you choose. You will receive a star map so that you can locate your little piece of the universe. Although professional astronomers do not recognize these names, your sweetheart will always think of you when she or he looks into the night sky and sees his or her namesake twinkling down.

Two companies that name stars are **The International Star Registry**: *starregistry.com* or (800)282-3333 and **Name a Star**: *nameastar.com* or (800)868-7800.

Little Women

Louisa May Alcott

Any young girl can imagine Amy's state of mind when she "took the stage" that night, leaning on Laurie's arm. She knew she looked well, she loved to dance, she felt that her foot was on her native heath in a ballroom, and enjoyed the delightful sense of power which comes when young girls first discover the new and lovely kingdom they are born to rule by virtue of beauty, youth, and womanhood. She did pity the Davis girls, who were awkward, plain, and destitute of escort, except a grim papa and three grimmer maiden aunts, and she bowed to them in her friendliest manner as she passed, which was good of her, as it permitted them to see her dress, and burn with curiosity to know who her distinguished-looking friend might be. With the first burst of the band, Amy's color rose, her eyes began to sparkle, and her feet to tap the floor impatiently, for she danced well and wanted Laurie to know it: therefore the shock she received can better be imagined then described, when he said in a perfectly tranquil tone, " Do you care to dance?"

"One usually does at a ball."

Her amazed look and quick answer caused Laurie to repair his error as fast as possible.

"I meant the first dance. May I have the honor?"

"I can give you one if I put off the Count. He dances divinely, but he will excuse me, as you are an old friend," said Amy, hoping that the name would have a good effect, and show Laurie that she was not to be trifled with.

"Nice little boy, but rather a short Pole to support 'A daughter of the gods, Divinely tall, and most divinely fair,' was all the satisfaction she got however.

The set in which they found themselves was composed of English, and Amy was compelled to walk decorously through a cotillion, feeling all the while as if she could dance the tarantella with a relish. Laurie resigned her to the "nice little boy," and went to do his duty to Flo, without securing Amy for the joys to come, which reprehensible want of forethought was properly punished, for she immediately engaged herself till supper, meaning to relent if he then gave any signs of penitence. She showed him her ball book with demure satisfaction when he strolled instead of rushed up to claim her for the next, a glorious polka redowa; but his polite regrets didn't impose upon her, and when she gallopaded away with the Count, she saw Laurie sit down by her aunt with an actual expression of relief.

That was unpardonable, and Amy took no more notice of him for a long while, except a word now and then when she came to chaperon between the dances for a necessary pin or a moment's rest. Her anger had a good effect, however, for she hid it under a smiling face, and seemed unusually blithe and brilliant. Laurie's eyes followed her with pleasure, for she neither romped nor sauntered, but danced with spirit and grace, making the delightsome pastime what it should be. He very naturally fell to studying her from this new point of view, and before the evening was half over, had decided that "little Amy was going to make a very charming woman."

It was a lively scene, for soon the spirit of the social season took possession of everyone, and Christmas merriment made all faces shine, hearts happy, and heels light. The musicians fiddled, tooted, and banged as if they enjoyed it, everybody danced who could, and those who couldn't admired their neighbors with uncommon warmth. The air was dark with Davises, and many Joneses gamboled like a flock of young giraffes. The golden secretary darted through the room like a meteor with a dashing Frenchwoman who carpeted the floor with her pink satin train. The Serene Teuton found the

supper table and was happy, eating steadily through the bill of fare, and dismayed the *garçons* by the ravages he committed. But the Emperor's friend covered himself with glory, for he danced everything, whether he knew it or not, and introduced impromptu pirouettes when the figures bewildered him. The boyish abandon of that stout man was charming to behold, for though he "carried weight," he danced like an India-rubber ball. He ran, he flew, he pranced, his face glowed, his bald head shone, his coattails waved wildly, his pumps actually twinkled in the air, and when the music stopped, he wiped the drops from his brow, and beamed upon his fellow men like a French Pickwick without glasses.

Amy and her Pole distinguished themselves by equal enthusiasm but more graceful agility, and Laurie found himself involuntarily keeping time to the rhythmic rise and fall of the white slippers as they flew by as indefatigably as if winged. When little Vladimir finally relinquished her, with assurances that he was "desolated to leave so early," she was ready to rest, and see how her recreant knight had borne his punishment.

It had been successful, for at three-and-twenty, blighted affections find a balm in friendly society, and young nerves will thrill, young blood dance, and healthy young spirits rise, when subjected to the enchantment of beauty, light, music, and motion. Laurie had a waked-up look as he rose to give her his seat; and when he hurried away to bring her some supper, she said to herself, with a satisfied smile, "Ah, I thought that would do him good!"

"You look like Balzac's *Femme peint par elle-même*," he said, as he fanned her with one hand and held her coffee cup in the other.

"My rouge won't come off." And Amy rubbed her brilliant cheek, and showed him her white glove with a sober simplicity that made him laugh outright.

"What do you call this stuff?" he asked, touching a fold of her dress that had blown over his knee.

"Illusion."

"Good name for it. It's very pretty-new thing, isn't it?"

"It's as old as the hills; you have seen it on dozens of girls, and you never found out that it was pretty till now—*stupide!*"

"I never saw it on you before, which accounts for the mistake, you see."

"None of that, it is forbidden. I'd rather take coffee than compliments just now. No, don't lounge, it make me nervous."

Laurie sat bolt upright, and meekly took her empty plate feeling an odd sort of pleasure in having "little Amy" order him about, for she had lost her shyness now, and felt an irresistible desire to trample on him, as girls have a delightful way of doing when lords of creation show any signs of subjection.

"Where did you learn all this sort of thing?" he asked with a quizzical look.

"As 'this sort of thing' is rather a vague expression, would you kindly explain?" returned Amy, knowing perfectly well what he meant, but wickedly leaving him to describe what is indescribable.

"Well-the general air, the style, the self-possession, the-the-illusion-you know," laughed Laurie, breaking down and helping himself out of his quandary with the new word.

Amy was gratified, but of course didn't show it, and demurely answered, "Foreign life polishes one in spite of one's self, I study as well as play, and as for this"—with a little gesture toward her dress—"why, tulle is cheap, posies to be had for nothing, and I am used to making the most of my poor little things."

Amy rather regretted that last sentence, fearing it wasn't in good taste, but Laurie liked her the better for it, and found himself both admiring and respecting the brave patience that made the most of opportunity, and the cheerful spirit that covered poverty with flowers. Amy did not know why he looked at her so kindly, nor why he filled up her book with his own name, and devoted himself to her for the rest of the evening in the most delightful manner but the impulse that wrought this agreeable change was the result of one of the new impressions which both of them were unconsciously giving and receiving. ♥

Let's Do It
(Let's Fall In Love)

COLE PORTER

When the little bluebird,
Who has never said a word,
Starts to sing "spring, spring"

When the little bluebell,
In the bottom of the dell,
Starts to ring: "ding, ding"

When the little blue clerk,
In the middle of his work,
Starts a tune to the moon up above,
It is nature, that's all,
Simply telling us to fall
In love.

And that's why
Birds do it, Bees do it,
Even educated fleas do it,
Let's do it, let's fall in love.
In Spain, the best upper sets do it,

Lithuanians and Let's do it,
Let's do it, let's fall in love.
The Dutch in old Amsterdam do it,
Not to mention the Finns,
Folks in Siam do it,
Think of Siamese twins.
Some Argentines, without means, do it,
People say, in Boston, even beans do it,
Let's do it, let's fall in love.

Romantic Sponges, they say, do it,
Oysters, down in Oyster Bay, do it,
Let's do it, let's fall in love.
Cold Cape Cod clams, 'gainst
their wish, do it,
Even lazy Jellyfish do it,
Let's do it, let's fall in love.
Electric eels, I might add, do it, Though it
shocks 'em I know.
Why ask if shad do it,
Waiter, bring me shad roe.
In shallow shoals, English soles do it,
Goldfish, in the privacy of bowls, do it,

Let's do it, let's fall in love.

The Best Singing Telegrams

Here's a unique gift for the man or woman who has it all: a singing telegram! Whether by phone, by e-mail or in the flesh, a singing telegram shows the one you love that you're willing to go the extra mile.

Luv-Grams Luv-Grams is a nationwide agency that offers singing telegrams either in person or by phone anywhere in the country. Choose from among more than two hundred characters and celebrity impersonators to sing your custom-written tune: *luv-grams.com* or (866) luv-grms (588-4767).

Western Onion Probably the best-known nationwide singing telegram agency, Western Onion has been delivering singing telegrams since 1978. The website also provides a referral service for flowers, balloons, or "Lobster-

Grams" to accompany your singing telegram: *western-onion.com*.

Teddybear and a Song Teddybear and a Song will send a phone-gram anywhere in the world incorporating your own text. The lucky recipient will get a teddy bear or flowers and a tape recording of the singing telegram. Free demonstration is available: *teddybear-and-a-song.com* or (877) 746-4496.

Acapellafella.com "Online singing telegrams are the wave of the future." So sayeth the Acapellafella, the number-one purveyor of video e-card singing telegrams. You can preview some of his "for-couples-only" creations, such as "Loving Loud" and "Hands Together," on line: *1onlinegreetingcards.com*.

Bubbygrams Unfortunately, this unique and humorous service is for the NY metro area only. You can send a singing Jewish grandmother with a bottle of Manischewitz or a heart of chopped liver to your lover, or "pick a schtick": a drag act, star impersonators, belly and hula dancers, or clowns. Bubby "does everything a real Jewish grandmother does—except sleep with your grandfather": *bubbygram.com* or (212) 353-3886.

Be My Mistress Short or Tall
Robert Herrick

Be my mistress short or tall
And distorted therewithall
Be she likewise one of those
That an acre hath of nose
Be her teeth ill hung or set
And her grinders black as jet
Be her cheeks so shallow too
As to show her tongue wag through
Hath she thin hair, hath she none
She's to me a paragon.

Sing Me A Love Song

A Brief History of Serenading

Birds do it, bees do it... even people in love do it. Wooing with song is a custom probably as old as humanity itself. The traditional serenade, however, dates back only to thirteenth-century Europe, when lute-strumming young men would indeed sing outside their beloveds' windows. The serenade, a word that has its root in the Italian word *serenata* ("evening song"), was originally an extension of chivalric ideas of romance. Medieval knights would compose love poems in homage to their ladies, and in time, the poems were set to music.

Before long, those less musically inclined were hiring professionals, known as *troubadours*, to do their wooing for them. The tradition of the serenade spread to the lower classes as well. France soon had its *jongleurs* and *minstrels*, Germany its *gauklers*, and England its *scops* and *gleemen*. These itinerant musicians would travel from town to town spreading the popular music of the day.

Serenades were originally simple, sensuous tunes sung by a single voice accompanied by a single instrument. The form eventually became part of the classical music tradition—Beethoven and Brahms composed serenades to be performed by choirs and orchestras. In today's terms, however, a serenade is simply a love song.

Top Ten Love Songs

Can't say it in words? Say it with a song. Here are ten classic love songs to inspire and delight:

1. **"I Will Always Love You"— Whitney Houston** Whitney Houston took this sweet Dolly Parton song, belted it into immortality, and made it one of the most popular ballads of this generation.

2. **"At Last"— Etta James** Sultry and understated, this song is a moody jazz favorite. Many have sung it since, but Etta's performance remains the definitive version.

3. **"Evergreen"— Barbara Streisand** If you've never understood why people go ga-ga over Barbara, listen to this soaring, bittersweet love song and you'll get it.

4. **"Just the Way You Are"— Billy Joel** The simple melody, the generous sentiment, and the no-frills rendition deliver the message we all want to hear.

5. **"Unforgettable"— Nat King Cole** Listening to this song is like being stroked by a velvet glove. It's a classic.

6. **"When a Man Loves a Woman"— Percy Sledge** Desperate! Crazy! Forgetful! No other song so eloquently articulates the power of love in a man's life.

7. **"Can't Get Enough of Your Love"— Barry White** Barry White's bedroom vocals never fail to ignite the fires of passion.

8. **"You Are So Beautiful"— Lionel Richie** For those of us who just can't find the right words, Lionel Richie has come to the rescue with this sincere and tender ballad.

9. **"Love Me Tender"— Elvis Presley** Elvis's deep, crooning, timeless appeal for love makes even the hardest hearts turn to jelly.

10. **"Wonderful Tonight"— Eric Clapton** Old "Slowhand's" classic has given couples the world over something touching and mesmerizing to dance to at their weddings.

Daisy Miller

HENRY JAMES

"I am afraid your habits are those of a flirt," said Winterbourne, gravely.

"Of course they are," she cried, giving him her little smiling stare again. "I'm a fearful, frightful flirt! Did you ever hear of a nice girl that was not? But I suppose you will tell me now that I am not a nice girl."

"You're a very nice girl, but I wish you would flirt with me, and me only," said Winterbourne.

"Ah! thank you, thank you very much; you are the last man I should think of flirting with. As I have had the pleasure of informing you, you are too stiff."

"You say that too often," said Winterbourne.

Daisy gave a delighted laugh. "If I could have the sweet hope of making you angry, I would say it again."

"Don't do that; when I am angry I'm stiffer than ever. But if you won't flirt with me, do cease at least to flirt with your friend at the piano; they don't understand that sort of thing here."

"I thought they understood nothing else!" exclaimed Daisy.

"Not in young unmarried women."

"It seems to me much more proper in young unmarried women than in old married ones," Daisy declared.

"Well," said Winterbourne, "when you deal with natives you must go by the custom of the place. Flirting is a purely American custom; it doesn't exist here. So when you show yourself in public with Mr. Giovanelli, and without your mother—"

"Gracious! poor mother!" interposed Daisy.

"Though you may be flirting, Mr. Giovanelli is not; he means something else."

"He isn't preaching, at any rate," said Daisy, with vivacity. "And if you want very much to know, we are neither of us flirting; we are too good friends for that; we are very intimate friends."

"Ah!" rejoined Winterbourne, "if you are in love with each other it is another affair."

She had allowed him up to this point to talk so frankly that he had no exception of shocking her by this ejaculation; but she immediately got up, blushing visibly, and leaving him to exclaim mentally that little American flirts were the queerest creatures in the world. ♥

Top Ten Romantic Hooky Days

Even the happiest affair can get into a "weekends-only" rut. Spending time together on a stolen Wednesday, however, can be just as good for putting the sparkle back in your love life as a trip to Paris. Escape from work and into your own private world. The following are a few suggestions for weekday adventures.

1. **Cycle Away** Take an all-day bike ride together. Find a restaurant in a far-off place and cycle there for lunch.

2. **Hooky on Ice** Most ice-skating rinks are practically empty on weekdays, so you can glide and stumble together to your heart's delight. Warm up with hot chocolate and each other afterward.

3. **Rainy Day Special** Pick a favorite actor or director, rent a bunch of their movies, and have your own film festival in bed. Make popcorn, eat junior mints, and sip your sodas with bendy straws.

4. **Bon Appétit!** Have lunch at the fanciest restaurant in town. You can enjoy the glamour while keeping the tab down.

5. **Rest and Relax** You see each other in all kinds of moods; take a day to get relaxed together. Visit your local beauty spa or stay home and give each other a massage!

6. **Be a Tourist** Visit a few of your town's most famous attractions. Looking at your town from the perspective of visitors can bring you closer together.

Love doesn't make the world go round. Love is what makes the ride worthwhile.

—FRANKLIN P. JONES

Dating Allowances

India's NIIT, a computer-training institute, offers a "dating allowance" to its employees, the better to encourage workers to marry one another. They even offer a wedding allowance for those who marry within the company.

7. **See a Psychic** Whether or not you believe in such things, it will be romantic to share your future, even if just for a day.

8. **His and Hers** Each pick one activity and do them both together. A day at the ballpark and a night at the ballet is a great way to share each other's passions.

9. **Time Machine** Relive your first date. Retracing the steps that brought you to-gether will bring back all that new-love giddiness.

10. **Road Trip!** Hop in a car and drive off in a random direction. The adventure you have together is sure to leave a lasting memory.

Test Your Love

There are so many kinds of love in the world. How can you tell if yours is the real thing? Is that hunk you hang out with worthy of you? When you marry your princess will she turn out to be a witch? Take these compatibility quizzes to find out the ultimate answer to that age-old question, "Should I stay or should I go?"

Compatibility Quiz

There are no "right" answers to this quiz. The trick is just to see how many answers you and your mate have in common (and whether the ones you disagree on matter to you). If you agree on all ten questions, you are truly compatible; eight out of ten signals healthy individuality; less than six in common, and we don't like your chances.

1. *The best way to spend an evening together is to:*
   a) go out with a bunch of friends
   b) stay home on the couch and watch a movie
   c) dine at the fanciest restaurant in town
   d) play Scrabble

2. *If we get into a terrible argument, we should:*
   a) spend some time apart to think things over
   b) call it quits
   c) contact a counselor
   d) each list three things we love about the other

3. *Washing the dishes is the responsibility of:*
   a) whoever did not prepare dinner
   b) whoever loses the coin toss
   c) whoever is most bothered by a sink full of dirty dishes
   d) whoever did not do them last time

4. *The perfect number of children to have is:*
   a) 0
   b) 1
   c) 2
   d) 3 or 4
   e) a baker's dozen

5. *If I say I want to lose weight, you should:*
   a) encourage me to do so at once
   b) tell me that I am fine the way I am
   c) help me work out a practical diet/exercise program
   d) challenge me to lose more than you in a set amount of time

6. *My idea of the ideal vacation is:*
   a) hiking in the Outer Hebrides
   b) lying on a tropical beach in the sun
   c) staying at the Ritz in Paris
   d) the Peace Corps

7. *The way to select a car is to:*
   a) find out what your boss is driving
   b) read *Consumer Reports*
   c) see how it handles at top speed
   d) go to a police auction

8. *The best thing to do with old clothes is to:*
   a) keep wearing them
   b) give them away to a charity
   c) sell them in a garage sale
   d) turn them into other things

9. *The ideal pet is:*
   a) furry
   b) scaly
   c) edible
   d) invisible

10. *When I die, I want you to:*
    a) wear black for the rest of your life
    b) mourn, then remarry
    c) throw yourself on my funeral pyre
    d) start dating my single best friend

"How Much Do You Know?" Quiz

This test gauges how much your mate has shared with you and how much you remember. Answer ten questions correctly and the gods rejoice at your union. Five out of ten and you may want to spend more time together. Less than three correct answers and you and your mystery mate should probably part. While you are taking this quiz, keep in mind your mate's potential answers about YOU—they're just as important as your own.

1. Who is his/her best friend?
2. What is the hardest thing he/she has ever had to do?
3. What's his/her favorite movie?
4. What is his/her favorite way to celebrate a birthday?
5. What is his/her least favorite body part?
6. What five items could he/she not live without? (Bonus points if one of them is you.)
7. What was the name of his/her childhood pet?
8. When was the last time he/she had a belly laugh?
9. What accomplishment is he/she proudest of?
10. How many kids does he/she want?

Fan Language

In the Victorian era, many women would communicate flirtatiously using a fan:
- *Slow fanning meant she was married.*
- *Fast fanning meant she was available.*
- *A fan wide open meant love.*
- *A fan open and then shut meant "kiss me."*

The Eggstasy of Love

A decorated egg is a common token of affection in many parts of the world. In China, a man will give a colorfully painted egg to a potential marriage partner, and in some European countries, decorated eggs will often have love notes painted on the side.

True (or False) Love Quiz

Answer these questions *true* or *false* to decide whether you really love your "cuddle bunny," or are just in love with love. If you answer ten out of ten true, you are definitely smitten; if six out of ten, there may be other fish in the sea for you; if three or fewer . . . what on earth are you sticking around for?

- I think he/she is always (okay, *almost* always) the most attractive person in the room.
- If the person who broke my heart when I was twenty wanted me back now, I wouldn't even consider it.
- No one has ever cared about me as much as he/she does.
- I look forward to finding out what he/she looks like at age seventy.
- I love being referred to as his/her boyfriend/girlfriend/spouse.
- If he/she were injured in an accident, I would want to be the first one at the hospital.
- Sometimes I feel guilty for getting so lucky.
- If I were in a crisis, he/she is the first person I'd call.
- I think he/she would make a great parent.
- I can't imagine my life without him/her.

The Rules: Time-Tested Secrets for Capturing the Heart of Mr. Right

Ellen Fein and Sherrie Schneider

Rule 1: Be a "Creature Unlike Any Other"
Rule 2: Don't Talk to a Man First (and Don't Ask Him to Dance)
Rule 3: Don't Stare at Men or Talk Too Much
Rule 4: Don't Meet Him Halfway or Go Dutch on a Date
Rule 5: Don't Call Him and Rarely Return His Calls
Rule 6: Always End Phone Calls First
Rule 7: Don't Accept a Saturday Night Date after Wednesday
Rule 8: Fill Up Your Time before the Date
Rule 9: How to Act on Dates 1, 2, and 3
Rule 10: How to Act on Dates 4 through Commitment Time
Rule 11: Always End the Date First
Rule 12: Stop Dating Him if He Doesn't Buy You a Romantic Gift
　　　　for Your Birthday or Valentine's Day
Rule 13: Don't See Him More Than Once or Twice a Week
Rule 14: No More than Casual Kissing on the First Date
Rule 15: Don't Rush into Sex and Other *Rules* for Intimacy
Rule 16: Don't Tell Him What to Do
Rule 17: Let Him Take the Lead
Rule 18: Don't Expect a Man to Change or Try to Change Him
Rule 19: Don't Open Up Too Fast
Rule 20: Be Honest but Mysterious
Rule 21: Accentuate the Positive and Other *Rules* for Personal Ads
Rule 22: Don't Live with a Man (or Leave Your Things in His Apartment)
Rule 23: Don't Date a Married Man
Rule 24: Slowly Involve Him in Your Family and Other *Rules* for Women with Children
Rule 25: Practice, Practice, Practice! (or, Getting Good at the *Rules*)
Rule 26: Even if You're Engaged or Married, You Still Need *The Rules*
Rule 27: Do *The Rules*, Even when Your Friends and Parents Think It's Nuts
Rule 28: Be Smart and Other *Rules* for Dating in High School
Rule 29: Take Care of Yourself and Other *Rules* for Dating in College
Rule 30: Next! And Other *Rules* for Dealing with Rejection
Rule 31: Don't Discuss *The Rules* with Your Therapist
Rule 32: Don't Break *The Rules*
Rule 33: Do *The Rules* and You'll Live Happily Ever After!
Rule 34: Love Only Those Who Love You
Rule 35: Be Easy to Live With

A woman has got to love a bad man once or twice in her life to be thankful for a good one.

—MAE WEST

Help, I'm Single!
Top Ten Romantic Advice Books

Love is wonderful, but only a lunatic would try to figure it all out on their own. Following is a list of some popular books that help navigate the glorious mystery of love and relationships.

1. *The Rules: Time-Tested Secrets for Capturing the Heart of Mr. Right*, by Ellen Fein and Sherrie Schneider— How to use old-fashioned know-how to snag a serious beau.

2. *The Fine Art of Flirting*, by Joyce Jillson— Become dangerously intriguing to all you meet.

3. *Zolar's Starmates*, by Zolar Entertainment—Use astrology to find and keep your perfect mate.

4. *Are You the One for Me?* by Barbara De Angelis— Find out what you really want in a mate, and how to get it.

5. *Extraordinary Relationships: A New Way of Thinking About Human Interactions*, by Roberta M. Gilbert— Make all your relationships healthy and productive.

6. *How to Attract Anyone, Anytime, Anyplace: The Smart Guide to Flirting*, by Susan Rabin and Barbara Lagowski— Release your inner charmer!

7. *Men are from Mars, Women are from Venus*, by John Gray— How to navigate the universe of love relationships.

8. *The Guide to Picking up Girls*, by Gabe Fischbarg— A humorous yet practical guide to feeling comfortable with women.

9. *Speed Dating: The Smarter, Faster Way to Lasting Love*, by Yaacov Deyo and Sue Deyo— Who has time to shop around? Find your true love in just seven minutes.

10. *Dating: A Survival Guide from the Frontlines*, by Josey Vogels— Did you know that talking about your contagious diseases on a first date is a no-no? If not, this book is for you.

Romeo and Juliet

WILLIAM SHAKESPEARE

ACT II, SCENE II

Romeo comes forward.

ROMEO. He jests at scars that never felt a wound.

Enter Juliet above.

But soft, what light through yonder window breaks?
It is the east and Juliet is the sun!
Arise fair sun and kill the envious moon
Who is already sick and pale with grief
That thou her maid art far more fair than she.
Be not her maid since she is envious,
Her vestal livery is but sick and green
And none but fools do wear it. Cast it off.
It is my lady, O it is my love!
O that she knew she were!
She speaks, yet she says nothing. What of that?
Her eye discourses, I will answer it.
I am too bold. 'Tis not to me she speaks.
Two of the fairest stars in all the heaven,
Having some business, do entreat her eyes
To twinkle in their spheres till they return.
What if her eyes were there, they in her head?
The brightness of her cheek would shame those stars
As daylight doth a lamp. Her eyes in heaven
Would through the airy region stream so bright
That birds would sing and think it were not night.
See how she leans her cheek upon her hand.
O that I were a glove upon that hand
That I might touch that cheek.

JULIET. Ay me.

Romeo. She speaks.
O speak again bright angel, for thou art
As glorious to this night, being o'er my head,
As is a winged messenger of heaven
Unto the white-upturned wondering eyes
Of mortals that fall back to gaze on him
When he bestrides the lazy-puffing clouds
And sails upon the bosom of the air.

JULIET. O Romeo, Romeo, wherefore art thou Romeo?
Deny thy father and refuse thy name.
Or if thou wilt not, be but sworn my love
And I'll no longer be a Capulet.

ROMEO. Shall I hear more, or shall I speak at this?

JULIET. 'Tis but thy name that is my enemy:
Thou art thyself, though not a Montague.
What's Montague? It is nor hand nor foot
Nor arm nor face nor any other part
Belonging to a man. O be some other name.
What's in a name? That which we call a rose
By any other word would smell as sweet;
So Romeo would, were he not Romeo call'd,
Retain that dear perfection which he owes
Without that title. Romeo, doff thy name,
And for thy name, which is no part of thee,
Take all myself.

ROMEO. I take thee at thy word.
Call me but love, and I'll be new baptis'd:
Henceforth I never will be Romeo.

JULIET. What man art thou that thus bescreen'd
    in night
So stumblest on my counsel?

ROMEO. By a name
I know not how to tell thee who I am:
My name, dear saint, is hateful to myself
Because it is an enemy to thee.
Had I it written, I would tear the word.

JULIET. My ears have yet not drunk a hundred words
Of thy tongue's uttering, yet I know the sound.
Art thou not Romeo, and a Montague?

ROMEO. Neither, fair maid, if either thee dislike.

JULIET. How cam'st thou hither, tell me, and wherfore?
The orchard walls are high and hard to climb,
And the place death, considering who thou art,
If any of my kinsmen find thee here.

ROMEO. With love's light wings did I o'erperch
    these walls,
For stony limits cannot hold love out,
And what love can do, that dares love attempt:
Therefore thy kinsmen are no stop to me.

JULIET. If they do see thee, they will murder thee.

ROMEO. Alack, there lies more peril in thine eye
Than twenty of their swords. Look thou but sweet

And I am proof against their enmity.

JULIET. I would not for the world they saw thee here.

ROMEO. I have night's cloak to hide me from their eyes,
And but thou love me, let them find me here.
My life were better ended by their hate
Than death prorogued, wanting of thy love.

JULIET. By whose direction found'st thou out this place?

ROMEO. By love, that first did prompt me to enquire.
He lent me counsel, and I lent him eyes.
I am no pilot, yet wert thou as far
As that vast shore wash'd with the farthest sea,
I should adventure for such merchandise.

JULIET. Thou knowest the mask of night is on my face,
Else would a maiden blush bepaint my cheek
For that which thou hast heard me speak tonight.
Fain would I dwell on form; fain, fain deny
What I have spoke. But farewell, compliment.
Dost thou love me? I know thou wilt say 'Ay,'
And I will take thy word. Yet, if thou swear'st,
Thou mayst prove false. At lovers' perjuries,
They say, Jove laughs. O gentle Romeo,
If thou dost love, pronounce it faithfully.
Or, if thou think'st I am too quickly won,
I'll frown and be perverse and say thee nay,
So thou wilt woo; but else, not for the world.
In truth, fair Montague, I am too fond,
And therefore thou mayst think my haviour light,
But trust me, gentleman, I'll prove more true
Than those that have more cunning to be strange.
I should have been more strange, I must confess,
But that thou overheard'st, ere I was ware,
My true-love passion; therefore pardon me,
And not impute this yielding to light love
Which the dark night hath so discovered.

ROMEO. Lady, by yonder blessed moon I vow,
That tips with silver all these fruit-tree tops—

JULIET. O swear not by the moon, th'inconstant moon,
That monthly changes in her circled orb,
Lest that thy love prove likewise variable.

ROMEO. What shall I swear by?

JULIET. Do not swear at all.
Or if thou wilt, swear by thy gracious self,
Which is the god of my idolatry,
And I'll believe thee.

ROMEO. If my heart's dear love—

JULIET. Well, do not swear. Although I joy in thee,

I have no joy of this contract tonight:
It is too rash, too unadvis'd, too sudden,
Too like the lightning, which doth cease to be
Ere one can say 'It lightens.' Sweet, good night.
This bud of love, by summer's ripening breath,
May prove a beauteous flower when next we meet.
Good night, good night. As sweet repose and rest
Come to thy heart as that within my breast.

ROMEO. O wilt thou leave me so unsatisfied?

JULIET. What satisfaction canst thou have tonight?

ROMEO. Th'exchange of thy love's faithful vow for mine.

JULIET. I gave thee mine before thou didst request it,
And yet I would it were to give again.

ROMEO. Wouldst thou withdraw it? For what
    purpose, love?

JULIET. But to be frank and give it thee again;
And yet I wish but for the thing I have.
My bounty is as boundless as the sea,
My love as deep: the more I give to thee
The more I have, for both are infinite.
I hear some noise within. Dear love, adieu.
Nurse calls within.
Anon, good Nurse—Sweet Montague be true.
Stay but a little, I will come again. *(Exit Juliet.)*

ROMEO. O blessed blessed night. I am afeard,
Being in night, all this is but a dream,
Too flattering sweet to be substantial.

Enter Juliet above.

JULIET. Three words, dear Romeo, and good
    night indeed.
If that thy bent of love be honourable,
Thy purpose marriage, send me word tomorrow
By one that I'll procure to come to thee,
Where and what time thou wilt perform the rite,
And all my fortunes at thy foot I'll lay,
And follow thee my lord throughout the world.

NURSE. *(Within.)* Madam.

JULIET. I come, anon—But if thou meanest not well
I do beseech thee—

NURSE. *(Within.)* Madam.

JULIET. By and by I come—
To cease thy strife and leave me to my grief.
Tomorrow will I send.

ROMEO. So thrive my soul—

JULIET. A thousand times good night. *(Exit Juliet.)*

ROMEO. A thousand times the worse, to want thy light.
Love goes toward love as schoolboys from their books,
But love from love, toward school with heavy looks.

    Enter Juliet (above) again.

JULIET. Hist! Romeo, hist! O for a falconer's voice
To lure this tassel-gentle back again.
Bondage is hoarse and may not speak aloud,
Else would I tear the cave where Echo lies
And make her airy tongue more hoarse than mine
With repetition of my Romeo's name.

ROMEO. It is my soul that calls upon my name.
How silver-sweet sound lovers' tongues by night,
Like softest music to attending ears.

JULIET. Romeo.

ROMEO. My nyas.

JULIET. What o'clock tomorrow
Shall I send to thee?

ROMEO. By the hour of nine.

JULIET. I will not fail. 'Tis twenty year till then.
I have forgot why I did call thee back.

ROMEO. Let me stand here till thou remember it.

JULIET. I shall forget, to have thee still stand there,
Remembering how I love thy company.

ROMEO. And I'll still stay to have thee still forget,
Forgetting any other home but this.

JULIET. 'Tis almost morning, I would have thee gone,
And yet no farther than a wanton's bird,
That lets it hop a little from his hand
Like a poor prisoner in his twisted gyves,
And with a silken thread plucks it back again,
So loving-jealous of his liberty.

ROMEO. I would I were thy bird.

JULIET. Sweet, so would I:
Yet I should kill thee with much cherishing.
Good night, good night. Parting is such sweet sorrow
That I shall say good night till it be morrow.

    Exit Juliet.

ROMEO. Sleep dwell upon thine eyes, peace in thy breast.
Would I were sleep and peace so sweet to rest.
The grey-ey'd morn smiles on the frowning night
Chequering the eastern clouds with streaks of light;
And darkness fleckled like a drunkard reels
From forth day's pathway, make by Titan's wheels.
Hence will I to my ghostly Sire's close cell,
His help to crave and my dear hap to tell.

    Exit. ♥

85

He Wishes for the Cloths of Heaven

William Butler Yeats

Had I the heavens' embroidered cloths,
Enwrought with golden and silver light,
The blue and the dim and the dark cloths
Of night and light and the half-light,
I would spread the cloths under your feet:
But I, being poor, have only my dreams;
I have spread my dreams under your feet;
Tread softly, because you tread on my dreams.

Sugar Cookie Valentines

These heart-shaped cookie cards are a unique (and delicious!) way to express affection for your sweetheart, family, and friends on Valentine's Day.

1 cup butter (2 sticks), at room temperature
1 cup sugar
2 eggs
1 teaspoon vanilla extract
3 cups flour

1. Cream the butter and sugar. Beat in the eggs and add the vanilla. Add the flour and mix well. Refrigerate for at least 2 hours.
2. Preheat the oven to 375°F and line baking sheets with parchment paper.
3. Roll the dough out on a lightly floured surface and cut out heart shapes with a cookie cutter.
4. Transfer the cookies with a spatula to cookie sheets and make two holes on the left side of each cookie large enough to string ribbon through (you can use a knife or straw depending on the thickness of the ribbon you have chosen).
5. Bake for approximately 10 minutes. When the cookies are beginning to brown, remove them from the oven and slide the parchment off the baking sheet. If necessary, redefine ribbon holes with a knife tip while cookies are still warm and pliable. Wait until they are completely cool before icing.

Makes approximately 6–10 Valentine's Day cards, depending on size and thickness.

Snow Icing

1 package (16 oz) confectioners' sugar
3 egg whites
1 tablespoon white vinegar
Assorted food coloring

1. Place the confectioners' sugar in a mixing bowl.
2. In a separate bowl, beat the egg whites lightly with a fork. Add them to the sugar and beat with an electric mixer on the lowest speed for 1 minute. Add vinegar and beat for 2 more minutes at high speed, or until the mixture is stiff and glossy, as for stiff meringue.
3. Divide the mixture into several small bowls and tint with different colors.

Assembling Your Valentine

red or pink ribbon up to a 1/4 inch wide, scissors, pastry bags, and assortment of decorative tips

1. It's time to be creative. One heart will be the cover of your card, another one the interior. Use the bags of icing to decorate the front of the card. Then, inside the card write a romantic message like "Be Mine," "I Love You," "Marry Me," or "I'm Sweet on You." Since you are writing with icing, you'll want to keep it short and simple, but if you have a more elaborate message in mind, or wish to include a poem or photograph, just cut it down to fit your card and attach it with a dab of icing.
2. When your cookies are decorated and the icing has hardened completely (overnight), cut two pieces of ribbon approximately 4 inches long and thread your card together. Tie loosely so that the "card" can be opened, and finish it off with bow ties.

Cookie cards can be refrigerated up to two weeks in an airtight container.

Ever wonder where the expression "wearing your heart on your sleeve" comes from? At Valentine's Day parties, each bachelor would draw the name of a young single lady from a hat and wear her name on his sleeve to claim her as his valentine.

A Brief History of
Valentine's Day

In ancient Rome, the date of February 14 was a holiday commemorating the queen of the Roman gods and goddesses, Juno. In honor of Juno, boys were matched with girls by drawing names from a lot. Also during the month of February, the Romans celebrated a feast named Lupercalia in honor of the god Lupercus, who protected the Roman shepherds and their flocks from wolves.

During early Christianity, Christian priests adopted the martyred bishop named Valentine as a replacement for Lupercalia, in the hope of diminishing the influence of Pagan rituals and practices. In A.D. 269, the Roman emperor Claudius II had Valentine, bishop of Interamna, imprisoned and later executed for disobeying his order to not allow any man or woman to be wed. The emperor felt that married men made poor soldiers due to their sentimental attachment to their wives. During his confinement, the bishop fell in love with the jailer's daughter and was known to write her romantic letters signed "Your Valentine."

In A.D. 496, Pope Gelasius officially outlawed the celebration of Lupercalia and replaced it with the celebration of the martyrdom of St. Valentine. Hence, St. Valentine's Day. The lottery that contained the names of the single women was replaced with the names of saints. The saint who was chosen on the slip of paper was meant to be honored and impersonated by the person who picked it.

Chocolicious Reading

Chocolatier magazine is a chocolate lover's dream—the perfect gift for the true chocoholic! Issues are jammed with recipes, interviews with famous chefs, sumptuous photographs, and the most recent chocolate trends. Search on line or write: Chocolatier Dept. A92, P.O. Box 333, Mt. Morris, IL 61054 USA.

Approximately 1 billion Valentine's Day cards are sent each year.

Be Mine, Sweetie

Conversation Hearts have been around since 1866, when they were first created by Daniel Chase, brother of NECCO founder, Oliver Chase. It wasn't long before these sweet little Valentines became a hit (today, no fewer than 8 billion Conversations Hearts are manufactured each year. That's enough to place them back to back across the United States, from New York to L.A. and back again!)

If you want a sweet twist for your own Valentine, NECCO will actually imprint a custom Conversation Heart message for you—that is, if you purchase a full production run, which is around 1.6 million hearts. But at three calories a pop, what better way is there to say "I love you" than with 3,500 pounds of candy? *necco.com.*

When you have once seen the glow of happiness on the face of a beloved person, you know that a man can have no vocation but to awaken that light on the faces surrounding him. In the depth of winter, I finally learned that within me there lay an invincible summer.

—ALBERT CAMUS

Top Ten Valentine's Gifts for Her

It can be difficult enough to find the perfect present for a friend, but what about the friend who is also your lover and soul mate? Take a deep breath, relax, and consider this list of sure-to-please valentines.

1. **Silk sheets.** (And a roll in them!)

2. **A locket with your picture in it.** Find an antique locket to make it unique; she'll carry your face with her everywhere.

3. **A spa treatment at home.** Massage, scented bath, lots of candles, and a little worship.

4. **A love letter.** People seldom write letters anymore; she'll treasure your sincere message of devotion forever.

5. **Two fine crystal glasses and a bottle of champagne.** A little bubbly goes a long way!

6. **Licorice ropes.** Licorice has aphrodisiac qualities. (And ropes can be fun!)

7. **Silk stockings.** Let your valentine know she's your glamour girl.

8. **A bouquet of anemones and bluebells.** These flowers stand for unfading love and constancy.

9. **A night in a great local hotel.** Take her on a mini-vacation, even if it's just around the corner!

10. **An indoor picnic.** Bring over a basket of delicious food and spread a tablecloth on the floor. Surround her with bunches of flowers for a real "outdoors" experience.

Now That's a Gift!

Next time you're trying to come up with a great gift for your sweetie, take inspiration from Mark Antony. In his attempt to win Cleopatra's affections, he gave her much of what is today the Middle East, including Phoenicia, Coele-Syria, Cyprus, and parts of Cilicia, Arabia, and Judea.

Move Over, Fabio!

Here's a one-of-a-kind gift for your loved one: a customized romance novel in which the two of you star as the hero and heroine! With four different plots to choose from—"Pirates of Desire," "Medieval Passion," "Tropical Treasure," or "Love's Next Door"—you just provide **Book By You** with your names, physical characteristics (a woman's figure options range from "slim" to "voluptuous" and a man's from "slim" to "cuddly"), favorite drinks, pets' names, home state, etc. The result? For little more than the price of a hardcover novel from a bookstore you'll have a fantastic personal romantic adventure to spice up the bedtime hour: *bookbyyou.com* or (877) 266-5298.

Love has nothing to do with what you are expecting to get—only with what you are expecting to give— which is everything.

—Katherine Hepburn

Valentine's Day Traditions Around the World

The day devoted to love in **China** is called *Qi Qiao Jie* or the "seventh eve." Two legends describe the origins of this holiday. In the first, seven daughters of the Goddess of Heaven were spotted bathing by a cowherd named Niu Lang, who ran off with their clothes. When the prettiest daughter, named Zhi Nu, asked for their return, the two fell in love and married, only to be separated years later. Forever after, the Goddess of Heaven reunited the couple once a year. The second legend says that Niu Lang and Zhi Nu were fairies from opposite sides of the sky brought together by the Jade Emperor, who then separated them because they were neglecting their work. Stargazers look to the constellation of Aquila and the star of Vega to see the two lovers in the night sky. In both stories, Niu Lang and Zhi Nu meet on the seventh day of the seventh moon in the Chinese calendar.

In **Denmark**, valentines consist of pressed flowers. Another custom is for a man to send a woman an anonymous "joke card" signed with a dot for every letter in his name. If the woman guesses the sender, she will receive an Easter Egg on Easter.

On Valentine's Day in **Italy**, superstition holds that if an unmarried woman rises before dawn and stares out her window, the first man she sees will become her husband within the year.

Valentine's Day in **Japan** promises lovebirds a double helping of amour—they celebrate it twice! The first holiday is just for women giving gifts to men. Chocolates are the most common present. However, these sweet tokens of love may not always be romantic in nature. Women give chocolates to many men in their lives, from their fathers and bosses to their beloved. In return, men give gifts to women a month later, on March 14, called "White Day."

International Women's Day is treated as a combination of Valentine's Day and Mother's Day in **Russia**. On March 8, men take the time to appreciate the women in their lives by giving them gifts and helping out around the house.

A traditional Valentine's Day gift in **Spain** is a single red rose and a novel.

DID YOU KNOW?

110 million roses (mostly red), will be sold for Valentine's Day. ♥ 15 percent of women in the United States send themselves flowers on Valentine's Day. ♥ *1 billion Valentine's Day cards are given every year.* ♥ Over 35 million heart-shaped boxes of chocolate are sold every Valentine's Day. ♥ *The first Valentine's Day candy box was invented by Richard Cadbury in the late 1800s.* ♥ Hallmark makes over 1330 different Valentine's Day cards. ♥ *To dream of her future husband, a single woman in the seventeenth century ate a hard-boiled egg and pinned five bay leaves to her pillow before going to sleep on Valentine's eve.* ♥ Verona, Italy, where Shakespeare's *Romeo and Juliet* is set, receives nearly a thousand Valentines addressed to Juliet every February.

A Brief History of the Heart's Shape

How did the body's main circulatory organ come to be represented as the cute rounded *V* that shapes cakes, jewelry and Valentine's Day cards? Some believe that the heart shape is an imitation of the Silphium plant's seedpod. Silphium, a giant relative of fennel, was an important commercial crop in Cyrene in the seventh century B.C. and is depicted on coins from this ancient North African city-state. Scholars speculate that this now extinct plant may have been used as a type of birth control, which would go a long way toward explaining the heart shape's link to erotic love.

Another theory suggests that the heart shape is really a combination of three different ideograms—namely the symbol for togetherness (two adjacent linked circles), the symbol for fire (a *V* with the edges curled outward) and the symbol for flight (a line drawing of a seagull).

Perhaps the well-known heart shape is really just a stylized version of the real thing. Whereas an actual ticker is lopsided and covered in veins, the heart icon is smooth, uniform in color, and symmetrical in shape.

Though the heart shape appears in cultures as diverse as the Hindu, Jewish, Roman, Greek, Christian, Taoist, and Aztec, it was the Victorians who took the heart to new heights of decorative excess. Since then, the heart shape has been unequivocally linked to romance, teenage crushes, Valentine's Day, and molded chocolates alike.

You have a heart of stone

Your heart doesn't belong to me any longer

You possess my heart

My heart is broken

My heart is occupied

You've Got Mail
The Best E-Cards

Nowadays it's hard to find a mate who does not have an on-line hookup. With that in mind, try this: Instead of sending your loved one tired jokes and annoying chain letters every morning, send a romantic e-card! We promise it'll make your sweetheart's day.

✉

bluemountain.com
Blue Mountain is a general e-card site with quirky and clever options, complete with animation and music. They have romantic cards for every type of relationship, including on-line ones. Try sending your loved one an e-hug or e-kiss! The first month is free.

✉

cards.lovingyou.com
Loving You is an all-purpose site for people in love. Besides gifts, "lovescopes," and heart-shaped chocolate chip cookies, the site provides a wide variety of free romantic e-cards.

✉

fukkad.com
Fukkad.com offers more than your average e-card. You can send e-flower bouquets, naughty notes, and even pranks, including a humorous animated one for pesky "stalkers" at work.

If love is the answer, could you rephrase the question?

—LILY TOMLIN

passionup.com
Passionup.com provides the tongue-tied romantic with e-cards and secret love letters. From tasteful to schmaltzy, Passionup's cards are even accompanied by tinkly music.

✉

supergreetingcards.com
This site offers free e-cards for every occasion from "Kiss Your Mate Day" to Ramadan. The love and romance e-cards run the gamut from gushing to cute.

✉

virtualkiss.com
Visit the e-kissing booth and send your loved one a personalized cyber kiss. You choose the color and style of the lips or select from their "pre-puckered" smooches like the Eskimo Kiss or Flamin' Lips Kiss.

Gift of Sight
Robert Graves

I had long known the diverse tastes
   of the wood,
Each leaf, each bark, rank earth from
   every hollow;
Knew the smells of bird's breath and of
   bat's wing;
Yet sight I lacked: until you stole upon me,
Touching my eyelids with light finger-tips.
The trees blazed out, their colors whirled
   together,
Nor ever before had I been aware of sky.

Playing Your Cards Right
Love Notes & Valentines

The next time you want to say "Be Mine" or "I Love You," make your message that much sweeter by giving your sweetheart a card that's out of the ordinary. You can send these creative love notes in the mail or hide them in special places where you know your mate will find them.

Romantic Fortune Card
Square piece of notepaper,
colored pens or pencils

1. Fold opposite corners together to make a triangle. Crease the paper at the fold.
2. Fold the triangle in half, bringing opposite corners together to make a smaller triangle. Crease the paper at the fold, then open up the paper.
3. Fold each corner to the center of the square to make a smaller square.
4. Flip the square over. As in Step 3, fold each corner to the center of the square to make an even smaller square.
5. On each of the eight triangles, write the name of a color.
6. Lift each triangular flap, and write a romantic note or message to correspond to each of the eight colors.
7. Turn the paper over and write one numeral on each of the triangular sections from 1 through 8. Fold the paper in half, creating a rectangle with the numbers on the outside.
8. Present the fortune card in person, or send it to your valentine with the following instruc-

tions: Slip your thumb and forefinger underneath the numbered flaps on both sides. Pick a number. Open and close the fortune card back and forth the chosen number of times. Pick a color. Lift the flap to read the message underneath.

Pressed Flower Card
Dried wildflowers, plain note card, glue,
vellum paper, scissors, thick book, lace or
decorative trim, pen or marker

1. Arrange dried flowers decoratively on the cover of a blank note card and glue in place.
2. Trim the vellum paper to fit on the cover of the note card. Put a drop of glue on each corner and place the vellum over the flowers.
3. Create a border for the vellum with lace or decorative trim, and glue in place. Once the card has dried, write your love note inside.

Picture Card
Cardboard, scissors, photograph, glue,
decorative trim, metallic pen

1. Measure and cut a piece of cardboard slightly wider than your photograph and twice as long.
2. Lightly score the cardboard in order to fold it in half lengthwise, with the scoring on the outside. Allowing the fold to be the top of the card, put a few drops of glue on the front of the card and affix the photograph.
3. Create a border around the picture with ribbon, beads, lace, or other trim, and glue in place.
4. On the outside back cover of the card, write a personal love note or poem.
5. Cut a 2- to 3-inch length of ribbon and glue each end to the center of the inside edge of each card flap. Allow to dry, then stand card upright.

Seal it with a Kiss

The practice of adding *X*s to the end of a letter to symbolize kisses may be related to the widespread illiteracy of the premodern era. In medieval Europe, people who could not write, signed documents with an *X* and kissed the page in front of witnesses to show sincerity. The *X* then became associated with the kiss. Another possibility is simply that the *X* resembles a puckered mouth.

TOKENS OF AFFECTION

Throughout history, there have been many ways to say "I love you" without actually choking out the words. Here are a few tried and true ways people have found to express their romantic feelings.

It is a Welsh tradition to give your beloved a wooden spoon with a handle that is carved with a key, keyhole, or heart and can be worn as a necklace. The gift represents the key to the giver's heart.

Amish couples give each other homemade household items to signal their wish to marry. Nothing says "I love you" quite like a cake pan!

In the Victorian era, a man would send a pair of gloves to a woman he wanted to marry. If she appeared in church the next Sunday with the gloves on, she had accepted.

Medieval knights would ride into battle with ladies' sleeves attached to their armor for good luck. The women gave the men the garments, which were detachable from their bodices, as tokens of love.

In many African cultures, lovers exchange small silver pendants made out of engraved

coins drilled with holes so that they can be worn around the neck. In the nineteenth century, African Americans sometimes used dimes for love tokens.

Italians have long regarded the gift of a pot of basil a love token, although ancient Greeks considered basil a sign of hatred.

Beginning in the late seventeenth century in Europe, men and women exchanged miniature portraits of themselves as tokens of love. The practice died out when photography was invented.

The *luckenbooth*, a love token traditional in Scotland since the seventeenth century, takes its name from the locked booths or cabinets where jewelers displayed the charms. Couples exchange the charms, which are in the shape of crowned hearts, as engagement gifts.

The *claddagh* is an ancient Irish symbol in which two hands hold a heart with a crown on top. The way in which a claddagh is worn indicates its wearer's romantic status. Worn on the right hand with the crown turned in means "I'm available"; right hand with the crown turned out means "I'm involved"; and left hand, heart turned out means "I'm committed."

Top Ten Valentine's Gifts for Him

Do men even LIKE Valentine's Day? Or do all the expectations overwhelm them? Items on this little list should help turn the fellows on to the holiday and all its benefits.

1. **A coupon book full of services you are willing to perform.** From darning his socks to knocking them off.

2. **Personalized boxer shorts.** Get a laundry pen, some white boxers, and write him a love letter he can (discreetly) wear.

3. **Breakfast in bed.** Even if it's just Cheerios and coffee, it's great to start the day knowing someone loves you.

4. **A mixed CD of your favorite love songs.** Now he will always know how to get you in the mood.

5. **A helicopter ride.** In most cities you can charter a private helicopter to take you on a romantic flight for two.

Nightcrawlers

On the island of Pohnpei in Micronesia, a couple will date in secrecy. In this ritual, called "nightcrawling," a young man will visit the home of the girl he is pursuing. If she returns his affections, they will sneak out together. If the community discovers that the couple is dating, they are considered married.

6. **A progressive meal.** Take him to one place for appetizers, another for the main course, a third for dessert, and home for a nightcap.

7. **A professional massage.** Many massage therapists will come to your home. While he still has his post-massage glow, treat him to his favorite homemade meal.

8. **Tickets to his favorite sporting event.** And if you offer to let him take his best friend, he'll certainly pick you.

9. **Flavored body paint.** You can take turns playing artist.

10. **A love list.** Write down all the things you adore about him. This is one that money can't buy.

She Walks in Beauty
Lord Byron

She walks in beauty, like the night
  Of cloudless climes and starry skies;
And all that's best of dark and bright
  Meet in her aspect and her eyes:
Thus mellowed to that tender light
  Which heaven to gaudy day denies.

One shade the more, one ray the less,
  Had half impaired the nameless grace
Which waves in every raven tress,
  Or softly lightens o'er her face;
Where thoughts serenely sweet express
  How pure, how dear their dwelling place.

And on that cheek, and o'er that brow,
  So soft, so calm, yet eloquent,
The smiles that win, the tints that glow,
  But tell of days in goodness spent,
A mind at peace with all below,
  A heart whose love is innocent!

Heart Art

If you've got a yen to create homemade valentines, add some extra love to your kitchen, or wrap up a gift with a little romance, make it with your heart—your personal heart stamp, that is. With simple potato or rubber stamps, you can easily decorate paper, cloth, or wood.

Potato Stamp
Potato, paring knife, heart-shaped cookie cutter (optional), tempera or other water-based paint, fabric paint (optional), plastic or styrofoam plate

1. Using the paring knife, cut the potato in half to create two flat surfaces.
2. Press a heart-shaped cookie cutter into one of the potato pieces about a half inch, or use the paring knife to carve a heart shape into the potato.
3. Cut away about a half inch of potato around the heart shape to create your stamp. When finished, you will have a raised, solid heart in the center of the potato.
4. Pour a thin layer of your chosen paint onto a plastic or styrofoam plate.
5. Dip the heart stamp into the paint and gently press onto the surface or fabric that you wish to decorate. Repeat to your heart's desire!

Rubber Stamp
Rubber eraser (approximately $1/2$" thick by $2^1/2$" long), pen or pencil, X-Acto knife, inkpad

1. Draw the outline of a heart on one side of the rubber eraser.
2. Using the X-Acto knife, carefully carve away about $1/4$-inch depth of eraser surrounding your outline, so the heart is in relief.
3. To make heart impressions, press the heart stamp onto an inkpad and then onto the paper surface you wish to decorate.

Never sign a valentine with your own name.

—CHARLES DICKENS

I ♥ Hearts

Now that you have the means, put your stamps into action with these fun ideas:

■ **Quick 'n' Easy Gift Bags** Save small plain brown paper bags and decorate them with various colored heart prints.

■ **Country Bread Boards** Adorn one side of a wooden cutting board with a heart motif using water-soluble paint. Use the plain side for cutting bread, then hang the board on the wall heart-side out to cheer up your kitchen.

■ **Romantic Notes** Use a rubber stamp to create a heart border on stationery or note cards. Seal your letters with a heart stamp on the back of an envelope.

■ **Lovely Fabrics** Add fun to T-shirts, pillow slipcovers, tablecloths, or other fabrics with heart-print potato stamps and fabric paint.

■ **Wrapped-up-in-Love Paper** In addition to decorating plain or solid-color wrapping paper with heart prints, try this: Dip the heart stamp into glue and press onto paper. Pour glitter over the glue prints. Allow to dry, and then shake off excess glitter.

Chocolate Ecstasy
The Best Chocolate

It's sweet. It's decadent. It's simply one of the most delicious and romantic gifts you can give. Move over diamonds, chocolate is a girl's best friend (and guys don't mind it either.) Milk, white, bittersweet, or dark, there's no denying that a dose of chocolate makes us all feel loved. Whether you're looking for a special box of truffles or an exotic mix for your hot cocoa, these chocolate vendors will fulfill your wildest cravings!

Chocophile Looking to try rare artisan chocolate? This website delivers the unusual from all over the world: *chocophile.com* or (914) 833-1596.

Fran's Chocolates Hailed by *The Book of Chocolate* as America's best chocolatier, Fran Bigelow remains intimately involved in all

> *All I really need is love, but a little chocolate now and then doesn't hurt!*
>
> —LUCY VAN PELT, *PEANUTS*

stages of the chocolate-making process, from choosing ingredients to tasting the results. Try her Brandied French Cherries, the chocolate-covered fruits, or one of her rich, indulgent chocolate tortes—the choices are wonderfully endless: *franschocolates.com* or (800) 422-FRAN.

Godiva Chocolatiers The name Godiva evokes both elegance and a naked woman on horseback. A classic in the world of chocolate, this Belgian import never disappoints a chocolate craving: *godiva.com* or (800) 9-GODIVA.

Joseph Schmidt The United States' premier confectioner produces the ultimate chocolate truffle: *jschmidtconfections.com* or (800) 861-8682.

La Maison du Chocolat Luscious, artistic chocolates are available through this French chocolatier's website. Click on the link for the English version of the site: *lamaisonduchoco-lat.com/index.php* or (212) 744-7117.

Lilac Choose from among their 5,000 chocolate molds, sublime lillipops, decadent truffles, chocolate covered strawberries, or most anything else your heart desires: (212) 242-7374.

Vosges Haut-Chocolat These exotic chocolates blend classic French confectionery craft with Far Eastern spices. The Vosges website offers the adventurous chocolate lover such exotic items as the "Black Pearl Bar," dark chocolate infused with ginger, wasabi, and black sesame seeds: *vosgeschocolate.com* or (888) 301-YUMM.

Homemade Box of Chocolates

This Valentine's Day, make the tradition of giving chocolate truly special by spoiling your sweetie with a batch of homemade truffles. Pack them in a heart-shaped tin with tissue paper and finish with a red satin or velvet ribbon.

12 oz. semisweet chocolate chips
⅓ cup heavy cream
⅓ cup unsalted butter
3 egg yolks
¼ teaspoon vanilla extract
1 cup unsweetened cocoa powder for dusting

1. Combine chocolate chips, cream, and butter in a small saucepan. Heat on low, stirring constantly, until smooth. Remove from heat.
2. In a small bowl, lightly whisk egg yolks, then add a small amount of the heated mixture and whisk. Add this to the saucepan.
3. Add vanilla and stir well.
4. Pour mixture into a small bowl and refrigerate until firm (about 3–4 hours).
5. Form teaspoonfuls into balls and roll in cocoa. Refrigerate until ready to serve.

Makes about 36 chocolate truffles

A Bittersweet Lust
A Brief History of Chocolate

More than 3,500 years ago, the Olmecs of ancient Mexico discovered the delights found in the heart of the cacao tree's fruit. The secret of transforming these beanlike seeds into a paste passed from the Olmecs to the Mayans—the first culture to establish cacao plantations—to the Toltecs, and throughout much of Central America.

It wasn't until the fifteenth century that the Spanish began to prepare chocolate as a hot beverage, adding sugar to counteract the beans' bitterness, and eventually preparing it with milk instead of water. By the mid-1500s, wellborn ladies all across Spain were beginning their days with this rich, steamy drink. But chocolate soon acquired a darker reputation. Its bitter flavor could be—and was!—used to disguise the taste of deadly substances. One *señora* did away with her unfaithful lover by using just such a cup of poisoned cocoa.

Others, however, turned to chocolate to inspire love—or at least lust. The infamous Marquis de Sade believed strongly in chocolate's erotic properties and featured it extensively in his writings. Casanova's gifts of chocolate were a successful aid to seduction, whereas Madame de Pompadour, the unenthusiastic mistress of Louis the XV, dosed herself with chocolate to help her stimulate passion for the king.

Today chocolate retains a reputation for, if not *inspiring* sexual cravings, then at least satisfying them. Much has been made of chocolate containing the chemical phenylethyamine (PEA), which the human body produces when in love—or when skydiving. Studies have shown, however, that eating foods laced with PEA doesn't translate into lusty feelings. And if it did, you'd be better off eating a cheddar-and-smoked salami sandwich (both cheddar and smoked salami contain higher levels of PEA than chocolate!).

Everything's Coming Up Roses!

The Best Rose Bouquets

Roses are usually available at your local florist. But if you're looking for something special or need to place an order out of your area code, here are some great sources:

✄

1-800-FLOWERS A reliable source for roses as well as other flowers, candy, and gift items: *1800flowers.com* or (800) 356-9377.

✄

All Roses, Roses, Roses Looking for roses in shades other than red? Here's a source that provides beautiful cut roses in every color of the rainbow: *allrosesrosesroses.com* or (800) 325-0877.

✄

Calyx & Corolla Beautiful flowers in elegant arrangements, plus gift items, are available through this premier merchant's website and catalogue: *calyxandcorolla.com* or (800) 800-7788.

✄

FTD Florists Order on line or use their search form (*florists.ftd.com*) to find an FTD florist in your area, or in 153 other countries around the world: *ftd.com* or (800) SEND-FTD.

✄

Martha's Flowers Martha Stewart's on-line "flower shop" offers uniquely arranged flowers of all kinds, including gorgeous roses: *proflowers.com/marthasflowers* or (800) 462-7842.

The Best Rosebushes

Give the gift that keeps on growing! If the object of your affection has outdoor space, try a twist on the tradition and send her a rosebush instead of cut roses. Here are some sources:

✄

The American Rose Society This organization offers rose information and a gift shop. All sales benefit the society: *ars.org* or (800) 637-6534.

✄

Jackson & Perkins This premier source of flowers, gardening equipment, and information also allows you to purchase roses to support a number of causes: *jacksonandperkins.com* or (877) 322-2300.

✄

Heirloom Roses A great source for unusual and antique roses: *heirloomroses.com* or (800) 820-0465.

✄

John's Miniature Roses Even if you don't have a garden, you can add roses to your life. These miniature bushes take up little space and are perfect for apartment dwellers with window boxes: *johnsminiatureroses.com* or (800) 820-0465.

A Brief History of the Rose

Roses, both red and white, first became linked with love in the myths of the ancient Greeks and Romans. In one story, it's Aphrodite, distraught over the death of her lover, Adonis, who creates a red rose from his blood. In a Roman myth, Cupid creates roses in an attempt to bribe his fellow gods to remain silent about his mother's many lovers.

When the rose took root in Europe, poets and playwrights—Shakespeare among them—took note of the flower's mythical meaning. Soon it was immortalized in song and story as a token of love. But it was the Victorians of the nineteenth century who solidified the rose's romantic reputation. The red rose, in the Victorian pantheon of flowers, was confirmed as a potent symbol of passion.

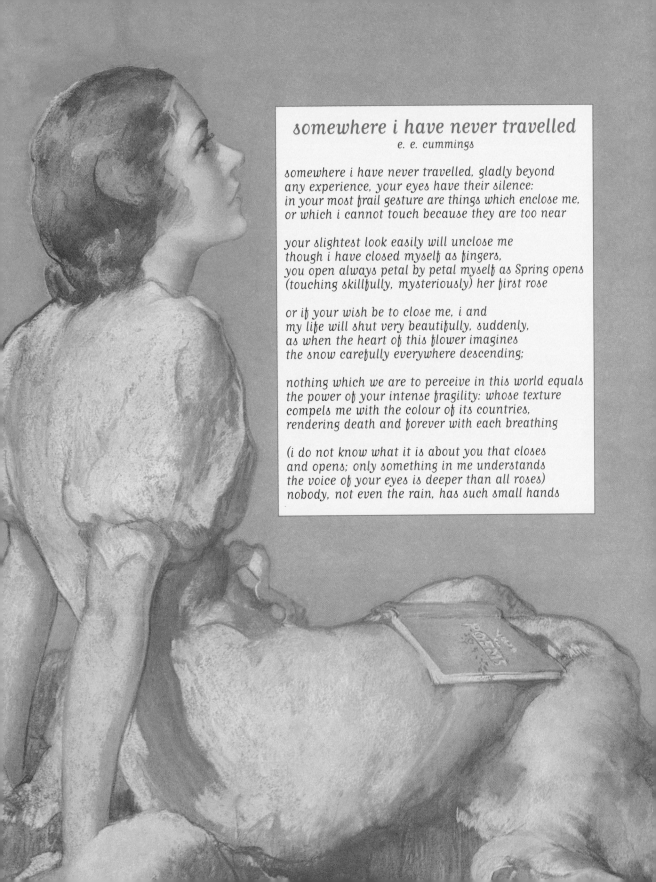

somewhere i have never travelled

e. e. cummings

somewhere i have never travelled, gladly beyond
any experience, your eyes have their silence:
in your most frail gesture are things which enclose me,
or which i cannot touch because they are too near

your slightest look easily will unclose me
though i have closed myself as fingers,
you open always petal by petal myself as Spring opens
(touching skillfully, mysteriously) her first rose

or if your wish be to close me, i and
my life will shut very beautifully, suddenly,
as when the heart of this flower imagines
the snow carefully everywhere descending;

nothing which we are to perceive in this world equals
the power of your intense fragility: whose texture
compels me with the colour of its countries,
rendering death and forever with each breathing

(i do not know what it is about you that closes
and opens; only something in me understands
the voice of your eyes is deeper than all roses)
nobody, not even the rain, has such small hands

Petal Talk
The Language of Flowers

Flowers, herbs, and even trees have held symbolic meaning from ancient times to the present, in cultures all around the globe. In fifteenth-century Turkey, *floriography*, which literally means "writing with flowers," was used for sophisticated communications, and not only about matters of the heart.

From Turkey, floriography spread to France; in fact, one of the first attempts to catalog flowers' meanings was Frenchwoman Charlotte de la Tour's *Le Langage des Fleurs* (*The Language of Flowers*) published in 1819. In 1879, during England's Victorian era, a "Miss Corruthers of Inverness" wrote another catalog that was widely used in both England and, later, the United States.

Next time you send your sweetheart a bouquet, refer to the list below, and choose your blooms carefully! To make sure your message is understood, attach a note with the names of the flowers that you've included and their hidden meanings.

FLOWER	MEANING
American linden	Matrimony
Asparagus fern	Fascination
Baby's breath	Innocence; sincerity
Basil	"I hate you"
Calla lily	Magnificent beauty
Camellia; pink	Longing
Camellia; red	"You're a flame in my heart"
Camellia; white	Adoration; perfection
Crocus; spring	Youthful gladness
Daisy	Innocence; loyal love
Dandelion	Faithfulness; happiness
Delphinium	Big-hearted; fun
Edelweiss	Daring; courage; noble purity
Forget-me-not	True love; memories
Forsythia	Anticipation
Foxglove	Falsehood; deception
Freesia	Innocence; trust
Gardenia	"You're lovely"; secret love
Garlic	Courage; strength; "Get well"
Ginger	Strength
Hibiscus	Delicate beauty
Henbane	Attracts female love
Honeysuckle	The bond of love
Iris	Faith; wisdom
Iris, yellow	Passion
Ivy	Wedded love; fidelity
Lady's slipper	Capricious beauty
Lilac, purple	First emotions of love
Lilac, white	Youthful innocence
Love-in-a-mist	"You puzzle me"
Mint	Virtue
Myrtle	Love; joy
Oak leaves	Bravery
Orange blossom	Eternal love; marriage
Phlox	Our souls are united
Poppy, red	Pleasure
Raspberry	Remorse
Rose of Sharon	Consumed by love
Rosemary	Remembrance
Sage	Wisdom; great respect
Sunflower, dwarf	Adoration
Sunflower, tall	False riches; pride
Sweet pea	"Good-bye"; departure
Sweet William	Gallantry
Tulip, variegated	Beautiful eyes
Tulip, yellow	Hopeless love
Tulip; red	Declaration of love
Violet	Modesty and simplicity
Violet, blue	Faithfulness
Violet, yellow	Modest worth
Water lily	Purity of heart
Wisteria	Welcome; "I cling to thee"

This bud of love, by summer's ripening breath,
May prove a beauteous flower when next we meet.

—WILLIAM SHAKESPEARE

One Perfect Rose
Dorothy Parker

A single flow'r he sent me, since we met.
All tenderly his messenger he chose;
Deep-hearted pure, with scented dew
    still wet—
One perfect rose.

I knew the language of the floweret;
'My fragile leaves,' it said, 'his heart
enclose.'
Love long has taken for his amulet
One perfect rose.

Why is it no one ever sent me yet
One perfect limousine, do you suppose?
Ah no, it's always just my luck to get
    One perfect rose.

When we find someone
whose weirdness is
compatible with ours,
we join up with them
and fall into mutually
satisfying weirdness—and
call it love—true love.

—ROBERT FULGHUM

Heart-Shaped Sachets

A familiar fragrance can awaken memories and enhance moods. The smell of a summer garden may be reminiscent of a romantic tryst. A whiff of spiced cider might inspire thoughts of cuddling by the fireplace. A tucked-away scented sachet can romance your senses every time you open your closet, trunk, or lingerie drawer. Try your hand at making your own potpourri with this spicy blend.

Materials: Tracing paper, pencil, scissors, pins, quilted fabric scraps or swatches, sewing machine or needle and thread, ribbon, lace, miniature silk rosebuds

Filling:

³⁄₄ cup lavender, ¹⁄₂ cup vetiver root or 2 drops vetiver essential oil, ¹⁄₄ cup oak moss, ¹⁄₄ cup orange blossoms, ¹⁄₄ cup sandalwood, 1¹⁄₂ teaspoons whole cloves, crushed cinnamon stick, ¹⁄₄ cup patchouli leaves or 1 drop patchouli essential oil, 3 drops musk oil

1. On tracing paper, draw a heart-shaped pattern about 6 inches wide.
2. Use the pattern to cut two identical fabric hearts from the swatches.
3. Pin the right sides of the fabric pieces together. Sew the edges with a sewing machine or stitch by hand with a backstitch. Leave a 3-inch opening at the top of the heart.
4. Turn the heart right side out. Blend filling ingredients to make potpourri and stuff heart sachet.
5. Cut 6 inches of ribbon and fold in half to make a loop. Pin the loop ends to the inside of the sachet opening at the top of the heart. Hand stitch the opening closed.
6. Pin lace around the edge of the sachet and hand stitch into place. Pin miniature silk rosebuds along the inside border of the lace and hand stitch into place.

The Chemistry of Love

Social researchers, evolutionary biologists, and all sorts of science-minded people have been trying for decades to pin down why we fall in—and out—of love. Beauty may be more than skin deep, but love, the experts say, starts with looks.

Symmetrical facial features are the first characteristic that humans unconsciously seek in a mate: It's a sign of good genes. Another factor is scent, especially for females. A woman can be powerfully attracted to a man's aroma, possibly because it may suggest he's a good genetic match.

But love's biology extends beyond looking good and smelling great. Once two people find themselves in a state of mutual attraction, a pharmacopoeia of chemicals floods the brain. The key chemicals include testosterone (for men), dopamine, and serotonin. All stimulate the brain's pleasure centers, producing a sense of euphoria.

As anyone who has been in a long-term relationship can attest to, this state of heightened excitement doesn't last forever. But eventually, the body produces a reward: oxytocin, "the cuddle hormone." Scientists believe that this chemical helps create a feeling of blissful affection, and may encourage selfless behavior—the perfect sustenance for lasting love.

We Should Talk about This Problem
Daniel Ladinsky

There is a Beautiful Creature
Living in a hole you have dug.

So at night
I set fruit and grains
And little pots of wine and milk
Beside your soft earthen mounds,

And I often sing.

But still, my dear,
You do not come out.

I have fallen in love with Someone
Who hides inside you.

We should talk about this problem—

Otherwise,
I will never leave you alone.

Great Romances
JOHN LENNON & YOKO ONO

The romance of John Lennon and Yoko Ono epitomized the free-loving liberal spirit of the decade in which they met and married: the sixties. Together, they shared a passion for creativity and peace and became well known for their activism and anti-war politics. Their most famous act of protest was the seven-day-long "bed-in" they staged on their honeymoon. Hundreds of members of the press were invited to their hotel suite to report the event and spread the word of peace. Their expressions of love were often considered eccentric—John legally changed his middle name from Winston to Ono, and the two regularly dressed alike, in matching white suits. Fixtures on New York's Upper West Side until John's tragic death in 1980, this couple's devotion is immortalized in the many love songs they wrote for each other.

Shall I Compare Thee to a Summer's Day
William Shakespeare

Shall I compare thee to a summer's day?
Thou art more lovely and more temperate:
Rough winds do shake the darling buds of May,
And summer's lease hath all too short a date:
Sometime too hot the eye of heaven shines,
And often is his gold complexion dimm'd;
And every fair from fair sometime declines,
By chance or nature's changing course untrimm'd;
But thy eternal summer shall not fade,
Nor lose possession of that fair thou owest;
Nor shall Death brag thou wander'st in his shade,
When in eternal lines to time thou grow'st:
So long as men can breathe, or eyes can see,
So long lives this, and this gives life to thee.

Summer

EDITH WHARTON

Charity's heart contracted. The first fall of night after a day of radiance often gave her a sense of hidden menace: it was like looking out over the world as it would be when love had gone from it. She wondered if some day she would sit in that same place and watch in vain for her lover. . . .

His bicycle-bell sounded down the lane, and in a minute she was at the gate and his eyes were laughing in hers. They walked back through the long grass, and pushed open the door behind the house. The room at first seemed quite dark and they had to grope their way in hand-in-hand. Through the window-frame the sky looked light by contrast, and above the black mass of asters in the earthen jar one white star glimmered like a moth.

"There was such a lot to do at the last minute," Harney was explaining, "and I had to drive down to Creston to meet someone who has come to stay with my cousin for the show."

He had his arms about her, and his kisses were in her hair and her lips. Under his touch things deep down in her struggled to the light and sprang up like flowers in sunshine. She twisted her fingers into his, and they sat down side by side on the improvised couch. She hardly heard his excuses for being late: in his absence a thousand doubts tormented her, but as soon as he appeared she ceased to wonder where he had come from, what had delayed him, who had kept him from her. It seemed as if the places he had been in, and the people he had been with, must cease to exist when he left them, just as her own life was suspended in his absence.

He continued, now, to talk to her volubly and gaily, deploring his lateness, grumbling at the demands on his time, and good-humoredly mimicking Miss Hatchard's benevolent agitation. "She hurried off Miles to ask Mr. Royall to speak at the Town Hall tomorrow: I didn't know till it was done." Charity was silent, and he

added: "After all, perhaps it's just as well. No one else could have done it."

Charity made no answer: She did not care what part her guardian played in the morrow's ceremonies. Like all the other figures peopling her meager world he had grown non-existent to her. She had even put off hating him.

"Tomorrow I shall only see you from far off," Harney continued. "But in the evening there'll be the dance in the Town Hall. Do you want me to promise not to dance with any other girl?"

Any other girl? Were there any others? She had forgotten even that peril, so enclosed did he and she seem in their secret world. Her heart gave a frightened jerk.

"Yes, promise."

He laughed and took her in his arms. "You goose—not even if they're hideous?"

He pushed the hair from her forehead, bending her face back, as his way was, and leaning over so that his head loomed black between her eyes and the paleness of the sky, in which the white star floated. . . . ♥

Chapter Three
Love & Marriage

Jane Eyre

CHARLOTTE BRONTË

It is a long way to Ireland, Janet, and I am sorry to send my little friend on such weary travels: but if I can't do better, how is it to be helped? Are you anything akin to me, do you think, Jane?"

I could risk no sort of answer by this time: my heart was full.

"Because," he said, "I sometimes have a queer feeling with regard to you—especially when you are near me, as now: it is as if I had a string somewhere under my left ribs tightly and inextricably knotted to a similar string situated in the corresponding quarter of your little frame. And if that boisterous channel, and two hundred miles or so of land come broad between us, I am afraid that cord of communion will be snapt; and then I've a nervous notion I should take to bleeding inwardly. As for you,—you'd forget me."

"That I never should, sir: you know"—impossible to proceed.

"Jane, do you hear that nightingale singing in the wood? Listen!"

In listening, I sobbed convulsively; for I could repress what I endured no longer; I was obliged to yield, and I was shaken from head to foot with acute distress. When I did speak, it was only to express an impetuous wish that I had never been born, or never come to Thornfield.

"Because you are sorry to leave it?"

The vehemence of emotion, stirred by grief and love within me, was claiming mastery, and struggling for full sway; and asserting a right to predominate: to overcome, to live, rise, and reign at last; yes,—and to speak.

"I grieve to leave Thornfield: I love Thornfield:—I love it, because I have lived in it a full and delightful life,—momentarily at least. I have not been trampled on. I have not been petrified. I have not been buried with inferior minds, and excluded from every glimpse of communion with what is bright and energetic, and high. I have talked, face to face, with what I reverence; with what I delight in—with an original, a vigorous, an expanded mind. I have known you, Mr. Rochester; and it strikes me with terror and anguish to feel I absolutely must be torn from you for ever. I see the necessity of departure; and it is like looking on the necessity of death."

"Where do you see the necessity?" he asked, suddenly.

"Where? You, sir, have placed it before me."

"In what shape?"

"In the shape of Miss Ingram; a noble and beautiful woman,—your bride."

"My bride! What bride? I have no bride!"

"But you will have."

"Yes:—I will!—I will!" He set his teeth.

"Then I must go:—you have said it yourself."

"No: you must stay! I swear it—and the oath shall be kept."

"I tell you I must go!" I retorted, roused to something like passion. "Do you think I can stay to become nothing to you? Do you think I am an automaton?—a machine without feelings? and can bear to have my morsel of bread snatched from my lips, and my drop of living water dashed from my cup? Do you think, because I am poor, obscure, plain, and little, I am soulless and heartless? You think wrong!—I have as much soul as you,—and full as much heart! And if God had gifted me with some beauty, and much wealth, I should have made it as hard for you to leave me, as it is now for me to leave you. I am not talking to you now through the medium of custom, conventionalities, or even of mortal flesh:—it is my spirit that addresses your spirit; just as if both had passed through the grave, and we stood at God's feet, equal,—as we are!"

"As we are!" repeated Mr. Rochester—"so," he added, enclosing me in his arms, gathering me to his breast, pressing his lips on my lips: "so, Jane!"

"Yes, so, sir," I rejoined: "and yet not so; for

you are a married man—or as good as a married man, and wed to one inferior to you—to one with whom you have no sympathy—whom I do not believe you truly love; for I have seen and heard you sneer at her. I would scorn such a union: therefore I am better than you—let me go!"

"Where, Jane? To Ireland?"

"Yes—to Ireland. I have spoken my mind, and can go anywhere now."

"Jane, be still; don't struggle so, like a wild, frantic bird that is rending its own plumage in its desperation."

"I am no bird; and no net ensnares me; I am a free human being with an independent will; which I now exert to leave you."

Another effort set me at liberty, and I stood erect before him.

"And your will shall decide your destiny," he said: "I offer you my hand, my heart, and a share of all my possessions."

"You play a farce, which I merely laugh at."

"I ask you to pass through life at my side—to be my second self and best earthly companion."

"For that fate you have already made your choice, and must abide by it."

"Jane, be still a few moments: you are over-excited: I will be still too."

A waft of wind came sweeping down the laurel-walk, and trembled through the boughs of the chestnut: it wandered away—away—to an indefinite distance—it died. The nightingale's song was then the only voice of the hour: in listening to it, I again wept. Mr. Rochester sat quiet, looking at me gently and seriously. Some time passed before he spoke: he at last said:—

"Come to my side, Jane, and let us explain and understand one another."

"I will never again come to your side: I am torn away now, and cannot return."

"But, Jane, I summon you as my wife: it is you only I intend to marry."

I was silent: I thought he mocked me.

"Come, Jane—come hither."

"Your bride stands between us."

He rose, and with a stride reached me.

"My bride is here," he said, again drawing me to him, "because my equal is here, and my likeness. Jane, will you marry me?"

Still I did not answer, and still I writhed myself from his grasp: for I was still incredulous.

"Am I a liar in your eyes?" he asked passionately. "Little sceptic, you shall be convinced. What love have I for Miss Ingram? None: and that you know. What love has she for me? None: as I have taken pains to prove: I caused a rumour to reach her that my fortune was not a third of what was supposed, and after that I presented myself to see the result; it was coldness both from her and her mother. I would not—I could not—marry Miss Ingram. You—you strange—you almost unearthly thing!—I love as my own flesh. You—poor and obscure, and small and plain as you are—I entreat to accept me as a husband."

"Mr. Rochester, let me look at your face: turn to the moonlight."

"Why?"

"Because I want to read your countenance; turn!"

"There: you will find it scarcely more legible than a crumpled, scratched page. Read on: only make haste, for I suffer."

His face was very much agitated and very much flushed, and there were strong workings in the features, and strange gleams in the eyes.

"Oh, Jane, you torture me!" he exclaimed. "With that searching and yet faithful and generous look, you torture me!"

"How can I do that? If you are true and your offer real, my only feelings to you must be gratitude and devotion—they cannot torture."

"Gratitude!" he ejaculated: and added wildly—"Jane, accept me quickly. Say Edward—give me my name—Edward—I will marry you."

"Are you in earnest?—Do you truly love me?—Do you sincerely wish me to be your wife?"

"I do; and if an oath is necessary to satisfy you, I swear it."

"Then, sir, I will marry you."

"Edward—my little wife!"

"Dear Edward!"

"Come to me—come to me entirely now," said he: and added, in his deepest tone, speaking in my ear as his cheek was laid on mine, "Make my happiness—I will make yours." ♥

Carl Jung from "Marriage as a Psychological Relationship," 1925

Psychiatrist Carl Gustav Jung met Emma Rauschenbach in 1893 and prophesied that they would marry. Ten years later, in 1903, they were, and stayed happily married for 52 years.

The young person of marriageable age does, of course, possess an ego-consciousness (girls more than men, as a rule), but, since he has only recently emerged from the mists of original unconsciousness, he is certain to have wide areas which still lie in the shadow and which preclude to that extent the formation of psychological relationship. This means, in practice, that the young man (or woman) can have only an incomplete understanding of himself and others, and is therefore imperfectly informed as to his, and their, motives. As a rule the motives he acts from are largely unconscious. Subjectively, of course, he thinks himself very conscious and knowing, for we constantly overestimate the existing content of consciousness, and it is a great and surprising discovery when we find that what we had supposed to be the final peak is nothing but the first step in a very long climb. The greater the area of unconsciousness, the less is marriage a matter of free choice, as is shown subjectively in the fatal compulsion one feels so acutely when one is in love.

My most brilliant achievement was my ability to be able to persuade my wife to marry me.

—WINSTON CHURCHILL

And One Shall Live in Two
Jonathan Henderson Brooks

Though he hung dumb upon her wall
And was so very still and small—
A miniature, a counterpart,
Yet did she press him to her heart
On countless, little loving trips,
And six times pressed him to her lips!
As surely as she kissed him six,
As sure as sand and water mix,
Sure as canaries sweetly sing,
And lilies come when comes the spring,
The two have hopes for days of bliss
When four warm lips shall meet in kiss;
Four eyes shall blend to see as one,
Four hands shall do what two have done,
Two sorrow-drops will be one tear—
And one shall live in two each year.

I Only Have Eyes for You
AL DUBIN AND HARRY WARREN

My love must be a kind of blind love,
I can't see anyone but you.
And dear, I wonder if you find love
An optical illusion too?

Are the stars out to night?
I don't know if it's cloudy or bright
'Cause I only have eyes for you, dear.
The moon may be high, but I can't
see a thing in the sky,
'Cause I only have eyes for you.

I don't know if we're in
a garden,
Or on a crowded avenue.
You are here, so am I,
Maybe millions of people go by,
But they all disappear from view,
And I only have eyes for you.

Letters of Love

John Middleton Murry and his wife, Katherine Mansfield

Katherine Mansfield, New Zealand-born British writer, married John Middleton Murry, English writer and critic, in 1918. They were together until her death, in 1923.

To Katherine   14 January 1918

. . . As I got up from my chair, I saw your letter lying on the little round table in front of me. I had to kiss it: then I stood by the fire and looked at the clock, and loved you so much that I thought my heart would burst. I wondered whether some thing would tell you that I was full of love of you, wanting you to know I loved you so deeply, at a quarter to twelve on Monday night. Then I got down your photograph. It's stuck in a corner of the looking glass. And I was knocked all of a heap by your beauty again. It's the photo where you have the black jacket on, and the marguerite on your button-hole. And there is all that wonderful, secret child-ness, trembling about that impossibly delicate mouth. You darling, darling, darling. That's only the first words of what I said to you. You exquisite, incredible woman.

To John   27 January 1918

My love for you tonight is so deep and tender that it seems to be outside myself as well. I am fast shut up like a little lake in the embrace of some big mountains. If you were to climb up the mountains, you would see me down below, deep and shining—and quite fathomless, my dear. You might drop your heart into me and you'd never hear it touch bottom. I love you—I love you— Goodnight. Oh, Bogey, what it is to love like this!

Infatuation is when you think that he's as sexy as Robert Redford, as smart as Henry Kissinger, as noble as Ralph Nader, as funny as Woody Allen, and as athletic as Jimmy Conners. Love is when you realize that he's as sexy as Woody Allen, as smart as Jimmy Conners, as funny as Ralph Nader, and as athletic as Henry Kissinger, and nothing like Robert Redford—but you'll take him anyway.

—JUDITH VIORST

Come, and Be My Baby
Maya Angelou

The highway is full of big cars going nowhere fast
And folks is smoking anything that'll burn
Some people wrap their lives around a cocktail glass
And you sit wondering
where you're going to turn
I got it.
Come. And be my baby.
Some prophets say the world is gonna end tomorrow
But others say we've got a week or two
The paper is full of every kind of blooming horror
And you sit wondering
What you're gonna do.
I got it.
Come. And be my baby.

Top Ten Ways to Propose

OK, the moment has arrived. She's The One. The only thing left to do is pop that famous question—and pray that the answer is YES! Here are some ideas for Where, When, and How to do it. You already know the Why.

1. **Traditional.** On bended knee, in a restaurant—hey, don't knock the classics.

2. **Send a telegram.** Really. In our high-tech world, bygone technologies take on a certain weight, reverence, and—especially—romance.

3. **By plane.** What list would be complete without a skywriting airplane? Take her out for a picnic in the park and wait for your proposal to fly by. A plane with a banner works too.

4. **Advertise.** Take out a full-page ad in her daily newspaper. Surprise her one morning with a romantic breakfast in bed and include the newspaper on the tray.

5. **In the seventh inning.** If she's a sports fan, have the question flashed across the jumbotron at her favorite arena during a game.

6. **Film buff?** Most movie theaters will let you purchase a short ad that plays onscreen before the feature. Invite your beloved to watch a romantic flick at your local cinema and surprise her with a big screen proposal!

7. **On a silver platter.** Visit one of those make-your-own-pottery studios and design a plate with the words "Will You Marry Me?" on the top. Then arrange with the wait staff at her favorite restaurant to have dessert served on the special plate and hope she's still hungry!

8. **By air.** Have The Question writ large, in lights, wooden planks, etc. Lay the letters out on the roof of your apartment building or house so they can be read from above. Rent a helicopter and fly over your sign.

9. **In her sleep.** Slip the ring on your sleeping beauty's finger in the middle of the night and watch her wake up the next morning and realize she's not dreaming!

10. **Ask her.** And hand her a ticket to Paris along with the ring. Again, don't knock the classics.

The Right Ring

The first step to finding the right engagement ring is going to the right jeweler. Here are a few great places to get you started:

♦

Tiffany & Co. The best of the best. When a girl is presented with a little blue box from Tiffany's, she knows she's receiving something spectacular: The name is synonymous with ultimate luxury. The world's most famous jeweler was the first to introduce the classic six-prong diamond engagement ring, in 1886. Prices range from about $1,000 to $1,000,000. Tiffany has stores throughout the United States, Europe, and Asia, as well as a website: *tiffanys.com* or (800) 843-3269.

♦

United Diamonds, Inc. One of several companies that allows you to "build your own" diamond engagement ring, choosing from a variety of cuts and settings. Prices range from about $500 to $10,000, and customers may design and order rings on line: *uniteddiamonds.com* or (888) 732-2258.

♦

The Clay Pot Located in Brooklyn, New York, the Clay Pot is well known as a source for unique styles of engagement rings made by independent artists. A great alternative for those looking for something a bit nontraditional. Prices range from about $400 to about $5000: *clay-pot.com* or (800) 989-3579.

A Brief History of the Engagement Ring

The tradition of engagement rings as we know them probably began in Ancient Greece, where men and women exchanged rings as tokens of friendship or as a promise to marry. In Roman times, prospective grooms gave their brides rings with keys on them to symbolize the fact that women became part owners of their husbands' property when they married. Ancient Celts, unimpressed by shiny objects, wore promise rings made from the braided hair of their loved ones. The first recorded gift of a diamond engagement ring was in Italy in 1477. In medieval times, rings were offered as part of a dowry or as a sign of the groom's honest intention to marry. While the diamond continued to be popular for engagement rings it only became the standard choice after 1939, when the De Beers family, who controlled the world's supply of diamonds, began an aggressive (and hugely successful) marketing campaign.

The time to be happy is now; the place to be happy is here.

—Robert G. Ingersoll

Couplehood

Paul Reiser

I remember officially proposing. Actually asking this woman to literally, legally, officially, marry me. I couldn't get the words out. I couldn't stop laughing. It felt so dopey. So cliché. "Asking for her hand in marriage." I felt like I was in some bad Ronald Colman movie.

And it was a moment, after all, I had started planning when I was four and saw a girl jump off the monkey bars and watched her hair bounce off her shoulders. I had given this moment a lot of thought. And suddenly, there it was.

I worried I might do it wrong. Should I be on my knee? Two knees? Should knees be involved? Should we be somewhere else? Should I have hired a band? Would someone else be doing this better?

But I asked. And for all the silliness, I was amazed when she actually said "Yes." I mean, not that I thought she'd say "No." We'd discussed it. We knew we would be doing this eventually, so popping the question wasn't a real risk. But still, there's something so powerful about a woman saying "Yes." The mutual agreement, the shared desire, the consent—it's staggering. ♥

18% *of men who pop the question propose on bended knee.*

Ka-Ching!

Q. How much should you spend on an engagement ring?

A. The rule of thumb is two months' salary, but many a man would argue that's just too pricey.

LOVE AND LETTERS: *Alex Tresniowski and Helene Stapinski*

The following article is reprinted from the New York Times

Skywriting? Been done. Engagement ring on the lobster claw? Boring. What Bill Gottlieb was searching for was the perfect way to propose to his sweetheart, Emily Mindel. And that's when Gottlieb got a clue. "Emily does the puzzle every day," said the twenty-seven-year-old New York City corporate lawyer, referring to the venerable *New York Times* crossword. "I thought that would be a romantic way to propose." So last October, Gottlieb called *Times* puzzle editor Will Shortz and asked him to play Cupid. "My reaction was, 'Wow, what a great idea!'" says Shortz, who agreed to weave a wedding proposal into the puzzle as "a onetime thing."

The puzzle ran on January 7. Gottlieb invited Mindel, a Brooklyn Law School student, to brunch. "I just said, 'Let's grab the paper,'" he recalls. "Very casual. But I was so nervous." Gottlieb feigned interest in the rest of the paper while Mindel, twenty-four and a crossword whiz, penciled in answers: 38 Across asked for a Gary Lewis and the Playboys hit ("This Diamond Ring"); 56 Across was a Paula Abdul song ("Will You Marry Me"). Other answers included "Emily," "BillG," and "Yes" (the hoped-for response to 56 Across). "I had the feeling the puzzle was saying something," says Mindel, no dummy. "My heart was racing, and I got all hot and flushed."

With only four squares undone, Mindel faced her beau and stammered, "This puzzle . . ." over and over.

"Her voice was all shaky," he says. "I smiled and asked, "Will you marry me?" Mindel's reply: an eight-letter phrase for absolutely ("Of course!"). Now the couple, fixed up by their families in 1995, are shopping for a ring and planning an intimate wedding (Shortz is on the guest list). When's the big day? Umm, they haven't a clue.

Love Puzzle

If the person you love always seems to be buried in a puzzle, if she shouts out the answers to clues at inappropriate moments, you have only one way to capture her attention: Get a clue and give your beloved cruciverbalist a personalized crossword.

Hire a wordsmith to compose a custom crossword puzzle. You can include all sorts of clues with special meanings that only your precious puzzler will know—romantic memories, personal jokes, even a marriage proposal! For between $125 and $300, depending on the number of clues and the difficulty of composition, these custom puzzle makers will perplex your mate in a way he or she will thoroughly enjoy.

For custom puzzles, contact **Gail Beckman** at *custompuzzles.com* or **Shierdelight** at *shierdelightcrossword.com*.

The Owl and the Pussy-Cat
Edward Lear

The Owl and the Pussy-Cat went to sea
    In a beautiful pea-green boat.
They took some honey, and plenty of money
    Wrapped up in a five-pound note.
The Owl looked up to the stars above,
    And sang to a small guitar,
"O lovely Pussy! O pussy, my love,
What a beautiful Pussy you are,
    You are,
    You are!
What a beautiful Pussy you are!"

Pussy said to the Owl, "You elegant fowl!
    How charmingly sweet you sing!
O let us be married! too long we have tarried:
    But what shall we do for a ring?"
They sailed away, for a year and a day,
    To the land where the Bong-Tree grows,
And there in a wood a Piggy-wig stood,
With a ring at the end of his nose,
    His nose,
    His nose!
With a ring at the end of his nose.

"Dear Pig, are you willing to sell for one shilling
    Your ring?" Said the Piggy, "I will."
So they took it away, and were married next day
    By the Turkey who lives on the hill.
They dined on mince, and slices of quince,
    Which they ate with a runcible spoon;
And hand in hand, on the edge of the sand
    They danced by the light of the moon,
    The moon,
    The moon,
They danced by the light of the moon.

Yes, let us now set forth one of the fundamental truths about marriage: the wife is in charge. Or, to put it another way, the husband is not. Now I can hear your voices crying out:

What patronizing nonsense.
What a dumb generalization.
What a great jacket for the Salvation Army.

LOVE AND MARRIAGE

BILL COSBY

Well, my proof of the point is a simple one. If any man truly believes that he is the boss of his house, then let him to this: pick up the phone, call a wallpaper store, order new wallpaper for one of the rooms in his house, and then put it on. He would have a longer life expectancy sprinkling arsenic on his eggs. Any husband who buys wallpaper, drapes, or even a prayer rug on his own is auditioning for the Bureau of Missing Persons.

Therefore, in spite of what Thomas Jefferson wrote, all men may be created equal, but not to all women, and the loveliest love affair must bear the strain of this inequality once the ceremony is over. When a husband and wife settle down together, there is a natural struggle for power (I wonder why he bothers); and in this struggle, the husband cannot avoid giving up a few things—for example, dinner.

To be fair, I must admit that Camille did wait a few years before allowing me to make this particular sacrifice. I had just sat down at the table one night with her and our three children when I happened to notice that my plate contained only collard greens and brown rice.

"Would you please donate this to the Hare Krishna and bring me my real meal," I said to the gentleman serving the food.

"You have it all," he replied.

"No, what I have is a snack for the North Korean Army. The meat must have slipped off somewhere. Why don't we try to find it together?"

"Mrs. Cosby said we are no longer eating meat."

"She did?" I looked down the table at Camille. "Dear, if I got a letter from the Pope, do you think I could—"

"Bill, meat is bad for us and we just have to cut it out. It's full of fat that could kill you. I'm sorry I forgot to tell you."

"So am I. I could've started eating out at a place where they don't mind who they kill."

"Honey, lots of people are vegetarians."

"And lots of people like to get hit with whips, but I've managed to be happy not joining them."

Nevertheless, I became a vegetarian. A husband should go with the flow of his marriage, even when that flow leads over a cliff.

About two years later, however, I sat down to dinner one night and a steak suddenly appeared on my plate.

"Look at this," I said to the gentleman serving the food. "Someone has lost a steak. Would you please return it to its owner."

"Mrs. Cosby said we are eating meat again," he told me.

"How nice to see the cows come home," I said. ♥

"Marry Me?" Dessert & Cocktail

The most delicious way to propose that we know of. Have a plate made that says "Will You Marry Me?" on it (see suggestion #7 in our Top Ten Ways to Propose on page 118.) Cover it up with this delicious recipe for Chocolate Mousse and serve it to your true love. When she scrapes the bottom of her plate, your proposal will be peeking out from underneath. How can anyone say "No" to a man who knows how to make mousse?

Chocolate Mousse

A double boiler
4 oz. (2 2-oz. squares) high-quality
 semisweet chocolate, chopped fine
2 eggs
2 teaspoons granulated sugar
2 tablespoons strong espresso
1 tablespoon dark rum (if desired)
a stainless steel mixing bowl,
 chilled in freezer 1 hour
½ cup (approximately ¼ pint) very cold
 heavy whipping cream
1 teaspoon sugar

1. Melt chocolate in double boiler.
2. Separate the eggs and put the yolks in a bowl together with two teaspoons sugar and beat until they become pale yellow and creamy. Add the melted chocolate, coffee, and rum and mix them with a wooden spoon until uniformly combined.
3. Take bowl out of the freezer and add the cream and one teaspoon sugar. Beat until high peaks form, and then fold into the chocolate/egg mixture.
4. Put the egg whites into a clean bowl, whip until they form stiff peaks, then fold gently but thoroughly into chocolate mousse.
5. Spoon the mousse into a bowl, cover with plastic wrap and refrigerate overnight.

Serve with whipped cream and raspberries
to fully cover your proposal.

Raspberry Kir

She said,"Yes!" Toast in celebration of your engagement with this delicious champagne cocktail.

½ cup raspberries
1 teaspoon sugar
1 tablespoon raspberry liqueur
1 bottle very good champagne
Fresh whole raspberries for garnish

1. In a blender, mix the ½ cup raspberries, sugar, and liqueur until pureed. Press through a strainer and refrigerate until needed.
2. To serve, spoon one tablespoon of the puree into each chilled champagne glass, fill with champagne, garnish with a few raspberries, and serve.

The best and most beautiful things in the world cannot be seen or even touched. They must be felt with the heart.

—HELEN KELLER

The Passionate Shepherd to His Love
CHRISTOPHER MARLOWE

Come live with me and be my love,
And we will all the pleasures prove
That hills and valleys, dales and fields
And all the craggy mountains yields.

There we will sit upon the rocks
And see the shepherds feed their flocks,
By shallow rivers to whose falls
Melodious birds sing madrigals.

And I will make thee beds of roses
With a thousand fragrant posies,
A cap of flowers and a kirtle
Embroidered all with leaves of myrtle.

A gown made of the finest wool
Which from our pretty lambs we pull;
Fair lined slippers for the cold,
With buckles of the purest gold;

A belt of straw and ivy buds,
With coral clasps and amber studs:
And if these pleasures may thee move,
Come live with me and be my love.

The shepherds' swains shall dance and sing
For thy delight each May morning:
If these delights thy mind may move,
Then live with me and be my love.

They're Playing Our Song
Top Ten Wedding Dance Songs

There are truly too many great love songs to choose from, but if you need some inspiration, here are our top picks for the first time you share the dance floor as husband and wife:

1. "The Way You Look Tonight" by Frank Sinatra
2. "Can't Help Falling in Love" by Elvis Presley
3. "Unchained Melody" by the Righteous Brothers
4. "Everything I Do" by Bryan Adams
5. "How Do I Live" by Trisha Yearwood
6. "Chances Are" by Johnny Mathis
7. "My Heart Will Go On" by Celine Dion
8. "At This Moment" by Billy Vera and The Beaters
9. "I Don't Want to Miss a Thing" by Aerosmith
10. "I'll Stand by You" by The Pretenders

Gone with the Wind

Clark Gable and Vivien Leigh, 1939

SCARLETT
You're a fool, Rhett Butler, when you know I shall always love another man.

RHETT
Stop it. Do you hear me, Scarlett? Stop it! No more of that talk! *(he kisses her)*

SCARLETT
Rhett, don't. I shall faint.

RHETT
I want you to faint. That's what you were meant for. None of the fools you've ever known have kissed you like this, have they? Your Charles or your Frank or your stupid Ashley! *(they kiss)*

RHETT
Say you're going to marry me. Say yes. Say it.

SCARLETT
Yes.

RHETT
Are you sure you meant it? You don't want to take it back?

SCARLETT
No.

RHETT
Look at me and try to tell me the truth. Did you say yes because of my money?

SCARLETT
Well, yes. Partly.

From the Writings of Charles Darwin

Celebrated naturalist Charles Darwin married Emma Wedgwood on January 29, 1839. Their lives together ended with his death, in 1882.

This is the Question

MARRY

Children—(if it please God)—constant companion, (friend in old age) who will feel interested in one, object to be beloved and played with—better than a dog anyhow—Home, and someone to take care of house—Charms of music and female chit-chat. These things good for one's health. Forced to visit and receive relations but terrible loss of time.

My God, it is intolerable to think of spending one's whole life, like a neuter bee, working, working and nothing after all.

—No, no won't do.—

Imagine living all one's day solitarily in smoky dirty London House.—Only picture to yourself a nice soft wife on a sofa with good fire, and books and music perhaps—compare this vision with the dingy reality of Grt. Marlboro' St. Marry—Marry—Marry Q.E.D.

NOT MARRY

No children, (no second life) no one to care for one in old age.—What is the use of working without sympathy from near and dear friends—who are near and dear friends to the old except relatives.

Freedom to go where one liked—Choice of Society and little of it. Conversation of clever men at clubs.—

Not forced to visit relatives, and to bend in every trifle—to have the expense and anxiety of children—perhaps quarrelling.

Loss of time—cannot read in the evenings—fatness and idleness—anxiety and respon-sibility—less money for books etc.—if many children forced to gain one's bread.—(But then it is very bad for one's health to work too much)

Perhaps my wife won't like London; then the sentence is banishment and degradation with indolent idle fool—

On the reverse side he wrote:

It being proved necessary to marry—When? Soon or Late. The Governor says soon for otherwise bad if one has children—one's character is more flexible—one's feelings more lively, and if one does not marry soon, one misses so much good pure happiness.—

But then if I married tomorrow: there would be an infinity of trouble and expense in getting and furnishing a house,—fighting about no Society—morning calls—awkwardness—loss of time every day—(without one's wife was an angel and made one keep industrious)—Then how should I manage all my business if I were obliged to go every day walking with my wife.—Eheu!! I never should know French,—or see the Continent,—or go to America, or go up in a Balloon, or take solitary trip in Wales—poor slave, you will be worse than a negro—And then horrid poverty (without one's wife was better than an angel and had money)—Never mind my boy—Cheer up—One cannot live this solitary life, with groggy old age, friendless and cold and childless staring one in one's face, already beginning to wrinkle. Never mind, trust to chance—keep a sharp look out.—There is many a happy slave—

I and Thou
Martin Buber

Feelings are "entertained": love comes
   to pass.
Feelings dwell in man; but man dwells
   in his love.
That is no metaphor, but the actual truth.
Love does not cling to the I in such a way
as to have the Thou only for its "content,"
its object; but love is between I and Thou. .
. . Love is responsibility
of an I for a Thou.

For one human being to
love another: that is
perhaps the most diffi-
cult of our tasks; the
ultimate, the last test
and proof, the work for
which all other work
is but preparation.

—RAINER MARIA RILKE

Letters of Love

Dylan Thomas to his wife, Caitlin

Welsh poet Dylan Thomas married his wife and fellow bohemian, Caitlin, in the summer of 1937. They were married until his death, in 1953.

April 7, 1950

Caitlin. Just to write down your name like that. Caitlin. I don't have to say My dear, My darling, My sweetheart, though I do say those words, to you in myself, all day and night. Caitlin. And all the words are in that one word. Caitlin, Caitlin, and I can see your blue eyes and your golden hair and your slow smile and your faraway voice. Your faraway voice is saying, now, at my ear, the words you said in your last letter, and thank you, dear, for the love you said and sent. I love you. Never forget that, for one single moment of the long, slow, sad Laugharne day, never forget it in your mazed trances, in your womb & your bones, in our bed at night. I love you. Over this continent I take your love inside me, your love goes with me up in the aeroplaned air, into all the hotel bedrooms where momentarily I open my bag—half full, as ever, of dirty shirts—and lay down my head & do not sleep until dawn because I can hear your heart beat beside me, your voice saying my name and our love above the noise of the night-traffic, above the neon flashing, deep in my loneliness, my love.

Great Romances

HUMPHREY BOGART & LAUREN BACALL

In a place called Hollywood, a "long-term" romance usually has the shelf life of most filming schedules. But for those couples who have beaten the odds (and the tabloids), the legacy of their love will last forever.

He was the man's man who scowled his way across the silver screen. She was the smoldering beauty who captured his heart. Humphrey Bogart and Lauren Bacall were one of Tinsel Town's royal couples. They met in 1944, while filming *To Have and Have Not*, and went on to make three more films together: *The Big Sleep* (1946), *Dark Passage* (1947), and *Key Largo* (1948). Their marriage lasted for twelve years, until Bogie's death, in 1957. In memory of their first film together, where she spoke those famous words, "You know how to whistle, don't you Steve? You just put your lips together and blow," Bacall placed a whistle in his casket. Its inscription read, "If you need me, whistle." Their romance truly was "the stuff that dreams are made of."

Top Ten Wedding Books

Whether you're planning your own wedding or have been asked to participate in someone else's, these books offer inspiration and advice on everything from toasts and traditions to etiquette and vows.

1. *The Knot Guide to Vows and Traditions* by Carley Roney contains a variety of wedding vows, wedding customs and traditions, quotes, and a great list of dance songs. A must have for any bride-to-be.

2. *Timeless Traditions: A Couple's Guide to Wedding Customs Around the World* by Susan Wales and Ann Platz is a great source of inspiration and information about the variety of rituals and traditions practiced by different cultures throughout history.

3. *The Little Book of Weddings* by Will Balliett is a great anthology of writings on weddings. From Princess Diana to Madame Bovary, find out what was behind the veil.

4. *The Little Big Book for Brides* by Katrina Fried and Lena Tabori contains wedding customs and traditions from around the world, touching literary excerpts, poems, recipes, fun facts and trivia, and of course, advice.

5. *The Oxford Book of Marriage* by Helge Rubinstein is a great collection of literary excerpts and poems on marriage and love.

6. *Emily Post's Wedding Etiquette: Cherished Traditions and Contemporary Ideas for a Joyous Celebration* by Peggy Post answers every imaginable question about etiquette. This how-to and what-if bible should be required reading for the couple AND their families.

7. *Legendary Brides: From the Most Romantic Weddings Ever, Inspired Ideas for Today's Brides* by Letitia Baldrige is a must for anyone woman who ever wished for a fairy tale wedding.

8. *A Wedding Ceremony to Remember: Perfect Words for the Perfect Wedding* by Marty Younkin offers great advice, from writing your own wedding vows to organizing your wedding party.

9. *Into the Garden: A Wedding Anthology: Poetry and Prose on Love and Marriage* by Robert Hass is a comprehensive collection of poetry and prose.

10. *Sacred Threshold: Rituals and Readings for a Wedding with Spirit* by Gertrud Mueller Nelson and Christopher Witt offers guidance on choosing the right place, participants, symbols, prayers, format, readings, and music for your wedding.

To My Dear and Loving Husband
Anne Bradstreet

If ever two were one, then surely we.
If ever man were loved by wife, then thee;
If ever wife was happy in a man,
Compare with me ye women if you can.
I prize thy love more than whole
    mines of gold,
Or all the riches that the East doth hold.
My love is such that rivers cannot quench,
Nor ought but love from thee,
    give recompence.
They love is such I can no way repay,
The heavens reward thee manifold I pray.
Then while we live, in love lets so persevere,
That when we live no more, we may live ever.

You're the Top

COLE PORTER

At words poetic, I'm so pathetic
That I always have found it best,
Instead of getting 'em off me chest,
To let 'em rest unexpressed.
I hate parading
My serenading
As I'll probably miss a bar,
But if this ditty
Is not so pretty,
At least it'll tell you
How great you are

You're the top!
You're the Colosseum.
You're the top!
You're the Louvre Museum.
You're a melody from a symphony
by Strauss,
You're a Bendel bonnet,
A Shakespeare sonnet,
You're Mickey Mouse.
You're the Nile,
You're the Tow'r of Pisa
You're the smile
On the Mona Lisa.
I'm a worthless check, a total wreck,
a flop,
But if, Baby, I'm the bottom,
You're the top!

Your words poetic are not pathetic
On the other hand, boy, you shine
And I can feel after every line
A thrill divine
Down my spine.
Now gifted humans like Vincent Youmans
Might think that your song is bad,
But for a person who's just rehearsin'
Well I gotta say this my lad:
You're the top!
You're Mahatma Gandhi.
You're the top!
You're Napoleon brandy.
You're the purple light of a summer
night in Spain,

You're the National Gall'ry,
You're Garbo's sal'ry,
You're cellophane.
You're sublime,
You're a turkey dinner,
You're the time
Of the Derby winner.

I'm a toy balloon that is fated soon
to pop,
But if, Baby, I'm the bottom
You're the top!

You're the top!
You're a Ritz hot toddy.
You're the top!
You're a Brewster body.
You're the boats that glide on the
sleepy Zuider Zee,
You're a Nathan panning,
You're Bishop Manning,
You're broccoli.
You're a prize,
You're a night at Coney,
You're the eyes
Of Irene Bordoni.
I'm a broken doll, a fol-de-rol,
a blop,
But if, Baby, I'm the bottom
You're the top!

You're the top!
You're an Arrow collar.
You're the top!
You're a Coolidge dollar.
You're the nimble tread of the feet
of Fred Astaire.

You're an O'Neill drama,
You're Whistler's mama,
You're Camembert.
You're a rose,
You're Inferno's Dante,
You're the nose
On the great Durante.
I'm just in the way, as the French
    would say
"De trop,"
But if, Baby, I'm the bottom
You're the top.

You're the top!
You're a Waldorf Salad.
You're the top!
You're a Berlin ballad.
You're a baby grand of a lady and
    a gent,
You're an old Dutch master,
You're Mrs. Astor,
You're Pepsodent.
You're romance,
You're the steppes of Russia,
You're the pants on a Roxy usher.
I'm a lazy lout that's just about
    to stop,
But if, Baby, I'm the bottom
You're the top.

You're the top!
You're a dance in Bali.
You're the top!
You're a hot tamale.
You're an angel, you, simply too, too,
    too diveen,
You're a Botticelli,
You're Keats
You're Shelley,
You're Ovaltine.
You're boon,
You're the dam at Boulder,
You're the moon over Mae West's
    shoulder.
I'm a nominee of the G.O.P.
Or GOP,
But if, Baby, I'm the bottom
You're the top.

You're the top!
You're the Tower of Babel.
You're the top!
You're the Whitney Stable.
By the River Rhine,
You're a sturdy stein of beer,
You're a dress from Saks's,
You're next years taxes,
You're stratosphere.
You're my thoist,
You're a Drumstick Lipstick,
You're da foist
In da Irish svipstick.
I'm a frightened frog
That can find no log
To hop,
But if, Baby, I'm the bottom
You're the top!

too eager to send the couple to bed, and assisted them in removing their clothes. Eventually, couples learned to throw the bride's garter to the crowd as a distraction.

Old, New, Borrowed, Blue . . . The superstition found in the old rhyme is rife with symbolism. The "old" represents the bride's family and her past; the "new", hope for the future; the "borrowed", friendship; and the "blue" represents purity, loyalty, and love. In ancient Israel, brides used to wear the color for that reason, and it became part of this folklore tradition.

Behind the Veil The tradition of the wedding veil arose independently in many cultures. In some cultures, such as ancient Rome, it was intended to protect the bride from the evil eye of jealous rivals. In other cultures, such as ancient Egypt, India, and China, where arranged marriages held sway, it was considered bad luck for the groom to see the bride, not merely on their wedding day, but ever before the ceremony. Korean brides forego veils, but ward off evil spirits by painting a large red dot on each cheek.

Crossing the Threshold The tradition of a bride being carried across the threshold has several origins. First, it was done to protect the bride from evil spirits lurking in the floor. Second, it was considered bad luck for the bride to fall as she walked through the door, so she was lifted instead. And third, it preserved the bride's reputation of maidenly modesty—it wouldn't be proper to look too eager to reach the marriage bed!

The Origins of Classic Wedding Traditions

Stealing the Bride The tradition of the groom standing to the right of his bride stems from a time when the bride was at risk of being kidnapped at the alter and her husband-to-be needed his right hand free to grab his sword in order to fend off any unwanted guests. If the groom required additional help, his best man and groomsmen were there to protect the wedding couple.

Who's Who? Bridesmaids and groomsmen wear matching clothes in order to trick any evil spirits who may wish to bother the bride and groom. It was believed the spirits would not be able to determine who was who and therefore would leave the newlyweds in peace.

Throwing the Garter Ever wonder why the bride's garter gets thrown to the crowd during the wedding reception? The post-wedding celebrations could get quite rowdy, and wedding guests would accompany the newlyweds to the bridal chamber. Sometimes guests were a little

The most expensive wedding was the $44 million nuptials of Mohammed, son of Shiek Rashid Ben Saeed Al Maktoum, to Princess Salama in Dubai, Saudi Arabia.

Did You Know ... Nine out of ten Americans will be married at some point in their lives. ♥ *The age of today's average bride is 25 and groom, 26.* ♥ The average cost of a wedding is a whopping $22,360. ♥ *80 percent of American men, and 50 percent of American women say they would marry the same person if they had it to do all over again.* ♥ Engagement and wedding rings are worn on the fourth finger of the left hand because it was once believed that a vein in that finger led directly to the heart. ♥ *The longest engagement lasted 67 years. The couple was eventually married at the age of 82.* ♥ The first diamond engagement ring is said to have been given by Archduke Maximillian of Austria to Mary of Burgundy in 1477. ♥ *In 1995, the largest mass wedding was held in Seoul, South Korea. Officiating the ceremony was Sun Myung Moon, who married 35,000 people at the Olympic Stadium— with an additional 325,000 people taking their vows via satellite around the world.*

Letters of Love

Thomas Woodrow Wilson to his wife, Ellen

Thomas Woodrow Wilson, twenty-eighth president of the United States, married his wife, Ellen Axson Wilson, on June 24, 1885. They were happily married for twenty-nine years.

May 9, 1886

. . . I've been reckoning up, in a tumultuous, heartful sort of way, the value of my little wife to me. I can't state the result—there are no terms of value in which it can be stated—but perhaps I can give you some idea of what its proportions would be if it were stated. She has taken all real pain out of my life: her wonderful loving sympathy exalts even my occasional moods of despondency into a sort of hallowed sadness out of which I come stronger and better. She has given to my ambitions a meaning, an assurance, and a purity which they never had before: with her by my side, ardently devoted to me and to my cause, understanding all my thoughts and all my aims, I feel that I can make the utmost of every power I possess. She has brought into my life the sunshine which was needed to keep it from growing stale and morbid: that has steadily been bringing back into my spirits their old gladness and boyhood, their old delight in play and laughter: —that sweetest sunshine of deep, womanly love, unfailing, gentle patience, even happy spirits, and spontaneous mirth, that is purest, swiftest tonic to a spirit prone to fret and apt to flag. She has given me that perfect rest of heart and mind of whose existence I had never so much as dreamed before she came to me, which springs out of assured oneness of hope and sympathy—and which, for me, means life and success. Above all she has given me herself to live for! Her arms are able to hold me up against the world: her eyes are able to charm away every care; her words are my solace and inspiration and all because her love is my life. . .

Night & Day

COLE PORTER

Like the beat, beat, beat of the tom-tom
When the jungle shadows fall,
Like the tick, tick, tock of the stately clock
As it stands against the wall,
Like the drip, drip, drip, of the raindrops,
When the summer show'r is through,
So a voice within me keeps repeating,
You, you, you.

Night and day you are the one,
Only you beneath the moon and under
    the sun,
Whether near to me or far,
It's no matter, darling, where you are,
I think of you, night and day.

Day and night why is it so,
That this longing for you follows
    wherever I go?
In the roaring traffic's boom,
In the silence of my lonely room,
I think of you, night and day.

Night and day under the hide of me,
    There's an, oh, such a
    hungry yearning,
        burning inside of me.
    And its torment won't
    be through
'Til you let me spend my
        life making love to you
Day and night, night and day.

*The secret of a happy
marriage remains a secret.*

—HENRY YOUNGMAN

136

Wild Weddings!

Looking for a less-traditional setting for your wedding ceremony? Your search is over. For the gal and guy who'd never dream of a classic church wedding, we've dug up some truly wild and even wacky ways to the tie the knot. These are guaranteed to leave a lasting memory of your Big Day.

Y'argh! How would you like your nuptials crashed by a bunch of sword-wielding, swash-buckling sea dogs? Will your beloved save you before you walk the plank? If a pirate wedding is what you're looking for, then come on board Treasure Island's HMS *Britannia*, a full-scale replica of a pirate ship! The package comes complete with fresh floral arrangements and access to the Buccaneer Bay Patio, where your guests can "y'argh" and "blarg" all they want!: *treasureislandlasvegas.com* or (800) 944-7444.

Meow! For only $200, you can get married in a wildlife sanctuary with 24 different species of felines, and maybe you'll find yourself purring, too: *wild-weddings.com* or (813) 920-4130.

Vroom! Vroom! Anyone who's ever had a Harley-Davidson can attest to how much they love their bikes. So shouldn't Harley be there on your special day? Now you can get married inside the Orlando Harley-Davidson First Factory dealership, complete with an old-fash-ioned gourmet barbecue reception: *orlandoharley.com/wedding* or (877) 740-3770.

Fairy Tales Can Come True Do you dream of looking like Cinderella on your wedding day? Do you long to be taken to the church in a glass coach? It's all possible if you get married at the Walt Disney Resorts in Florida, which offers a wide variety of Disney-themed weddings. Be wed as Beauty and the Beast or Pocahontas at Fort Wilderness—you can even turn your wed-ding into a tea ceremony with the Mad Hatter: *disneyweddings.com* or (407) 828-3400.

Sizzle! Want a steamy start to your marriage? Then head over to White Island, off the coast of New Zealand, and say your vows against the spectacular backdrop of an active volcano! Clink champagne glasses next to sulfur-laden jets; toss the bouquet on a field of pumice and obsidian; lock lips as man and wife with a seismic rumble! The package includes gas masks and helmets: *chc-weddings.co.nz/index*.

Yippee! Have you ever felt like saying your vows thousands of feet up in the air with a sky-diving minister? Of course you have. For $1,200, you get the private use of a plane, jump masters, pictures, a video, and of course, champagne and flowers: *weddingdreams.com* or (888) 293-3658.

Brrrrrr! A winter wonderland of crystalline pillars, windows, and sculptures, the Icehotel is rebuilt from ice and snow anew every year. Between Christmas Day and late April, you can get married inside this ephemeral palace's chapel in the village of Jukkasjärvi in northern Lapland, Sweden, for a truly unique wedding, before it all melts back into the Torne River. After the ceremony, you and your loved ones can go dogsledding, take a snowmobile tour, or even relax in an outdoor sauna beneath the Northern Lights: *icehotel.com*.

Take the Plunge! Nothing gets rid of those wedding-day jitters like free-falling 175 feet! For the truly adventurous, exchange your vows in midair as you bungee-jump, hand in hand, off a tower: *weddingdreams.com* or (888) 293-3658.

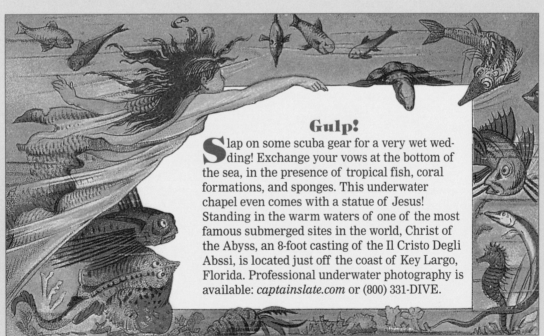

Gulp!

Slap on some scuba gear for a very wet wedding! Exchange your vows at the bottom of the sea, in the presence of tropical fish, coral formations, and sponges. This underwater chapel even comes with a statue of Jesus! Standing in the warm waters of one of the most famous submerged sites in the world, Christ of the Abyss, an 8-foot casting of the Il Cristo Degli Abssi, is located just off the coast of Key Largo, Florida. Professional underwater photography is available: *captainslate.com* or (800) 331-DIVE.

Forty percent of wedded Americans are married to their first love.

A Very Vegas Wedding
The Best Las Vegas Chapels

In a hurry to get hitched? A Las Vegas wedding may be just the thing for you. There's no blood test, no waiting period, and it only costs $35 for a marriage license! Just about any hotel on the strip worth its salt has a wedding chapel, but these are the cream of the crop:

♥ At **Cupid's Wedding Chapel** you can add live music or celebrity impersonators to your ceremony to make your special day exceptional. In addition to your garden-variety civil and religious weddings, Cupid's offers traditional Jewish ceremonies: *cupidswedding.com* or (800) 543-2933.

♦ If you're one of those people who feel that Vegas isn't Vegas without Elvis, then **Graceland Wedding Chapel** is the wedding chapel for you. In the tradition of Jon Bon Jovi and Lorenzo Lamas and their mates, tie the knot, drink champagne, and enjoy a first-class Elvis entertainer on your wedding day: *gracelendchapel.com* or (800) 824-5732.

Vegas Baby!

Feel like a quickie Vegas wedding? You'll be in some famous company. Some of the more notable nuptials that have taken place in Sin City are: Dennis Rodman and Carmen Electra, Angelina Jolie and Billy Bob Thornton, Jon Bon Jovi and Dorothea Hurley, Paul Newman and Joanne Woodward, Elvis and Priscilla Presley, Frank Sinatra and Mia Farrow, Mickey Rooney and Ava Gardner *and* Betty Jane Rase *and* Martha Vickers *and*... well, you get the point.

> *My wife Mary and I have been married for forty-seven years and not once have we had an argument serious enough to consider divorce; murder, yes, but divorce, never.*
>
> —JACK BENNY

♣ Elvis fans may recognize **The Hitching Post** from his *Viva Las Vegas* video clip. On the scene for seventy-five years, this famous chapel boasts multilingual wedding services and is open twenty-four hours a day for those 3-a.m. elopements: *hitchingpostwedd@aol.com* or (800) 572-5530.

♠ This is the one that started it all. When it opened, in 1942, **The Little Church of the West** was the first on the Vegas strip. Mickie Rooney loved this strange timber chapel so much, he got married in it eight times! *littlechurchlv.com* or (800) 821-2452.

♥ **The Little White Wedding Chapel** offers hot-air balloon, helicopter, and drive-through ceremonies. Tops on their roster of famous clientele are Natalie Maines of the Dixie Chicks and pro wrestler Stone Cold Steve Austin: *alittlewhitechapel.com* or (800) 545-8111.

> *Never go to bed angry. Stay up and fight.*
>
> —PHYLLIS DILLER

Wedding Customs Around the World

Bound Together The term "tying the knot" comes from the Celtic tradition where the bride and groom's hands are tied together.

Loosen Up! In Syria, it is thought that if the groom marries with a knot in his clothing, he will become impotent.

Body Paint Henna Tattoos or Mehendi are a traditional adornment in Hindu and Muslim weddings. The dark brown color of the Mehendi is a symbol of prosperity and luck. Mehendi is worn by the bride and sometimes the groom on the hands and feet.

Some Like It Hot The traditional color of the Chinese wedding dress is red.

The Men You've Loved
David Ignatow

The men you've loved are one man.
The women I've known are one woman:
I hold your hand and look
into your face with love, in peace.
We lie down together
and nothing matters
but making each of us
the first and the last.

Make a Wish After a wedding ceremony in Croatia, guests circle a well three times, in honor of the Trinity, and toss in apples to wish the couple fruitful life.

Mazeltof! The breaking of the glass in Jewish wedding ceremonies symbolizes the destruction of the Temple of Jerusalem. It is also said to represent the fragility of life.

Now That's Friendship In Latvia, the engaged couple will often pick another married couple, usually friends, to plan the wedding for them.

From the Altar to the Grave In Austria, the shirt the groom wears to his wedding is given to him by the bride. After the big day, he stores it in a safe place and when he dies, he is dressed and buried in his wedding shirt.

Love is the only thing you get more of by giving it away.

—TOM WILSON

If the Shoe Fits It is considered good luck in England for a bride to carry a horseshoe adorned with ribbons and flowers on her way to the church.

Those Glasses are Toast The Greeks aren't the only ones who break things at their weddings. In Russia, it is tradition to throw champagne glasses on the floor after the wedding toast.

Cone Heads In Iran, it is tradition for the crumbs of a decorated sugar cone to be shaved over the heads of the newlyweds after they exchange their vows.

Bird Walk In Korea, it is not uncommon to include ducks and geese, who mate for life, in the wedding procession.

Sweet Feet In Scotland, friends of the bride and groom will wash and perfume the feet of the newlywed couple in order to set them on a new path.

Thinking About Eloping?

Twenty-six U.S. states allow you to get married the same day your wedding license is issued (see list below). The caveat is that there may be a month's wait from the time you apply for the license until its receipt. The legal age for marriage varies from state to state, as do the requirements for proof of identity and age. As tempting as it may be to climb down the rose trellis and drive off into the night, make sure you plan ahead (just a little)!

Alabama, Arizona, Arkansas, California, Colorado, Connecticut, Georgia, Hawaii, Idaho, Kentucky, Montana, Nebraska, Nevada, New Mexico, North Carolina, North Dakota, Ohio, Oklahoma, Rhode Island, South Dakota, Tennessee, Utah, Vermont, Virginia, West Virginia, Wyoming

The Gift of Gold In Mexico, it is traditional for the groom to give his bride 13 gold coins as a symbol of trust and devotion.

A Leap of Faith It is an African-American wedding custom for the bride and groom to jump over a broom, a symbol for brushing away malevolent spirits. This tradition originated in the time of slavery when slaves were not permitted to legally marry and therefore sought a symbolic sanction of their union.

A Hot Bouquet The bride's bouquet is set on fire in Switzerland to symbolize the end of her maidenhood.

Pin Money At Cuban weddings, each man must dance with the bride and pin money on her dress. In the Philippines, both men and women are "pinned."

Love One Another
Kahlil Gibran

Love one another, but make not a bond of love:
Let it rather be a moving sea between the
    shores of your souls.
Fill each other's cup but drink not from one cup.
Give one another of your bread but eat not
    from the same loaf.
Sing and dance together and be joyous, but
    let each one of you be alone,
Even as the strings of a lute are alone
    though they quiver with the same music.
Give your hearts, but not into each
    other's keeping.
For only the hand of Life can contain
    your hearts.
And stand together yet not too near together:
For the pillars of the temple stand apart,
And the oak tree and the cypress grow not
    in each other's shadow.

A Brief History of the Wedding Cake

The origins of the wedding cake can be found in a friendly assault on the bride. In ancient Rome, well-wishers showered brides with grains of wheat to symbolize fertility. In later years, the wheat was baked into small cakes, which also were thrown at the bride or, in a gentler tradition, crumbled over the couple's head. Medieval English wedding feasts featured the piling of sweet buns in front of the happy couple. If they could kiss over the top of the pile, they were assured a happy life together. In the seventeenth century, a French chef came up with the idea of securing the precarious heap of cakes with icing, although the first tiered cake was not served until 1859 at the wedding of one of Queen Victoria's daughters. In the nineteenth century, rice replaced wheat as the symbolic grain tossed at the bride, although now many wedding parties prefer to toss birdseed (since rice injures wild birds who eat it) or blow bubbles, which symbolize happy wishes for the couple.

The oldest groom on record is Harry Stevens, who at the age of 103 married 83-year-old Thelma Lucas.

Top This!

Cake toppers became popular in the decoration-obsessed Victorian era. They were first made of flour paste and sometimes included lucky horseshoes. Others featured wedding bells hung on the stems of flowers. In the 1920s, whimsical toppers became fashionable as bakers placed kewpie-doll couples on top of cakes. A popular cake topper of the 1940s featured a man in uniform with a bride in white. By the 1960s, couples were putting whole wedding dioramas on their cakes, with little figures representing the bride, groom, bridesmaids, ushers, and clergy. Larger cakes had to be made—some as big as 6 feet in diameter—to accommodate the crowd.

"I Love You" Birthday Cake

With bright pink frosting and fresh raspberries for decoration, this heart-shaped birthday cake will turn even the most cynical heart to mush.

Cake

2$\frac{1}{4}$ cups white flour, sifted
1$\frac{1}{2}$ cups sugar
3 teaspoons baking powder
1 teaspoon salt
8 tablespoons (1 stick) butter
$\frac{2}{3}$ cup milk
1 tablespoon vanilla
$\frac{1}{3}$ cup milk
2 eggs

Icing

1 box confectioners' sugar
2 tablespoons milk
8 tablespoons (1 stick) butter
1$\frac{1}{2}$ cups raspberries, rinsed and patted dry

1. Preheat oven to 350° F. Butter and flour two heart-shaped cake pans and set aside.
2. In a large bowl, mix together flour, sugar, baking powder, and salt.
3. Continue to mix, slowly adding butter, $\frac{2}{3}$ cup milk, and vanilla. Beat vigorously.
4. Add another $\frac{1}{3}$ cup milk and eggs. Beat for two minutes, then pour into baking pans. Bake 30 to 35 minutes. Let cool in pans.
5. To make icing, combine sugar, milk and softened butter in a bowl. Slowly beat in 1 cup raspberries, mashing them as you go, until smooth. Add milk as needed.
6. When cake layers are completely cool, turn them out of the pans, and turn one layer upside down on cake platter. Ice what is now the flat top of this layer, stack other layer on top, and finish icing cake. Garnish with remaining $\frac{1}{2}$ cup raspberries, spelling "I ♥ U" on the top.

It Was A Quiet Way
Emily Dickinson

It was a quiet way
He asked if I was his.
I made no answer of the tongue
But answer of the eyes.

And then he bore me high
Before this mortal noise,
With swiftness as of chariots
And distance as of wheels.

The world did drop away
As countries from the feet
Of him that leaneth in balloon
an ether street.

The gulf behind was not—
The continents were new.
Eternity it was—before
Eternity was due.

No seasons were to us—
It was not night nor noon,
For sunrise stopped upon the place
And fastened it in dawn.

Marriage is the alliance of two people, one of whom never remembers birthdays and the other who never forgets.

—OGDEN NASH

Top Ten Honeymoon Destinations

Whether you're looking for rest and relaxation or the adventure of a lifetime, there's something on this list for every taste. All our picks have one quality in common: the perfect setting for romance.

1. **Hawaii** With its exquisite weather, rockin' nightlife, breathtaking volcanoes, valleys, waterfalls, and black-sand beaches, Hawaii is THE dream-come-true honeymoon destination for newlyweds.

2. **Walt Disney World, Orlando, Florida** Get ready to be a kid again. Any one of the great honeymoon packages offers deluxe accommodations at a select Disney resort and unlimited passes to any of the fun-filled theme parks.

3. **Tahiti** With towering mountain peaks, lush valleys, and rain forests, "The Island of Love" provides the intimate backdrop for an unforgettable tropical romance.

4. **Italy** Take a gondola ride in Venice. Bask in the Renaissance beauty of Florence. Rent a villa on Lake Como. No matter what your destination is, Italy will not disappoint.

5. **Greece** Spend a few days among the ruins in the classical city of Athens, followed by a cruise to the spectacular islands of Mykonos and Santorini. You won't want to come home!

6. **U.S. Virgin Islands** The three major islands that make up this U.S. territory, St. Croix, St. John, and St. Thomas, all offer exquisite accommodations, beautiful beaches, and activities that cater to every interest.

7. **Peru** Adventurous couples will enjoy hiking the Inca Trail. Revel in the majestic beauty of Machu Picchu, perched high in the Andes Mountains—a memory to last your whole lives together.

8. **Paris** The City of Light is not called the most romantic place for nothing! Stroll along the Seine, take in a museum, and have a romantic dinner at one of the hundreds of brasseries. Paris really is for lovers!

9. **Thailand** For those whose taste runs to the more exotic, Phuket, Thailand, is a must. This tropical paradise offers pristine beaches, great sightseeing, and appropriately wild nightlife.

10. **Niagara Falls** Take a heart-pounding ride on the *Maid of the Mist* in the gorge beneath the majestic falls (slickers provided), and kiss in the Cave of the Winds, behind the rushing water. No wonder Niagara Falls is a longtime traditional favorite for honeymoons.

The Origin of the Honeymoon

The word honeymoon comes from the ancient European tradition of drinking ale brewed from honey (known as bride-ale) for the month after marriage. According to legend, Attila the Hun drank so much of this honey wine at his wedding feast that he died. By the eighteenth century, the term had come to mean a trip that the bride and groom took together after their wedding, usually lasting about two weeks.

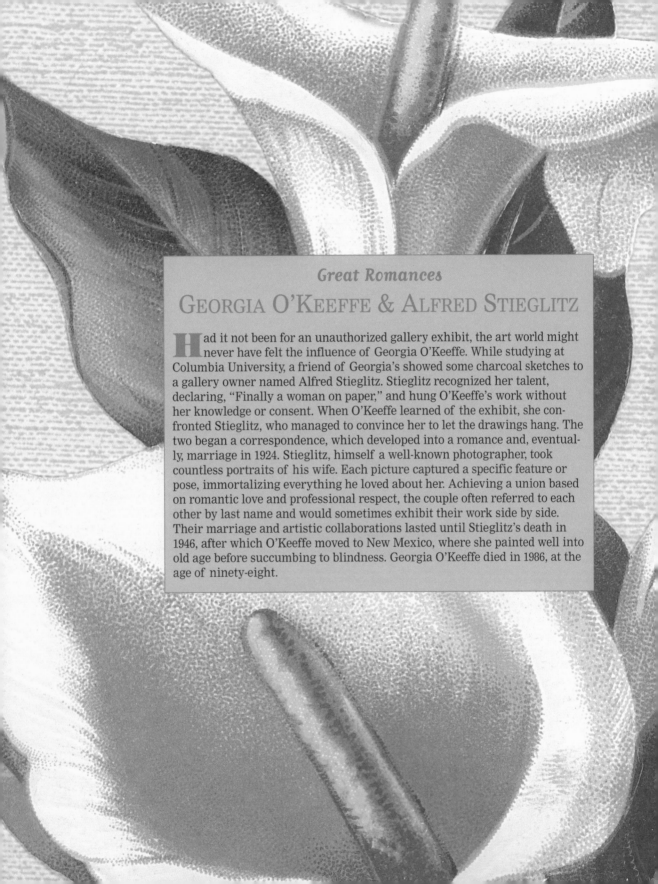

GEORGIA O'KEEFFE & ALFRED STIEGLITZ

Had it not been for an unauthorized gallery exhibit, the art world might never have felt the influence of Georgia O'Keeffe. While studying at Columbia University, a friend of Georgia's showed some charcoal sketches to a gallery owner named Alfred Stieglitz. Stieglitz recognized her talent, declaring, "Finally a woman on paper," and hung O'Keeffe's work without her knowledge or consent. When O'Keeffe learned of the exhibit, she confronted Stieglitz, who managed to convince her to let the drawings hang. The two began a correspondence, which developed into a romance and, eventually, marriage in 1924. Stieglitz, himself a well-known photographer, took countless portraits of his wife. Each picture captured a specific feature or pose, immortalizing everything he loved about her. Achieving a union based on romantic love and professional respect, the couple often referred to each other by last name and would sometimes exhibit their work side by side. Their marriage and artistic collaborations lasted until Stieglitz's death in 1946, after which O'Keeffe moved to New Mexico, where she painted well into old age before succumbing to blindness. Georgia O'Keeffe died in 1986, at the age of ninety-eight.

An Ancient Institution
A Brief History of Marriage

There are probably no human traditions older than marriage. Originally, the institution was created to cement ties between families and to provide support for children. It was not until the late eighteenth century in Europe that romantic love even became central to the process. Before that, love was expected to develop over time between married people, but not to be the basis for forming a union.

Throughout the ages there have been many variations on the theme and across the continents. Some cultures have practiced polygamy, in which one man may take many wives, while the Nyinba people of western Nepal practice a form of fraternal polyandry, in which one woman marries a group of brothers. In ancient Hebrew communities, a man was expected to marry the widow of his deceased brother in order to keep family wealth intact. In feudal China, each of a man's multiple wives occupied a different status within the household. Traditional culture in Dahomey allowed two women to marry each other, one becoming the "father" of the children her wife bore with secret lovers.

Some of the first laws relating to marriage and divorce were codified several thousand years ago in the ancient *Mesopotamian Code of Hamurabi*. These laws included provisions about returning a bride's wedding gifts if she proved infertile, whom a widow might marry, and how a man's concubines might appear in public.

Although today marriage is often thought of as a civil union involving laws of the state, for many centuries it was a matter of religious and community sanction. In ancient Jewish custom, a man simply brought his bride from her father's house to his, and the couple received the spoken blessings of his parents and their guests. In the ninth century, the Christian church began sanctifying the marriages of men and women who presented themselves at the church door.

Until the era of the Enlightenment in Europe, most marriages were arranged by family members and included property exchange, or a dowry. In the case of aristocratic families, large areas of land might be included in the deal. For more common folk, a goat or piece of furniture might change hands. The American custom of the "hope chest," in which a woman collects objects she will need when she is married, is a survivor of this tradition.

Even after personal choice became the main factor in marriage, it remained traditional for a man to ask a woman's father for her hand. It is also a longstanding and widespread practice for fathers to "give away" their daughters at the altar. Until the mid-nineteenth century in Europe and America, laws defined married women as *femme couverts*—literally, "covered women." This meant that they ceased to exist legally as individuals and became the possessions of their husbands.

Marriage has come a long way since then. Modern weddings focus much more on the notion of partnership. Many church rituals no longer use the term obey in the bride's part of the liturgy, and couples commonly write their own vows, often including personal words of affection and commitment as well as romantic readings and poetry. Though arranged marriages are still practiced in some parts of the world, love has certainly evolved into the number-one reason for tying the knot.

Queen Victoria started the tradition of wearing bridal white when she married Albert in 1840.

The River-Merchant's Wife: A Letter

Rihaku (Li T'ai Po), translated by Ezra Pound

While my hair was still cut straight across my forehead
I played about the front gate, pulling flowers.
You came by on bamboo stilts, playing horse,
You walked about my seat, playing with blue plums.
And we went on living in the village of Chokan:
Two small people, without dislike or suspicion.

At fourteen I married My Lord you.
I never laughed, being bashful.
Lowering my head, I looked at the wall.
Called to, a thousand times, I never looked back.

At fifteen I stopped scowling,
I desired my dust to be mingled with yours
Forever and forever and forever.
Why should I climb the look out?

At sixteen you departed,
You went into far Ku-to-en, by the river of swirling eddies,
And you have been gone for five months.
The monkeys make sorrowful noise overhead.

You dragged your feet when you went out.
By the gate now, the moss is grown,
        the different mosses,
Too deep to clear them away!
The leaves fall early this autumn,
        in wind.
The paired butterflies are already
        yellow with August
Over the grass in the West garden;
They hurt me. I grow older.
If you are coming down through the
        narrows of the river Kiang,
Please let me know beforehand,
And I will come out to meet you
        As far as Cho-Fu-Sa.

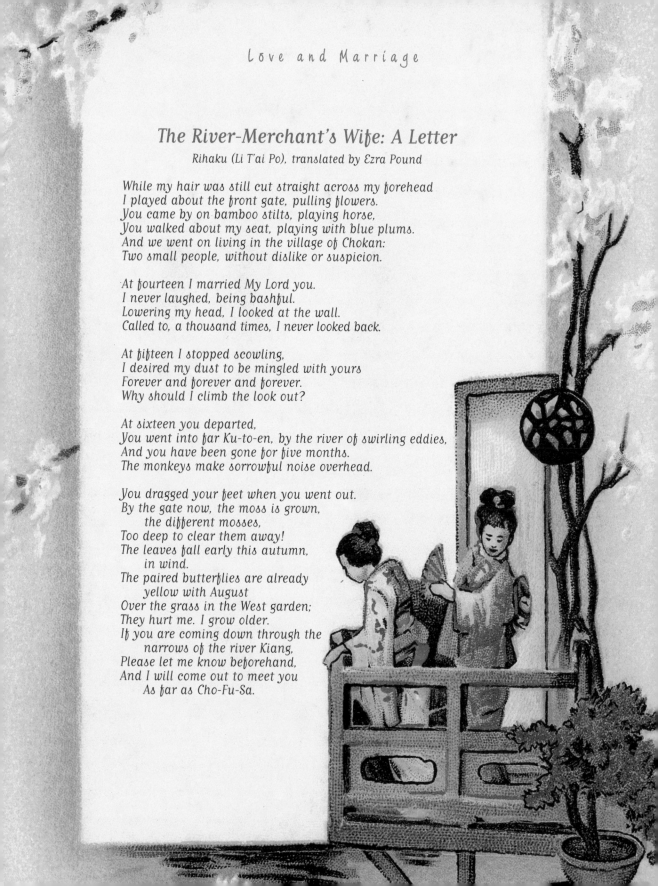

The Diary of Adam and Eve

Mark Twain

When I look back, the Garden is a dream to me. It was beautiful, surpassingly beautiful, enchantingly beautiful; and now it is lost, and I shall not see it any more.

The Garden is lost, but I have found him, and am content. He loves me as well as he can; I love him with all the strength of my passionate nature, and this, I think, is proper to my youth and sex. If I ask myself why I love him, I find I do not know, and do not really much care to know; so I suppose that this kind of love is not a product of reasoning and statistics, like one's love for other reptiles and animals. I think that this must be so. I love certain birds because of their song; but I do not love Adam on account of his singing—no, it is not that; the more he sings the more I do not get reconciled to it. Yet I ask him to sing, because I wish to learn to like everything he is interested in. I am sure I can learn, because at first I could not stand it, but now I can. It sours the milk, but it doesn't matter; I can get used to that kind of milk.

It is not on account of his brightness that I love him—no, it is not that. He is not to blame for his brightness, such as it is, for he did not make it himself; he is as God made him, and that is sufficient. There was a wise purpose in it, that I know. In time it will develop, though I think it will not be sudden; and besides, there is no hurry; he is well enough just as he is.

It is not on account of his gracious and considerate ways and his delicacy that I love him. No, he has lacks in these regards, but he is well enough just so, and is improving.

It is not on account of his industry that I love him—no, it is not that. I think he has it in him, and I do not know why he conceals it from me. It is my only pain. Otherwise he is frank and open with me, now. I am sure he keeps nothing from me but this. It grieves me that he should have a secret from me, and sometimes it spoils my sleep, thinking about it, but I will put it out of my mind; it shall not trouble my happiness, which is otherwise full to overflowing.

It is not on account of his education that I love him—no, it is not that. He is self-educated, and does really know a multitude of things, but they are not so.

It is not on account of his chivalry that I love him—no, it is not that. He told on me, but I do not blame him; it is a peculiarity of sex, I think, and he did not make his sex. Of course I would not have told on him, I would have perished first; but that is a peculiarity of sex, too, and I do not take credit for it, for I did not make my sex.

Then why is it that I love him? Merely because he is masculine, I think.

At bottom he is good, and I love him for that, but I could love him without it. If he should beat me and abuse me, I should go on loving him. I know it. It is a matter of sex, I think.

He is strong and handsome, and I love him for that, and I admire him and am proud of him, but I could love him without those qualities. If he were plain, I should love him; if he were a wreck, I should love him; and I would work for him, and slave over him, and pray for him, and watch by his bedside until I died.

Yes, I think I love him merely because he is mine and is masculine. There is no other reason, I suppose. And so I think it is as I first said; that this kind of love is not a product of reasonings and statistics. It just comes—none knows whence—and cannot explain itself. And doesn't need to.

It is what I think. But I am only a girl, and the first that has examined this matter, and it may turn out that in my ignorance and inexperience, I have not got it right. ♥

The oldest bride on record is Minnie Monroe, who married Dudley Reid at the tender age of 102.

Top Ten Romantic Gifts for Him

Looking for a gift that says "I love you" for your guy? Forget about all the he-man stuff and reach out to the softie inside. Here are some suggestions for gifts that speak right from—and to—the heart.

1. **A first edition of his favorite book.** Several on-line services will search for first editions and books that are out of print. Try *biblos.com* or *bibliofind.com* for starters.

2. **A framed movie poster** from the first flick you saw together. Don't worry if it was *Tommy Boy*—it's the thought that counts.

3. **A day of rest and relaxation.** Let him sleep late, do all his chores or errands, and spoil him silly with treats like breakfast in bed and a massage.

4. **A tent that sleeps two** and a map of a nearby campground.

5. **A wristwatch** with an engraved message of love on the back.

6. **A limousine ride to work.** Hire a car on a random day of the week to take him to work and make him feel like the superstar he is to you.

7. **A stack of his favorite comic books** from childhood. Let him know he's still the "boy" you fell in love with.

8. **A night on the town.** Reserve a table at a restaurant he's been dying to try, followed by an evening of live theater, music, or sports.

9. **A trip to the ASPCA.** Let him pick out that puppy or kitten he's been whimpering for. Nothing says "I love you" like the gift of loyalty.

10. **A case of wine.** Handpick twelve varieties, one for each month of the year, and attach a note to each that says "To be enjoyed by us together on [fill in a date] for a stay-at-home dinner for two."

*I never hated
a man enough
to give him his
diamonds back.*

—ZSA ZSA GABOR

Top Ten Romantic Gifts for Her

Finding the perfect gift for the woman you love is no easy task. The most romantic presents are those that express intimacy and thoughtfulness. Here are some great gift suggestions that are sure to make your partner feel loved and adored.

1. **A charm bracelet.** Personalize this with charms that relate to things you have done together—i.e., a bicycle, a sailboat, the Eiffel tower, etc.

2. **A scrapbook of your relationship.** Take pictures and collect souvenirs of all the places that have been important to the two of you and arrange them in a nice album.

3. **A picnic basket filled with goodies.** And an invitation to spend an afternoon in a park with you.

4. **Three dozen of her favorite flowers.** A classic. An abundant bouquet never fails to please. Think beyond red roses and show your originality.

5. **A postcard every day for a week.** A reminder that she's always in your thoughts.

6. **A poem.** Choose and memorize a poem that expresses your love. After you woo her with your recitation, give her an inscribed copy of the book.

7. **A basket of all her favorite "guilty pleasure" foods.** This one says, "Indulge and enjoy yourself—I love you the way you are."

8. **A sexy item of clothing.** You want her to know that you think she's gorgeous, but not to worry that you are trying to change her, so pick something just slightly more daring than what she might normally wear.

9. **A leather jacket.** Make her feel warm and adored! If you don't know exactly what she wants, ask her girlfriends or family, and err on the side of classic.

10. **A pair of silk pajamas.** Luxurious and comfortable, this is a gift that will make her feel pampered and appreciated every time she puts them on.

HUSBANDS AND BOYFRIENDS

ANNA QUINDLEN

I watched *Gone With the Wind* on television recently. It's my favorite movie. It's hokey, it's predictable, the color's lurid, I throw balled-up tissues at Olivia de Haviland when she's on screen. I love it. Each time I see it I notice something new.

This time, I noticed that in some ways it perfectly illustrates one of the great truths about men. Most men fall into one of two categories for the purpose of relationships: Husband or Boyfriend. These are not literal classifications based on marital status, just the best I can do. (I once classified them as the Good Guy and the Louse, which was an oversimplification made when I was depressed, menwise, and before I had admitted that I found the Lice much more interesting than their nobler brothers.)

Ashley Wilkes is a classic Husband: upright, dependable, prone neither to wild partying nor to gross flirtation. He will show up for dinner on time and be the kind of father a kid can depend on for lots of meaty talks about life and honor.

Rhett Butler is, of course, vintage Boyfriend: entertaining, unprincipled, with a roving eye and a wickedly expressive brow above it. I've watched Scarlett turn around and see him for the first time at the bottom of the staircase at Twelve Oaks plantation at least a hundred times. "He looks as if—as if he knows what I look like without my shimmy," she says, one of the few insightful things she says in the first half of the film, before she eats the radish and swears that she'll never be hungry again. And still my heart stops and I have trouble breathing. Give a damn? You bet I do.

This is because, unlike the obtuse Scarlett, I have never had any difficulty deciding between the Boyfriend and the Husband. Perhaps it is the way I was raised. My mother told me I should marry someone who could dance and who would make me laugh. She never said a word about a good provider. It was good advice, as far as it went, but since my mother had married a Boyfriend, it only went so far.

Of course, I married a Boyfriend, too, fell for him like a ton of bricks the first time I saw him wearing a sport coat with blue jeans and a wicked grin. I can't say I've never regretted it, because there have been times when I've wanted to turn him in for Ward Cleaver. But the truth is that if I had it to do over again, I would do it exactly the same way.

It's sometimes hard to accept this, although God knows why. Boyfriends rarely pretend to be Husbands. But lots of women fall for someone who is the life of the party, a dancing fool who has a weak spot for women, and then become enraged when they find themselves married to someone who is the life of the party, a dancing fool who has a weak spot for women. They expect matrimony to turn Jack Nicholson into Alan Alda. Yet they know that if they woke up in bed one morning with Alan Alda, they'd soon yearn with all their hearts for just a little Sturm und Drang, a little rock 'n' roll.

I don't mean to sound so down on Husbands. I think these are good times for them, with women marrying later in life and actively seeking stability and maturity in a man. Teenage girls have no interest in anything but Boyfriends, and women who marry early are often overly enamored of the kind of man who looks great in wedding pictures and passes the maid of honor his telephone number. But women who have been around a bit are, I think, more likely to see the virtues in a Husband.

A Husband provides a shoulder to lean on; when you lean on a Boyfriend's shoulder he may very well say, "You're wrinkling my jacket." You know what you are getting with a Husband, and at a time in your life when you've had too many unpleasant surprises—a man who demanded a commitment and then moved to L.A. the minute he got one, another who insisted he wanted to get married and then married his ex-girlfriend the day after you split—knowledge is power. You think you know what you are getting with a Boyfriend, but they're a little like kaleidoscopes: infinite permutations, many of them garish.

Men can work their own alchemy on the mix, too. The most obvious manifestation of the much ballyhooed midlife crisis is that the longtime Husband turns into a Boyfriend, starts driving a red car, wearing leather pants, and talking knowledgeably about the kinds of bands that generally hit the Top 10 with songs with only three words in them ("Yeah," "Love," and "Baby"). There are also a few documented cases of Boyfriends turning into Husbands, although not many. These can usually be linked to career changes, promotions, and fatherhood. (Even Rhett started to act pretty straight after Bonnie was born.)

My husband, a bred-in-the-bone Boyfriend, was terrified of this aspect of having children, convinced that on the morning after our first son was born he would awaken with a drawerful of pajamas and cardigan sweaters and the urge to say things like, "Now, son, I think we should have a little talk about that." Not a chance. His most recent foray into fatherhood was to teach both his children the words to "You Give Love a Bad Name." The eldest can also play air guitar along with the song. On the one hand, I hate "You Give Love a Bad Name," although my children sing it rather well. On the other hand, my husband would not think twice about scandalizing a Confederate ball by bidding $150 in gold to dance with me. And, like Scarlett, when someone said, "She will not consider it, sir," I know what I would say without a moment's hesitation: "Oh, yes, I will." ♥

Top Ten Marital Advice Books

In the words of André Maurois, "Marriage is an edifice that must be rebuilt every day." And while the rewards of a lifelong partnership are profound, so is the effort it takes to keep the relationship strong. When you need some advice or inspiration, here's our list of recommended reading:

1. *The Rules for Marriage* by Ellen Fein and Sherrie Schneider

2. *Advice for a Happy Marriage: From Miss Dietz's Third Grade Class* by Debi Dietz Crawford

3. *Advice to a Young Wife from an Old Mistress* by Michael Drury

4. *365 Reflections on Marriage: Advice, Whimsy, and Wisdom for You and Your Mate* by Eva Shaw

5. *Couple Care: Advice for a Healthy Relationship* by Liya Oertel

6. *Relationship Rescue: A Seven-Step Strategy for Reconnecting with Your Partner* by Phillip C. McGraw

7. *Ten Stupid Things Couples Do to Mess up Their Relationship* by Laura C. Schelssinger

8. *Starting Your Marriage Right: What You Need to Know In the Early Years to Make It Last a Lifetime* by Dennis and Barbara Rainey

9. *Getting the Love That You Want: A Guide for Couples* by Harville Hendrix

10. *The Complete Idiot's Guide to The Perfect Marriage* by Hillary Rich and Helaina Laks Kravitz

Once a woman has forgiven her man, she must not reheat his sins for breakfast.

– MARLENE DIETRICH

A Forgiveness Brunch

When you're really in the doghouse and a simple apology just won't suffice, a homemade brunch for your honey is a pretty good bet. Start the coffee for the café au lait first. Then slice the strawberries and make your waffles. (The whipped cream can be made ahead of time.) While the milk heats, assemble the waffles and mix the mimosas. Add the milk to the coffee and serve with a handwritten note of apology and single stem of your love's favorite flower.

Cinnamon Belgian Waffles
1 cup flour
1 teaspoon double-acting baking powder
a pinch of salt
1½ tablespoons sugar
2 tablespoons cinnamon
2 tablespoons butter
1 cup milk
1 egg
1 tablespoon vanilla
nonstick cooking spray
1½ cups sliced strawberries

1. Combine dry ingredients in a large bowl and mix well. In a separate bowl, mix butter, milk, egg, and vanilla. Add to dry ingredients and mix well.
2. Spray your waffle iron with a nonstick cooking spray and cook waffles according to directions. Serve hot topped with sliced strawberries, whipped cream, and maple syrup or powdered sugar.

Whipped Cream
1 small container whipping cream
1 tablespoon sugar
1 teaspoon vanilla

Combine ingredients in a bowl and beat with an electric mixer on high until stiff peaks form.

Mimosas
1 part champagne, chilled
1 part fresh orange juice

Café au Lait
1 part coffee
1 part hot milk (do not allow to boil)

Great Romances
ELIZABETH TAYLOR & RICHARD BURTON

They may have redefined the meaning of the "love/hate" relationship, but Elizabeth Taylor and Richard Burton shared the romance of a lifetime. Their torrid affair began on the set of *Cleopatra*, as did the media circus that would hound them throughout their years together. Following the film's release—and divorces from their respective spouses—they were married in 1964. A permanent fixture in the gossip columns, Taylor and Burton's relationship, with all its ups and downs, was often on public display. In 1974, the couple divorced, only to remarry in 1975, and divorce again a year later. Both struggled with substance abuse and career highs and lows. Although Taylor has been married a total of eight times (twice to Burton), she says that Richard was the great love of her life. At charity events, you can still spot her wearing the diamond-and-emerald earrings and necklace that Richard gave her so many years ago.

For two days we circled each other—very wary, very polite. On the third day, we had a fight. Then we knew that we were ourselves again.

—RICHARD BURTON ON HIS 2ND MARRIAGE TO ELIZABETH TAYLOR

Making Amends
Top Ten Ways to Apologize

For those who know that the saying, "Love means never having to say you're sorry," is just, well, wrong, we present the following tips for making amends.

1. **Flowers.** Always good. But if used more than once, vary the selection. Red roses are great, but lose their meaning if they become routine. Tip: There is no such thing as too many flowers.

2. **Simple note.** Enclose, along with a small but thoughtful gift, a note that simply reads, "I'm sorry. You were right." Sometimes the most direct approach is the most appreciated.

3. **Personal chef.** Cook her/his favorite dinner, AND clean up.

4. **Go public.** If you're really in the dog-house, take out an ad in your local newspaper's classified section expressing your regret. A public declaration of fault can go a long way!

5. **Put pen to paper.** Write your partner a love poem.

6. **Go for the sweet tooth.** Stock the freezer with your lover's favorite ice cream.

7. **Rub away the tension.** Give her/him a back massage every night for a week.

8. **Make-up music.** Make a mix tape or CD of songs that express how you feel about him/her and call it "My Apology."

9. **Make a list.** Write a top-ten list of reasons why she/he is wonderful.

10. **Make a fashion statement.** Make a T-shirt that says "I'm sorry. I was wrong" and wear it until he/she says not to. (Warning: Depending on the severity of the offense, this may dramatically hamper your wardrobe choices for the foreseeable future.)

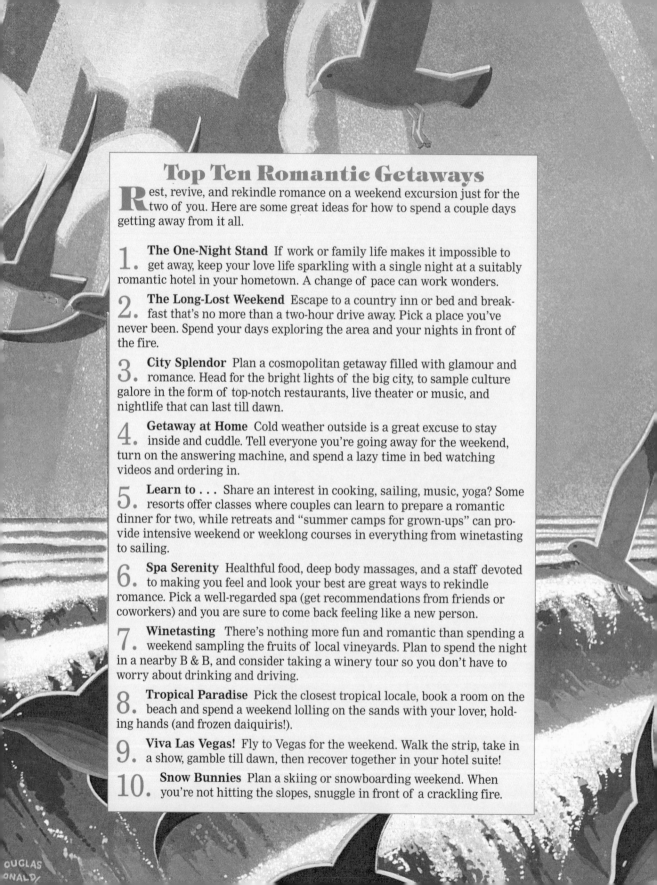

Top Ten Romantic Getaways

Rest, revive, and rekindle romance on a weekend excursion just for the two of you. Here are some great ideas for how to spend a couple days getting away from it all.

1. **The One-Night Stand** If work or family life makes it impossible to get away, keep your love life sparkling with a single night at a suitably romantic hotel in your hometown. A change of pace can work wonders.

2. **The Long-Lost Weekend** Escape to a country inn or bed and breakfast that's no more than a two-hour drive away. Pick a place you've never been. Spend your days exploring the area and your nights in front of the fire.

3. **City Splendor** Plan a cosmopolitan getaway filled with glamour and romance. Head for the bright lights of the big city, to sample culture galore in the form of top-notch restaurants, live theater or music, and nightlife that can last till dawn.

4. **Getaway at Home** Cold weather outside is a great excuse to stay inside and cuddle. Tell everyone you're going away for the weekend, turn on the answering machine, and spend a lazy time in bed watching videos and ordering in.

5. **Learn to . . .** Share an interest in cooking, sailing, music, yoga? Some resorts offer classes where couples can learn to prepare a romantic dinner for two, while retreats and "summer camps for grown-ups" can provide intensive weekend or weeklong courses in everything from winetasting to sailing.

6. **Spa Serenity** Healthful food, deep body massages, and a staff devoted to making you feel and look your best are great ways to rekindle romance. Pick a well-regarded spa (get recommendations from friends or coworkers) and you are sure to come back feeling like a new person.

7. **Winetasting** There's nothing more fun and romantic than spending a weekend sampling the fruits of local vineyards. Plan to spend the night in a nearby B & B, and consider taking a winery tour so you don't have to worry about drinking and driving.

8. **Tropical Paradise** Pick the closest tropical locale, book a room on the beach and spend a weekend lolling on the sands with your lover, holding hands (and frozen daiquiris!).

9. **Viva Las Vegas!** Fly to Vegas for the weekend. Walk the strip, take in a show, gamble till dawn, then recover together in your hotel suite!

10. **Snow Bunnies** Plan a skiing or snowboarding weekend. When you're not hitting the slopes, snuggle in front of a crackling fire.

Above It All

Here's to romance that defies gravity! Hot-air balloons are available for chartering throughout the United States. So if you're planning to visit any of the locations below, share a bird's-eye view of the world with your loved one.

■ **Above the Clouds, Inc** in Middletown, New York: *abovethecloudsinc.com* or (845) 692-2556.

■ **Above the Wine Country Ballooning** in Sonoma County, California: *balloontours.com* or (888) 238-6359.

■ **Great Adventure Balloon Tours** in Winter Park, Colorado: *grandadventureballoon.com* or (888) 887-1340 .

■ **Hot Air Expeditions** in Phoenix, Arizona: *hotairexpeditions.com* or (800) 831-7610.

■ **Rainbow Ryders Hot Air Balloon Company** in Albuquerque, New Mexico: *rainbowryders.com* or (800) 725-2477.

■ **Smoky Mountain Balloon Adventures** in Dandridge, Tennessee: *smokymtnballoons.com* or (423) 318-8991.

Love Song
Pablo Neruda

I love you, I love you, is my song
and here my silliness begins.

I love you, I love you my lung,
I love you, I love you my wild grapevine,
and if love is like wine:
you are my predilection
from your hands to your feet:
you are the wineglass of hereafter
and my bottle of destiny.

I love you forwards and backwards,
and I don't have the tone or the timbre
to sing you my song,
my endless song.

On my violin that sings out of tune
my violin declares,
I love you, I love you my double bass,
my sweet woman, dark and clear,
my heart, my teeth,
my light and my spoon,
my salt of the dim week,
my clear windowpane moon.

The Odyssey

HOMER

"What a strange creature!" he exclaimed. "Heaven made you as you are, but for sheer obstinacy you put all the rest of your sex in the shade. No other wife could have steeled herself to keep so long out of the arms of a husband she had just got back after nineteen years of misadventure…"

"You too are strange," said the cautious Penelope. "I am not being haughty or indifferent…But I have too clear a picture of you in my mind as you were when you sailed from Ithaca in your long-oared ship. Come, Eurycleia, make him a comfortable bed outside the bedroom that he built so well himself. Place the big bed out there, and make it up with rugs and blankets, and with laundered sheets."

This was her way of putting her husband to the test. But Odysseus flared up at once and rounded on his loyal wife. "Penelope," he cried, "you exasperate me! Who, if you please, has moved my bed elsewhere? Short of a miracle, it would be hard even for a skilled workman to shift it somewhere else, and the strongest young fellow alive would have a job to budge it. For a great secret went into the making of that complicated bed; and it was my work and mine alone. Inside the court there was a long-leaved olive-tree, which had grown to full height with a stem as thick as a pillar. Round this I built my room of close-set stone-work, and when that was finished, I roofed it over thoroughly, and put in a solid, neatly fitted, double door. Next I lopped all the twigs off the olive, trimmed the stem from the root up, rounded it smoothly and carefully with my adze and trued it to the line, to make my bedpost. This I drilled through where necessary, and used as a basis for the bed itself, which I worked away at till that too was done, when I finished it off with an inlay of gold, silver, and ivory, and fixed a set of purple straps across the frame.

"There is our secret, and I have shown you that I know it. What I don't know, madam, is whether my bedstead stands where it did, or whether someone has cut the tree-trunk through and shifted it elsewhere."

Her knees began to tremble as she realized the complete fidelity of his description. All at once her heart melted. Bursting into tears she ran up to Odysseus, threw her arms round his neck and kissed his head. "Odysseus," she cried. "do not be cross with me, you who were always the most reasonable of me. All our unhappiness is due to the gods, who couldn't bear to see us share the joys of youth and reach the threshold of old age together. But don't be angry with me now, or hurt because the moment when I saw you first I did not kiss you as I kiss you now. For I had always had the cold fear in my heart that somebody might come here and bewitch me with his talk…But now all's well. You have faithfully described our token, the secret of our bed, which no one ever saw but you and I and one maid…You have convinced your unbelieving wife."

Penelope's surrender melted Odysseus' heart, and he wept as he held his dear wife in his arms, so loyal and so true. Sweet moment too for her, sweet as the sight of land to sailors struggling in the sea, when the Sea-god by dint of wind and wave has wrecked their gallant ship. What happiness for the few swimmers that have fought their way through the white surf to the shore, when, caked with brine but safe and sound, they tread on solid earth! If the is bliss, what bliss it was for her to see her husband once again! She kept her white arms round his neck and never quite let go. ♥

> We two form a multitude.
>
> —OVID

Chapter Four
Passion

The Truest Pleasure

ROBERT MORGAN

The work in the sun and the sunburn acted like a spur to our lovemaking. It was as if the heat of July and August stored up in our veins and skin as a fever to be quenched by love in the house of darkness. Never had I seemed to need less sleep. After he got home each evening, milked and washed and had supper, Tom counted the money he had made. The coins shined like little flames and faces in the hearth. The bills crackled as he smoothed them in booklets. Afterwards he put the money in the cigar box.

As he counted the money, we talked about what we needed to buy for winter, for the children and for the place. Jewel would start school that fall, and needed new clothes. "You have to dress your girls nicer than boys," Tom said.

As soon as the children was asleep Tom and me went to bed ourselves. Pa was reading in the kitchen, and we tried not to disturb him. When Locke come on furlough for a week he slept on the couch and we tried to be careful not to bother him as we giggled in the dark and tried to keep the bed from creaking.

It was as if we was not ourselves some nights, but bigger and more powerful, more perfect, as we would want to be. The day had been a long delay and build-up of fever toward the summer night. And it felt like we couldn't do anything wrong. Every place we touched was right, and every pause was right. Everything we did in the dark led to something new and better.

As a girl I would not have thought a man of forty was capable of such exertions, or a woman of thirty-four for that matter. At moments of joy I felt this was what all the feeling of my life had been tending toward, includ-

ing my shouting and dancing at meetings. It was all just a preparation for this.

But I put such thoughts out of my mind for they was blasphemous. I may have felt them, but I didn't want to think them, least of all to say them. Long as I didn't put my feelings in words they was innocent. Kept at the edge of thought they couldn't hurt.

And I told myself lovemaking was also worship and praise. I told myself it was through love we take part in God's creation.

I remember one night in August special. We had picked beans in the far end of the bottom and Tom sold them by the bushel to women in the village. I reckon he had made more than ten dollars. But on the way home the axle of the wagon broke. I don't know why it broke. Maybe the extra hauling had wore it out. Tom had stuck in a sapling to hold up the wheel till he got home. The new axle would cost ten dollars, so the day had been wasted, he felt.

Now I have noticed that loving is best when you're feeling real good, or sometimes when you're feeling a little bad. If you're feeling mite low you resist lovemaking at first, and then it comes like a blessing. And your body takes over and reminds you of things you had forgot. The body has its own wisdom and its own will, and sometimes it knows what you need most.

That night I saw Tom needed to be cheered up. I took a full bath in the tub in the bedroom, and made myself rosy and soft. I put on powder and rubbed on cologne. By the time I had finished Tom had already gone to bed. I knowed he was tired, and when you want to forget some loss or bad news nothing is as comforting as sleep. In fact, I think he might already have been asleep when I put out the lamp and got in bed.

But as I slipped under the covers I could feel him waking. First, it was the way he stirred and was quiet in his breathing. Then he pushed against me a little, just enough to show it was intended. It's strange how much a little pressure tells you.

Well I won't go into detail. Folks got no right to hear what married couples do. But it was a time I never forgot. The katydids was out, loud in the woods beyond the orchard. And there was crickets in the yard, meadow moles

with their mellow note. After the heat of the day the house was cracking and knocking.

But I soon forgot the sounds in the dark. Time got big and magnified. The dark was lit with purple fires. I could feel colors through my fingertips and through every place I touched.

And we had so much time. Every instant was stretched out, and stretched further. Our bodies was big as landscapes and mountains and we had all the time in the world to climb and cross them. There was no hurry, never had been. There was years for a kiss.

It was also like a patient waiting. We was in no hurry because we knowed something would be give to us. I thought about the beans we had picked that day, and how beans get hard when they are ready to pick. You could pick beans just by the feel of them. With your fingers you could tell the pulses in a bean, and then count the beans into a basket.

I thought of Solomon again. "I am my beloved's, and his desire is toward me," I whispered. The words seemed perfect in the dark. "I am a wall, and my breasts are like towers: then was I in his eyes as one that found favor," I said.

We did some things new that night. Don't matter exactly what, but they was new to us. It was like we found out more things about each other. I guess it was like climbing way up a beautiful mountain past ridges and hollers. Laboring up a slope you think you are almost at the top, but when you get there see it is a false peak, and the real summit is higher and further.

The smells of the body are thrilling, the scent of armpits and sweat on skin. The skin has its own savors and salts. It is the salt of memory and wit and laughter. There is the salt that wakes you up, and the salt like the taste of rocks deep in the ground.

"Tom," I said. I had never been one to talk much while making love. Before, it had felt better to be hushed. "Tom," I said again, "This is the best thing, ain't it?"

He didn't say anything. He was waiting for me to say more.

"Tom," I said, "we won't never know anything this real."

It was like the dark was smoothing out in

contours of pasture hills and deep valleys lined with fur and velvet.

"I can see where the sky touches the ground," I said, "and it's smooth as milk."

There was rivers of sparks in the soil and they swirled through the dark and spread in wind to the end of the earth. It was a warm Nile flooding out of soil, lifting higher and higher.

"This is the place," I said, "ain't it?"

Tom still didn't say anything. He was waiting for me to go on. He never liked to waste a single word. It was for me to say things to him.

"This is the place it all starts," I said. "This is the place of creation."

And then in the dark I could see Tom's face. I don't know how I did in the pitch dark. Maybe there was heat lightning, or maybe a meteor outside. But I saw Tom's face, and his eyes was looking right into mine, like he saw what I was thinking and feeling. He could see and feel any part of me. Even if he laid still he could feel every inch of me that was moving.

"Tom!" I said. And then I knowed my talking made another kind of sense. It wasn't daylight talk with its words and sentences. It was a higher kind of talk. And it come to me I was speaking in tongues. It was the first time I had spoke in tongues outside a service. I didn't know what I was saying, but I saw what was visited upon me was a gift. "Tom!" I said, and my mouth flew like a bird and my tongue soared. I gripped and sung out and didn't hardly know what I was doing. I was on a long journey that went on and on over banks and gullies, valleys and mountains of flowers. The whole world was coming to us in the dark.

And then I saw what we had been going toward. Everything swung around like compass needles pointing in the same direction. It was in the eye of a dove setting high on a tree at the mountaintop. The eye was still as a puddle with no wind. It was still at the center of the whirl and clutter of things.

"This is what was meant," I said.

Tom still didn't say anything.

"This is really the place," I said. "Ain't it?"

"Yeah," Tom said. It was all he said, but it was enough. ♥

Tub for Two

Can aphrodisiacs really make the heart beat faster and get us in the mood for love? Absolutely. The secret recipe for romance is to awaken the limbic system—the part of our brain we use for matters of the heart. One way to do that is with essential oils. Their fragrance can arouse powerful feelings of pleasure and stir the libido. Certain scents, such as rose and jasmine, have been linked to romance for ages. Ylang-ylang, clary sage, and patchouli also are known aphrodisiacs. Place a few drops of these essential oils in a heated dish of water and disperse a sensual fragrance throughout the room, or add some drops to your bathwater for the ultimate love soak.

Romantic Scents
Small dish, warming stand, small candle, 3 drops of each of the following essential oils: benzoin, caraway, orange peel, patchouli

Fill the small dish with water and set it on the warming stand over lit candle. Add essential oils to the water. As the water warms, the fragrance will diffuse into the room.

Essential Love Bath
A half dozen roses (or so), 3 drops ylang-ylang essential oil, 2 drops jasmine essential oil, 5 drops palma rose essential oil, 2 drops clary sage essential oil

Fill the tub with very warm water. Stir in essential oils. Remove the petals from the roses and sprinkle over the water. Soak with your lover for at least 30 minutes.

The Kama Sutra

Vatsyayana

THE DIFFERENT KINDS OF LOVE

Scholars define four kinds of love:

1. Love that results from the execution, constant and continued, of a certain act is known as Love acquired through Constant Practice and Habit. For example, the love of sexual intercourse, the love of alcohol, gambling and sports.
2. Love that is felt for things out of the ordinary, and which is entirely based on the imagination or intellect, is called Love as the result of Imagination. For example, the love certain men or women feel for oral intercourse, and the love everyone feels for kisses, caresses, etc.

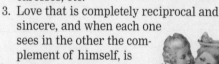

3. Love that is completely reciprocal and sincere, and when each one sees in the other the complement of himself, is known as Love as the result of Faith.
4. Love as a result of the Perception of Exterior Objects is known to everyone, as the sight of a beautiful woman has moved more poets to verse, and lovers to madness than any other form of love.

THE KINDS OF EMBRACES

The embrace is the bodily contact which reflects the joy of a man and woman united in love. The old writings state that there are four kinds of embrace:

1. When a man, feeling the hard bite of desire, touches a woman's body with his own (generally using some pretext or excuse, for this is the most elementary of all bodily contacts), it is known as the Embrace of Touch.
2. If, in some secluded room, a woman bends down to pick something up, and in doing so her breasts gently pierce her lover's body and are at once seized by him—it is known as the Embrace of Penetration.

These two forms of bodily contact are used only by lovers who are not yet sure of their mutual feelings and intentions.

3. When two lovers slowly walk together down some quiet shaded garden gently rubbing their bodies, one against the other, it is known as the Embrace of Friction.
4. But when one presses his body strongly and passionately against that of his lover it is known as the Embrace of Pressure.

These last two are used by those who have already succumbed to the arrows of Kama, and who are willing to float together on the stormy sea of desire.

Body of a Woman
Pablo Neruda

Body of a woman, white hills, white thighs,
you look like a world, lying in surrender.
My rough peasant's body digs in you
and makes the sun leap from the depth of the earth.

I was alone like a tunnel. The birds fled from me,
and night swamped me with its crushing invasion.
To survive myself I forged you like a weapon,
like an arrow in my bow, a stone in my sling.

But the hour of vengeance falls, and I love you.
Body of skin, of moss, of eager and firm milk.
Oh the goblets of the breast! Oh the eyes of absence!
Oh the roses of the pubis! Oh your voice, slow and sad!

Body of my woman, I will persist in your grace.
My thirst, my boundless desire, my shifting road!
Dark river-beds where the eternal thirst flows
and weariness follows, and the infinite ache.

Seduction Dinner

The notion that foods could both nourish and stimulate the libido first came from the Greeks in the first century A.D., when Pliny and Dioscordes documented the ancient diets that were said to increase potency. Foods were often selected as aphrodisiacs because of shape, texture, origin, or nutritional value. The Latin name for the walnut genus is Juglans, or "glans of Jupiter." Aztecs called the avocado tree Ahuacuati, or "testicle tree" because of the way the fruit hangs in pairs. In Mediterranean cultures, pine nuts have a long reputation as a powerful sexual stimulant. Fennel, likewise, is believed to have libido-inspiring properties. Dionysus, the Greek god of fertility and procreation, wore a crown of fennel.

So next time you want to ignite the passions of your loved one, light some candles and try serving this delicious aphrodisiac-laden dinner.

Artichokes with Lime Butter

2 large artichokes
1/2 cup butter, melted
juice of 1/2 lime

1. Steam 2 artichokes, stems up, in a covered pot for 30–40 minutes, depending on their size.
2. Test for doneness by piercing the stems with a fork; they will give easily.
3. Serve with melted butter with lime juice

Passionate Salad

1 15-oz. can black beans
1 avocado
1 papaya
2 teaspoons Hawaiian salt
2 tablespoons cilantro leaves, finely chopped
2 teaspoons cracked pepper
1 tablespoon fresh lime juice
2 shallots, finely chopped
1 8-oz. can crushed pineapple in its
*   own juice*

1. Divide the black beans and arrange on each of two salad plates.
2. Peel and cut slices of avocado and papaya, placing half of each fruit on the beans in each plate.
3. Crush salt, cilantro leaves, and pepper in a small bowl with the back of a spoon.
4. Add lime juice, shallots, and pineapple; mix. Spoon over the beans and fruit.

Linguini with Pesto Sauce

1 1/2 cups fresh basil leaves
2 cloves garlic
1/4 cup pine nuts
1/2 cup grated parmesan cheese
1/2 cup extra virgin olive oil
1/2 lb fresh linguine
salt and pepper

1. In a food processor, blend basil leaves, garlic, and pine nuts until coarsely chopped. Add parmesan cheese until mixture becomes a thick paste. Gradually blend in olive oil until mixture is creamy. Add salt and pepper to taste.
2. Toss with freshly cooked linguini and serve hot.

Honey Figs

1 tablespoon honey
6 figs, cut in half lengthwise
3 oz. whipping cream
1/2 teaspoon vanilla
1 teaspoon honey

1. Melt 1 tablespoon honey in a small heavy-bottom pan.
2. Place figs cut-side down on the hot honey.
3. Cook, shaking the pan often, until honey begins to caramelize (bubble and brown).
4. Whip the cream; add vanilla and 1 teaspoon honey.
5. Serve the figs cut-side up, topped with whipped cream and vanilla cookies.

I admit, I have a tremendous sex drive. My boyfriend lives forty miles away.

—PHYLLIS DILLER

The belief that pine nuts are potent aphrodisiacs dates back nearly 2000 years. An ancient Arabic love manual (circa 130-200 A.D.) called The Perfumed Garden prescribes "a glass of thick honey, plus 20 almonds and 100 pine nuts" at bedtime for three consecutive nights to revive a man's sexual abilities.

Wedding guests in some southern European countries throw figs instead of rice at the exiting newlyweds, as a sign of fertility.

Avocados were believed to be so sexually potent in the Aztec culture that virgins were forbidden to touch them.

Catherine d'Medici, who married Henry II of France at the age of 14, appalled the French Court with her voracious appetite for artichokes, a well-known aphrodisiac of the time.

FOOD FOR LOVE

Creating, or sustaining, that loving feeling has produced more than a few odd dietary regimens, some based on strange interpretations of human biology. Galen, a Greek physician, believed that flatulence-inspiring foods were a recipe for love because bodily gases were what caused the male member to "inflate." In other medical traditions, it was believed that eating foods that resembled an erect male organ would sustain lovemaking. Even today, rhinoceros horns are ground to a powder for men to ingest for just this reason.

Not all legendary aphrodisiacs, however, are without real amorous powers. None, perhaps, can inspire love or even lust, but some contain vitamins, minerals, or other chemicals that act as aids to romance. Others may not have a chemical-biological effect on the body, but indulging in them with a lover can create just the right atmosphere for intimacy.

Some of the items listed below were renowned for their properties before science could justify their reputation. Asparagus and bananas, in particular, initially gained their reputation based on their shape. Psychologists also point out that the mind has a power all its own: The belief that a food is an aphrodisiac may produce a "placebo effect" that induces the desired results.

Asparagus It and other vegetables containing high quantities of vitamin E help generate both male and female sex hormones.

Bananas They contain potassium and B vitamins, which also stimulate sex hormone production.

Chili Peppers Apsaicin, the chemical responsible for the pepper's "heat," also causes the pulse to rise, nerve endings to tingle, and the body to sweat. It's unproven, but it may cause the body to release endorphins, creating a natural high that can be put to "other" uses.

Chocolate contains phenylethylamine, the same chemical that causes feelings of love and sexual attraction.

Chocolate Energy-producing chocolate also contains two stimulants: theobromine and caffeine—not to mention that it tastes great and melts at body temperature.

Oysters Shellfish in general are rich in zinc and iron. Iron helps the blood carry oxygen efficiently, and men need zinc as a building block for testosterone.

Strawberries This delicious fruit is packed with all sorts of nutritive benefits, and its shape, texture, and color are all arousing.

Kissing Trivia

On September 15, 1990, Alfred Wolfram from New Brighton, Minnesota, kissed 8,001 people in eight hours at the Renaissance Festival—that's over 16 people a minute!

The longest known kiss in history: 30 hours and 45 minutes! This record was set by a couple in Israel at a kissing contest on April 5, 1999.

A kiss every day keeps the dentist away! Well it can help, anyway. Kissing encourages the production of saliva, which helps clean food from the teeth and lowers the level of the acid that causes tooth decay.

Under the Mistletoe

Ever wonder why we're supposed to pucker up when we pass underneath a sprig of mistletoe? The tradition first arose in ancient Scandinavia. According to Nordic mythology, the mischief-maker Loki fashioned a spear from mistletoe and tricked the god Hother into killing Balder (the god of vegetation) with it, thus bringing on the start of winter. With Balder's later resurrection, the gods pronounced mistletoe sacred—a plant of peace instead of death. Soon it became a tradition for any two people who happened to pass under the shrub to kiss in celebration of Balder's return. The mystical power of mistletoe was considered so strong that its presence was capable of inducing two enemies to drop their weapons and maintain a truce until the next day.

It takes a lot of experience for a girl to kiss like a beginner.
—LADIES HOME JOURNAL, 1948

Top Ten Movie Kisses

They stare into each other's eyes, the music swells, they dive into each other's arms, and finally, they're locking lips. Let's be honest: Most of us learned how to kiss from watching movies, and could still pick up a tip or two from these classic on-screen smooches.

1. ***From Here to Eternity*** The image of Deborah Kerr and Burt Lancaster lying on the beach, kissing as the waves roll over them is one of the most iconic in movie history.

2. ***The Thomas Crown Affair*** Faye Dunaway and Steve McQueen's kiss at the end of this romantic adventure may be the longest in cinema history.

3. ***Notorious*** Hitchcock managed to outwit the censors, who had a strict limit on how long a filmed kiss could last. Cary Grant and Ingrid Bergman prolong this memorable and sensual smooch by interrupting it with sexy whispers about having chicken for dinner.

4. ***Gone with the Wind*** How's this for a pick-up line: "Never mind about loving me. You're a woman sending a soldier to his death with a beautiful memory. Scarlett, kiss me, kiss me once." Rhett Butler (Clark Gable) grabs up a coy Scarlett O'Hara (Vivien Leigh) in his arms and plants one on her as Atlanta burns behind them. Of course, it's not long before Scarlett steps back and slaps him, but by that time, movie magic has been made.

5. ***The English Patient*** This epic wartime romance has it all: mystery, an exotic locale, and a love triangle. The first kiss in their adulterous affair knocks Almásy (Ralph Fiennes) and Katherine (Kristin Scott Thomas) to their knees, it's that passionate.

6. ***Don't Look Now*** Donald Sutherland and Julie Christie play a married couple who prove that even those who've locked lips a thousand times before can still share a kiss full of steamy passion and touching intimacy.

7. ***Casablanca*** Though brief, Rick (Humphrey Bogart) and Ilsa's (Ingrid Bergman) reunion kiss is so loaded with history that it has unparalleled dramatic force. One of the greatest romances ever brought to the screen, *Casablanca* is a must-see.

8. ***To Have and Have Not*** There's real chemistry on screen in Lauren Bacall and Humphrey Bogart's first movie together. Slim plops herself right onto Harry Morgan's lap and takes a smacker on the lips. Nothing tops this movie for flirty, sexually tinged verbal sparring.

9. ***Spiderman*** They're in an alley. It's raining. Kirsten Dunst's T-shirt is, well, soaked. Spiderman (Toby McGuire) hangs upside down by his feet from a fire escape, lifts just the bottom of his mask to plant a kiss on dripping Mary Jane, and a new classic on-screen smooch is born.

10. ***Cinema Paradiso*** OK, so it isn't one kiss. But when Salvatore (Jacques Perrin) sits in that theater and watches the montage of kisses the old projectionist, Alfredo (Philippe Noiret) compiled over the years, there isn't a dry eye in the house.

The Kisstory of Kissing

Why do we kiss? Scientists once believed it was due to the pleasurable sensation (how astute!) of a slight electrical charge created when lips made contact. Although that theory has since been disproved, it is well known that the act of kissing releases hormones into the blood that can turn the exploration of another's mouth into an enjoyable tactile experience.

But how did the custom of kissing originate? The Romans were among the first to regard the kiss as a sign of social status (noblemen were permitted contact with the emperor's lips, whereas plebeians had to be satisfied with his feet.) Russian czars would later dispense kisses as the ultimate sign of respect for their recipients. Today, the French frequently greet their friends with a double kiss—one on each cheek—whereas for the Dutch, three times is the charm.

However, the romantic kiss as we know it first evolved appropriately enough in 6th century France. With the growing popularity of figure dancing, it became fashionable for partners to close each dance with a kiss on the lips. The rest, as they say, is kisstory.

A ROMANTIC MOVIE MOMENT

Some Like It Hot

Starring Marilyn Monroe and Tony Curtis, 1959

SUGAR
Have you ever tried American girls?

JOE
Why? *(they kiss)*

SUGAR
Was it anything?

JOE
I'm not quite sure. Can we try it again? *(they kiss)*

JOE
I've got a funny sensation in my toes, like someone was barbecuing them over a slow flame.

SUGAR
Let's throw another log on the fire. *(they kiss)*

JOE
I think you're on the right track.

SUGAR
I must be. Your glasses are beginning to steam up. *(they kiss)*

JOE
I never knew it could be like this. *(he removes his glasses)*

SUGAR
Thank you.

JOE
They told me I was kaput, finished, all washed up. And here you are making a chump out of all those experts...Where did you learn to kiss like that?

SUGAR
I used to sell kisses for the milk fund. *(they kiss)*

JOE
Tomorrow, remind me to send a check for a hundred thousand dollars to the milk fund.

JOE *(much later)*
How much do I owe the milk fund so far?

SUGAR
Eight hundred and fifty thousand dollars.

174

Top Ten Female Sex Symbols

These luscious women have made many heads turn and tongues hang to the floor. Diva, goddess, tramp—call her what you want, the female sex symbol is an intrinsic fixture of human culture and an inspiration to both men and women.

1. **Pamela Anderson** The scandalous sex video, her appearances as a member of the Baywatch cast, and—let's face it—those boobs! She's every teenage boy's fantasy. Her outrageous rock 'n' roll lifestyle firmly entrenched, Anderson can make even motherhood look sexy.

2. **Jean Harlow** The original "blonde bombshell," platinum-haired Harlow made thirty-six movies before her untimely death at the tender age of twenty-six. The first actress to really work her blondeness, Jean introduced that now-clichéd line, "Would you be shocked if I changed into something more comfortable?" in the Howard Hughes film *Hell's Angels*.

3. **Farrah Fawcett** *Charlie's Angels* made Farrah Fawcett a superstar, and the ultimate 1970s pin-up. All shaggy hair, legs, and big white smile, her poster was a fixture on the bedroom walls of teenage boys the world over.

4. **Mae West** With lines like, "Is that a gun in your pocket or are you just happy to see me?" West proved herself as a brassy broad who was as witty as she was brazen. Decades ahead of her time, this busty blonde used innuendo (and lots of it!) to get past the Hollywood censors.

5. **Jennifer Lopez** J.Lo's derriere has been the subject of unprecedented interest ever since she stripped in front of George Clooney

Sex appeal is 50 percent what you've got and 50 percent what people think you've got.

—SOPHIA LOREN

My wife is a sex object— every time I ask for sex, she objects.

—LES DAWSON

in *Out of Sight*. Her much-publicized romances with hotties P. Diddy and Ben Affleck, and her suggestive music videos, have cemented her place in the modern pantheon of sex goddesses.

6. **Brigitte Bardot** The French "sex kitten" was one of the 1960s most drooled over women. With her pouty lips, kohl-encircled eyes and bodacious curves, this bleached blonde became a worldwide sensation after her breakthrough film *And God Created Woman*.

7. **Sophia Loren** With her high cheekbones, big almond-shaped eyes, and voluptuous body, Sophia Loren drove men wild. A dark Italian beauty, Sophia rose from abject poverty in her hometown of Naples to international fame and critical acclaim, including a lifetime achievement Oscar. One of the world's most beloved actresses, Sophia Loren's appeal, both sexual and otherwise, is timeless.

8. **Josephine Baker** This African-American expatriate made huge waves in Paris in the flapper era. Nicknamed "Black Venus," Baker both exploited and challenged stereotypical notions of black women's sexuality with her wild dancing and flamboyant personality. The French were helpless to resist her exotic appeal.

9. **Madonna** Madonna's sexuality is in-your-face, dangerous, and commercially lucrative. Here's a woman who used her head to market her sex appeal and become one of the most successful female performers of all time.

10. **Marilyn Monroe** Norma Jean Baker came to Hollywood and transformed herself into Marilyn Monroe, the physical embodiment of feminine allure. Her breathy voice, blonder-than-blonde hair, and curvy figure made her every man's dream. Monroe's tragic demise highlighted the pitfalls of "the glamorous life" of a Hollywood sex symbol.

i like my body when it is with your body
e. e. cummings

i like my body when it with your
body. It is so quite new a thing.
Muscles better and nerves more.
i like your body. i like what it does,
i like its hows. i like to feel the spine
of your body and its bones, and the trembling
-firm-smooth ness and which i will
again and again and again
kiss, i like kissing this and that of you,
i like, slowly stroking the, shocking fuzz
of your electric fur, and what-is-it comes
over parting flesh...And eyes big love-crumbs,

and possibly i like the thrill

of under me you so quite new

Champagne & Strawberries Under the Stars

Once dinner is done, slip out to the yard or up to the roof for a little romantic stargazing. This decadent combination of chocolate-covered strawberries and champagne cocktails is certain to ignite passions and set the mood for romance.

Champagne Cocktails
2 champagne glasses
crème de cassis
2 strawberries, cleaned and hulled
1 bottle of great champagne, chilled

Into each glass, pour a dash of crème de cassis and add a strawberry. Then fill with champagne.

Chocolate-Dipped Strawberries
12 long-stemmed strawberries
1/2 cup semisweet chocolate
5 tablespoons half-and-half
1/4 teaspoon vanilla
1/2 teaspoon corn syrup

1. Rinse strawberries and carefully pat dry with a clean dishtowel.
2. Combine chocolate and half-and-half in a small saucepan. Heat on low, stirring constantly, until chocolate melts and mixture is fully blended. Do not allow mixture to boil.
3. Remove saucepan from heat and stir in vanilla and corn syrup. Dip strawberries into the mixture one at a time. Place them on a tray of wax paper in the refrigerator to harden.
4. Serve these the same day: Strawberries won't last long without becoming soggy.

When I Am with You
Rumi

When I am with you, we stay up all night.
When you are not here, I can't go to sleep.
Praise God for these two insomnias!
And the difference between them.

The Best Champagne

Champagne is the sparkling wine pro-duced from a mixture of Pinot Noir and Chardonnay grapes in the Champagne region of France. It was first served toward the end of the seventeenth century and has been enjoyed as the ultimate romantic beverage ever since. Other regions may produce sparkling wine, but only those from Champagne are allowed to carry the famous name. Most experts prefer dry cham-pagnes, favoring those from the Marne Valley. Among the most famous champagnes are Moët & Chandon, Perrier Jouet, Bollinger, and Tattinger. Some of the most highly regarded (and most expensive) champagnes in recent vintage are:

Dom Perignon, 1990 This is a slightly sweet, creamy champagne with a fruity fla-vor. About $100 per bottle.

Krug Grand Cuvee NV (No vintage, made from a mixture of years) This is a hearty champagne with almond flavors. About $100 per bottle.

Veuve Clicquot Brut Rose La Grande Dame, 1990 If you want to try a rose cham-pagne, this is a very fine one with overtones of spice and cherry. About $200 per bottle.

To order champagne: *primewines.com* or (888) 867-9463; *wine.com* or (877) 289-6886; *sendchampagne.com* or (877) 736-3547.

Rachel Felix and Prince de Joinville, 1840

Prince de Joinville sent this note to actress Rachel Felix after seeing one of her performances. Their relationship lasted eight years.

> To Rachel
>> Where?
>> When?
>> How Much?

> To the Prince
>> Your place.
>> Tonight.
>> Free.

We are all mortal until the first kiss and the second glass of wine.

—EDUARDO GALEANO

179

Letters of Love

Charles Kingsley to his wife, Fanny

Charles Kingsley, preacher and canon at Westminister Abbey, first courted his wife, Fanny, in the summer of 1839. After a four-year courtship, they were married at Trinity Church in Bath on January 10, 1844. They were together until he died, in 1875.

To Fanny   24 July 1857

Oh that I were with you, or rather you with me here. The beds are so small that we should be forced to lie inside each other, and the weather is so hot that you might walk about naked all day, as well as night—*cela va sans dire!* Oh, those naked nights at Chelsea! When will they come again? I kiss both locks of hair every time I open my desk—but the little curly one seems to bring me nearer to you.

A Taste of Luxury
The Best Caviar

Caviar, the eggs of the sturgeon fish, is considered one of the most romantic and extravagant foods, often costing more than $100 per ounce. A gift of caviar, for someone who likes it, is a mark of special favor. Caviar comes in three colors—black, red, and gold—and a range of sizes. The largest and lightest "berries" are considered the best. Although tastes differ, Iranian caviar is widely regarded as the finest variety. Russian caviar, which comes in several varieties including Sevruga, Oestra, and Beluga (in that order of quality) also is considered excellent. Caviar is best served on a small piece of toast or *blini* (buckwheat pancake) with a glass of champagne.

To order exquisite caviar: **Caviarteria**, *caviarteria.com* or (212) 759-7410; **Russ and Daughters**, *russanddaughters.com* or (212) 475-4880.

When We Have Loved
from The Sanskrit

When we have loved, my love,
Panting and pale from love,
Then from your cheeks, my love,
Scent of the sweat I love:
And when our bodies love
Now to relax in love
After the stress of love,
Ever still more I love
Our mingled breath of love.

I kissed my first girl and smoked my first cigarette on the same day. I haven't had time for tobacco since.

—ARTURO TOSCANINI

Steaming up the Screen
Top Ten On-Screen Love Scenes

Hollywood is good for nothing if not acting out our innermost fantasies. Whether you're in the mood for something hot and heavy, sweet and mushy, or light and fluffy, there's something on this list for every sexual appetite.

1. ***Body Heat*** Who can forget the sexual charge sparked by Ned Racine (William Hurt) as he circles the house of femme fatale Matty Walker (Kathleen Turner), looking for a way in to possess her? Matty watches as Ned tries every door in the house and, finding them locked, hurls a chair through the glass—anything to be with the object of his desire. Whew! And that's all before the sex!

2. ***Thelma and Louise*** When Thelma (Geena Davis) reunites with cutie-pie cowboy, J. D. (Brad Pitt), at a motel on a rainy night, she discovers what great sex is supposed to be: hot, steamy, fun, and spontaneous. Sure, he steals all her money, but most women would agree that it was worth it!

3. ***Bull Durham*** After an hour and a half of rising sexual tension, Crash (Kevin Costner) and Annie (Susan Sarandon) finally hook up in the climactic scene of this romantic comedy masquerading as a sports film. First, they do it on the bedroom floor. Then, they do it on the kitchen table (after Costner ruggedly tosses his Wheaties into the sink.) And finally, they do it in a claw-footed tub surrounded by dozens of candles. . . . Now that's a love scene.

4. ***9½ Weeks*** Sex is the name of the game in this hopeless tale of Elizabeth's (Kim Basinger) erotic affair with John (Mickey Rourke). You can take your pick of spicy sex scenes (Elizabeth's strip tease to Joe Cocker's "You Can Leave Your Hat On" is a serious contender) but the food orgy on the kitchen floor gives a whole new meaning to "oral pleasure."

5. **Basic Instinct** The hottest scene in this famous thriller wasn't Catherine's (Sharon Stone) "dirty dance" with her gal pal or even the infamous interrogation scene where Stone uncrosses her legs to reveal a brazen lack of underwear. No, the most arousing moment has got to be when hunky Detective Nick Curran (Michael Douglas) sexually gratifies the woman who just may be a cold-blooded murderer.

6. **About Last Night** In this classic eighties movie about budding romance penned by David Mamet, Danny (Rob Lowe) and Debby (Demi Moore) embark on the rocky road to love. Buff encounters abound, but the wet, drippy bathroom montage wins our award for Best Bathtub Sex.

7. **Monster's Ball** Lauded by the critics, *Monster's Ball* stirred controversy due to the film's graphic depiction of sex between Leticia (Halle Berry) and Hank (Billy Bob Thornton). This notorious sex scene is notable for its length, variety of positions, and the lack of music, which gives it a raw, gritty edge.

8. **Risky Business** When Joel's (Tom Cruise) hooker friend Lana (Rebecca De Mornay) convinces him that there's nothing quite like making love on a train, we are in for a steamy ride. Helped by slo-mo camerawork and Phil Collins' hit song "In the Air Tonight," this sensual public encounter is a classic.

9. **An Officer and a Gentleman** After enduring a weekend of near torture at the hands of his sadistic drill sergeant, Zack (Richard Gere) gets some sexual healing from doting local girl, Paula (Debra Winger). Both tender and masculine, this scene is most memorable for featuring Gere at his peak of sexiness.

10. **The Postman Always Rings Twice** With Cora's (Jessica Lange) husband out, Frank (Jack Nicholson) wastes no time making his move. After a brief but vicious fight, Cora lies on the flour-covered kitchen table where she's been kneading dough all morning, throws her freshly baked loaves to the floor, and challenges Frank to "C'mon!" What follows is too lurid to print here. . . . Rent it.

Song
Liu Yung

*She lowers her fragrant curtain,
wanting to speak her love.*

*She hesitates, she frowns—
the night is too soon over!*

*Her lover is first to bed,
warming the duck-down quilt.*

*She lays aside her needle,
drops her rich silk skirt,*

*eager for his embrace.
He asks one thing:*

*that the lamp remain lit.
He wants to see her face.*

There is something that happens between men and women in the dark that seems to make everything else unimportant.

—Tennessee Williams, *A Streetcar Named Desire*

Variation
Federico García Lorca

*That still pool of the air
under the branch of an echo.*

*That still pool of the water
under a frond of bright stars.*

*That still pool of your mouth
under a thicket of kisses.*

Quietly
Kenneth Rexroth

*Lying here quietly beside you,
My cheek against your firm, quiet thighs,
The calm music of Boccherini
Washing over us in the quiet,
As the sun leaves the housetops and goes
Out over the Pacific, quiet-
So quiet the moves beyond us,
So quiet as the sun always goes,
So quiet, our bodies, worn with the
Times and the penances of love, our
Brains curled, quiet in their shells, dormant,
Our hearts slow, quiet, reliable
In their interlocked rhythms, the pulse
In your thigh caressing my cheek. Quiet.*

*Love is the answer, but
while you're waiting for
the answer, sex raises
some pretty good questions.*

—WOODY ALLEN

Fondue For Two

Casual and sexy, this is a meal in front of the fire with some heavenly Mozart, a wonderful Chardonnay and no place to go. You do need a fondue pot that sits over a Sterno or a tea light and fondue forks or wooden skewers.

Cheese Fondue
*½ clove of garlic
¾ cups dry white wine (6 oz)
½ tablespoon cornstarch
1 tablespoon kirsch brandy
⅓ lb Emmental cheese, coarsely grated
⅓ lb Gruyere cheese, coarsely grated
Freshly ground pepper and nutmeg to taste
1 loaf of French bread cut into 1-inch cubes*

1. Rub the inside of a casserole or heavy pot with the garlic, and then discard. Add wine and bring to a simmer.
2. Blend the cornstarch and the kirsch together in a small bowl.
3. Gradually add cheese to the pot and cook, stirring constantly to keep the cheese from balling up. Do not boil.
4. Add cornstarch mixture into the pot and stir. Bring fondue to a simmer.
5. Continue stirring for 5–6 minutes, until thick.
6. Transfer hot cheese mixture into fondue pot. Set pot over a flame immediately and serve with the bread for dipping and a salad of your choosing.

Chocolate Fondue
*6 oz. of your favorite dark chocolate
⅓ cup heavy cream
1 tablespoon kirsch brandy or Cointreau
6 large strawberries, 2 bananas, ½ of a
    pineapple, 1 apple, and 1 pear, cut
    into bite size chunks*

1. Break the chocolate into separate pieces and combine with heavy cream and brandy in a saucepan. Stir over low heat until everything is melted and smooth.
2. Transfer melted chocolate mixture into fondue pot and serve over a flame with a platter of assorted fruit for dipping.

Serves 2

LOVE:
the irresistible desire to
be irresistibly desired.

— MARK TWAIN

Top Ten Male Sex Symbols

Every generation has its own take on what's hot and what's not, but these sexy men have withstood the test of time, graciously providing women of all ages with a focus for their fantasies and desires. We dream about them; we poster them to our bedroom walls, office cubicles, and lockers; we wish they were ours.

1. **Sean Connery** Sean Connery is one of those burly, ultra-masculine Scottish men who just keep improving with age. Whether as James Bond, the sophisticated and seductive secret agent, or as Daniel Dravot in *The Man Who Would Be King*, or even as the Spanish immortal Juan Sanchez Villa-Lobos Ramirez in *Highlander*, Sean Connery's allure is unmistakable.

2. **Richard Gere** Richard Gere's reign as one of America's leading sex symbols is still going strong despite his silvering hair and Zen preoccupations. With provocative movies like *An Officer and a Gentleman* and *American Gigolo* early in his career, and more recently, *Unfaithful* and *Pretty Woman*, gorgeous Gere has captivated female audiences for years with his easy charm and unparalleled good looks.

3. **George Clooney** Since bursting onto the TV screen in the hit show *ER*, George Clooney's naughty smile and salt-and-pepper hair have made him a major object of desire worldwide. A stunning profile and a good sense of humor give this bewitching male lead lasting star power.

> *Women need a reason to have sex; men just need a place.*
>
> —BILLY CRYSTAL, *CITY SLICKERS*

4. **Mick Jagger** In his prime, he was the ultimate rock 'n' roll bad boy as front man for the Rolling Stones. Notorious for his sexual exploits and those juicy lips, Mick Jagger has fueled many a teenage fantasy over his long career.

5. **Frank Sinatra** No one could suck you into a song like the "Chairman of the Board." His seductive, evocative crooning made "Ol' Blue Eyes" a hit with the ladies and a figure of admiration for men.

6. **Marlon Brando** Brooding and brutish, Brando makes this list for his sheer animal magnetism. From *Streetcar Named Desire* to *Last Tango in Paris*, Brando's intensity and talent made him irresistible to women.

7. **Humphrey Bogart** Hard on the outside but tender on the inside, Bogart cemented his place as America's #1 romantic leading man, performing in such films as *Casablanca* and *To Have and Have Not*. His love affair with Lauren Bacall piqued the public's imagination and only added to his "strong and silent" mystique.

8. **Brad Pitt** Ever since he lit up the screen as an outlaw in *Thelma and Louise*, Brad Pitt has been at the top of many girls' Most Wanted lists. Cocky, charismatic, and oh-so-cute, even as a married man he continues to preoccupy women of all ages.

9. **James Dean** He was the embodiment of the expression "Live fast, die young and leave a nice-looking corpse." James Dean was just hitting his stride as an actor when a car accident tragically took his life. He had a sexy mix of youthful angst and tough-guy swagger, all packaged up with just the prettiest face.

10. **Elvis** Women adored him and men wanted to be him. Elvis Presley was and still is "the King" of many women's hearts, with his beautiful eyes, deep, blues-y voice, and some shockingly suggestive dance moves. When "Elvis the Pelvis" hit the 1950s scene, he scared conservative American parents and made young girls scream and swoon with desire.

I Want You
Arthur L. Gillom

I want you when the shades of eve are falling
   And purple shadows drift across the land;
When sleepy birds to loving mates are calling—
   I want the soothing softness of your hand.

I want you when the stars shine up above me,
   And Heaven's flooded with the bright moonlight;
I want you with your arms and lips to love me
   Throughout the wonder watches of the night.

I want you when in dreams I still remember
   The ling'ring of your kiss—for old times' sake—
With all your gentle ways, so sweetly tender,
   I want you in the morning when I wake.

I want you when the day is at its noontime,
   Sun-steeped and quiet, or drenched with sheets of rain;
I want you when the roses bloom in June-time;
   I want you when the violets come again.

I want you when my soul is thrilled with passion;
   I want you when I'm weary and depressed;
I want you when in lazy, slumbrous fashion
   My senses need the haven of your breast.

I want you when through field and wood I'm roaming;
   I want you when I'm standing on the shore;
I want you when the summer birds are homing—
   And when they've flown—I want you more and more.

I want you, dear, through every changing season;
   I want you with a tear or with a smile;
I want you more than any rhyme or reason—
   I want you, want you, want you—all the while.

The Greeks

JOHN BARTON AND KENNETH CAVANDER

Once long ago
in the mountains of the northland
lived a man named Peleus.
He was a master wrestler.
He fell in love with a sea-nymph,
Thetis, who was so fair
that the gods themselves
wanted her in their bed.
Peleus decided to try and capture her,
so he waited by the sea.
And one full-moon night, he saw her,
swimming shorewards, her body touched
with silver.
So when she was high and dry,
shaking out her hair, a free thing,
Peleus leapt out and seized her.
He tried every trick he knew as a wrestler.
She used every trick a sea-nymph knows.
She changed shape.
She became water—and soaked him.
She became fire—and singed him.
She became a lioness—and bit him.
She became a serpent—and stung him.
She became a cuttlefish—and squirted him
with purple ink all over.
She became a bird—and she tried to fly.
And she slipped and slid through his fingers.
Then just as he was tiring
he saw in his hands
A little silver fish,
wet, delicate, and tender.
It gasped, and arched its back
like a loving woman.
And he knew, that it was
the girl he so wanted.
So he stroked her,
and took her,
and loved her,
and they wrestled, as the dawn broke in sky.

Breakfast in Bed

Breakfast in bed is one of life's great simple luxuries. Rise early and surprise your sweetie with a romantic morning meal under the covers. You can make the strawberry butter the night before, and the popovers take just moments to put in the oven. While they bake, set the tray and scramble the eggs. Serve with fresh orange juice, the daily paper, and, of course, a single red rose.

Strawberry Butter

¹/₂ stick butter, softened
2 tablespoons sugar
¹/₄ cup rinsed, cleaned, and mashed
*   strawberries*

1. Cream together butter and sugar, then add mashed strawberries and mix until color is uniform.
2. Spoon into a small serving dish or butter mold and refrigerate for about a half hour, or until firm.

Popovers

1 cup flour
¹/₄ teaspoon salt
1 tablespoon sugar
1 tablespoon butter, melted
3 large eggs

1. Preheat oven to 400° F. Thoroughly grease a muffin pan.
2. Combine flour, salt, and sugar. Add butter and eggs, and beat with an electric mixer on high for 4 minutes.
3. Fill muffin cups halfway and bake for 30 minutes, until tops are a dark golden brown. Do not open oven while baking, or popovers will fall. When done, turn out of muffin pan and serve hot.

When Bad is Good

Caffeine might be a no-no for the health conscious, but coffee drinkers claim to have more frequent—and more enjoyable sex than those who do not drink coffee.

Scrambled Herb Eggs

6 large eggs
2 tablespoons milk
1 tablespoon of each of the following fresh
*   chopped herbs: dill, parsley, chives,*
*   and oregano*
salt and pepper to taste
2 tablespoons butter

1. Whisk eggs and milk together until frothy, then mix in chopped herbs and seasonings.
2. Melt butter in a nonstick skillet. Add eggs, stirring constantly, until cooked through and fluffy.

My Mistress' Eyes Are Nothing Like the Sun
William Shakespeare

My mistress' eyes are nothing like the sun;
Coral is far more red than her lips' red:
If snow be white, why then her breasts are dun;
If hairs be wires, black wires grow on her head.
I have seen roses damaskt, red and white,
But no such roses see I in her cheeks;
And in some perfumes is there more delight
Than in the breath that from my mistress reeks.
I love to hear her speak, yet well I know
That music hath a far more pleasing sound;
I grant I never saw a goddess go;
My mistress, when she walks, treads on
*   the ground.*
*   And yet, by heaven, I think my love as rare*
*   As any she belied with false compare.*

The Web and the Rock

Thomas Wolfe

Autumn was kind to them, winter was long to them—but in April, late April, all the gold sang.

Spring came that year like magic and like music and like song. One day its breath was in the air, a haunting premonition of its spirit filled the hearts of men with its transforming loveliness, working its sudden and incredible sorcery upon grey streets, grey pavements, and grey faceless tides of manswarm ciphers. It came like music faint and far, it came with triumph and a sound of singing in the air, with lutings of sweet bird cries at the break of day and the high, swift passing of awing, and one day it was there upon the city streets with a strange, sudden cry of green, its sharp knife of wordless joy and pain.

Not the whole glory of the great plantation of the earth could have outdone the glory of the city streets that Spring. Neither the cry of great, green, fields, nor the song of the hills, nor the glory of young birch trees bursting into life again along the banks of the rivers, nor the oceans of bloom in the flowering orchards, the peach trees; the apple trees, the plum and cherry trees—not all of the singing and the gold of Spring, with April bursting from the earth in a million shouts of triumph, the visible stride, the flowered feet of the Springtime as it came on across the earth, could have surpassed the wordless and poignant glory of a single tree in a city street that Spring.

Monk had given up his tiny room in the dingy little hotel and had taken possession of the spacious floor in the old house on Waverly Place. There has been a moment's quarrel when he had said that from that time on he would pay the rent. She had objected that the

> *The prerequisite for making love is to like someone enormously.*
>
> —HELEN GURLEY BROWN

place was hers, that she had found it—she wanted him to come, she would like to think of him as being there, it would make it seem more "theirs"—but she had been paying for it, and would continue, and it didn't matter. But he was adamant and said he wouldn't come at all unless he paid his way, and it the end she yielded.

And now each day he heard her step upon the stairs at noon. At noon, at high, sane, glorious noon, she came, the mistress of that big, disordered room, the one whose brisk, small step on the stairs outside his door woke a leaping jubilation in his heart. Her face was like a light and like a music in the light of noon: it was jolly, small, and tender, as delicate as a plum, and as rosy as a flower. It was young and good and full of health and delight; its sweetness, strength, and noble beauty could not be equaled anywhere on earth. He kissed it a thousand times because it was so good, so wholesome, and so radiant in its loveliness.

Everything about her sang out with hope and morning. Her face was full of a thousand shifting plays of life and jolly humor, as swift and merry as a child's, and yet had in it always, like shadows in the sun, all of the profound, brooding, and sorrowful depths of beauty.

Thus, when he heard her step upon the stairs at noon, her light knuckles briskly rapping at the door, her key turning in the lock, she brought the greatest health and joy to him that he had ever known. She came in like a cry of triumph, like a shout of music in the blood, like the deathless birdsong in the first light of the morning. She was the bringer of hope, the teller of good news. A hundred sights and magical colors which she had seen in the streets that morning, a dozen tales of life and work and business, sprang form her merry lips with the eager insistence of a child.

She got into the conduits of his blood, she began to sing and pulse through the vast inertia of his flesh, still heavied with great clots of sleep, until he sprang up with the goat cry in his throat, seized, engulfed, and devoured her, and felt there was nothing on earth he could not conquer. She gave a tongue to all the exultant music of the Spring whose great pulsations trembled in the gold and sapphire singing of the air. Everything—the stick-candy whippings of a flag, the shout of a child, the smell of old, worn plankings in the sun, the heavy, oily, tarry exhalations of the Spring-warm streets, the thousand bobbing and weaving colors and the points of light upon the pavements, the smell of the markets, of fruits, flowers, vegetables, and loamy earth, and the heavy shattering baugh of a great ship as it left its wharf at noon on Saturday—was given intensity, structure, and a form of joy because of her.

She had never been as beautiful as she was that Spring, and sometimes it drove him almost mad to see her look so fresh and fair. Even before he heard her step upon the stair at noon he always knew that she was there. Sunken in sleep at twelve o'clock, drowned fathoms deep at noon in a strange, wakeful sleep, his consciousness of her was so great that he knew instantly the moment when she had entered the house, whether he heard a sound or not.

She seemed to be charged with all the good and joyful living of the earth as she stood there in the high light of noon. In all that was delicate in her little bones, her trim figure, slim ankles, full, swelling thighs, deep breast and straight, small shoulders, rose lips and flower face, and all the winking lights of her fine hair, jolliness, youth, and noble beauty—she seemed as rare, as rich, as high and grand a woman as any on earth could be. The first sight of her at noon always brought hope, confidence, belief, and sent through the huge inertia of his flesh, still drugged with the great anodyne of sleep, a tidal surge of invincible strength.

She would fling her arms around him and kiss him furiously, she would flight herself down beside him on his cot and cunningly, insinuate herself into his side, presenting her happy, glowing little face insatiably to be kissed, covered, plastered with a thousand kisses. She was fresh as morning, as tender as a plum, and so irresistible that he felt he could devour her in an instant and entomb her in his flesh forever. And then, after an interval, she would rise and set briskly about the preparation of a meal for him.

These is no spectacle on earth more appealing that that of a beautiful woman in the act of cooking dinner for someone she loves. Thus the sight of Esther as, delicately flushed, she bent with the earnest devotion of religious ceremony above the food she was cooking for him, was enough to drive him mad with love and hunger.

In such a moment he could not restrain himself. He would get up and begin to pace the room in a madness of wordless ecstasy. He would lather his face for shaving, shave one side of it, and then begin to walk up and down the room again, singing, making strange noises in his throat, staring vacantly out of the window at a cat that crept along the ridges of the fence; he would pull books from the shelves, reading a line or page, sometimes reading her a passage from a poem as she cooked, and then forgetting the book, letting it fall upon the cot or on the floor, until the floor was covered with them. Then he would sit on the edge of the cot for minutes, staring stupidly and vacantly ahead, holding one sock in his hand. Then he would spring up again and begin to pace the room, shouting and singing, with a convulsion of energy surging through his body that could find no utterance and that ended only in a wild, goatlike cry of joy.

From time to time he would go to the door of the kitchen where she stood above the stove, and for a moment he would draw into his lungs the maddening fragrance of the food. Then he would fling about the room again, until he could control himself no longer. The sight of her face, earnestly bent and focused in its work of love, her sure and subtle movements, and her full, lovely figure—all that was at once both delicate and abundant in her, together with the maddening fragrance of glorious food, evoked an emotion of wild tenderness and hunger in him which was unutterable. ♥

Song
Tzu Yeh

Winter skies are cold and low,
with harsh winds and freezing sleet.

But when we make love beneath our quilt,
we make three summer months of heat.

I Want to Breathe
James Laughlin

*you in I'm not talking about
perfume or even the sweet*

*odour of your skin but of the
air itself I want to share*

*your air inhaling what you
exhale I'd like to be that*

*close two of us breathing
each other as one as that*

*Of all parts of the body
that can be caressed or
kissed, the brow is the
most accessible and the
most mysterious, just
as sensual as more
celebrated body parts
but less frightening. It
hides only the mind.*

—MARCELLE CLEMENTS

Letters of Love

Zelda to F. Scott Fitzgerald

Novelists Zelda and F. Scott Fitzgerald married in 1920. Their lifelong love affair was notoriously passionate and tempestuous.

I look down the tracks and see you coming—and out of every haze and mist your darling rumpled trousers are hurrying to me—Without you, dearest dearest I couldn't see or hear or feel or think—or live—I love you so and I'm never in all our lives going to let us be apart another night. It's like begging for mercy of a storm or killing Beauty or growing old, without you. I want to kiss you so—and in the back where your dear hair starts and your chest—I love you—and I can't tell you how much—To think that I'll die without your knowing—Goofo, you've got to try [to] feel how much I do—how inanimate I am when you're gone—I can't even hate these damnable people—Nobody's got any right to live but us—and they're dirtying up our world and I can't hate them because I want you so—Come Quick—Come Quick to me—I could never do without you if you hated me and were covered with sores like a leper—if you ran away with another woman and starved me and beat me—I still would want you I know—Lover, Lover, Darling—Your Wife.

F. Scott Fitzgerald & Zelda Sayre

F. Scott Fitzgerald first met Zelda Sayre in 1918. The beautiful southern belle caught the eye of the handsome aspiring writer at a local dance in Alabama, where F. Scott's army unit was stationed. But Zelda refused to marry her suitor until he could support her financially. After repeated attempts, Scott finally published his first novel, and he and Zelda were wed in 1920. They enjoyed a rich and decadent lifestyle, soon becoming the iconic couple of the Jazz Age. Their drinking, lavish parties, and outrageous antics were the stuff of legends. Whether jumping into the fountain at the Plaza Hotel or riding on the hood of a taxicab, their passion for each other was palpable. But their life of frivolity, volatility, and privilege eventually caught up with them. Zelda struggled for years to make her mark as an artist in her own right, but was beset by several mental breakdowns; and the years of drinking took its toll on F. Scott, at times leaving him bedridden. Though their marriage finally deteriorated, for a time F. Scott and Zelda shared the kind of mad, deep love that most of us only dream about.

Pillow Talk
Top Ten Sex Advice Books

If you're looking to add some spice to your sex life or just want a little how-to advice, here are some great books that will answer all your burning questions and offer a wealth of ideas for under-the-covers fun.

1. Read *Satisfaction: The Art of the Female Orgasm* by sexy *Sex and The City* star Kim Cattrall and her husband Mark Levinson.

2. Re-ignite that lost spark with *The Sex Starved Marriage: A Couple's Guide to Boosting Their Marriage Libido* By Michele Weiner-Davis.

3. Unleash your inner sex goddess with *The Good Girls Guide to Bad Girl Sex* by Barbara Keesling. We all know she's in there!

4. *How to Give Her Absolute Pleasure: Totally Explicit Techniques Every Woman Wants Her Man to Know* by Lou Paget. Take notes fellas. If you need to keep the book next to you on the night stand, do it.

5. *The Joy of Sex Series* by Alex Comfort. This classic sex manual may seem dated at times, but is still worth a peek.

6. *Ultimate Sex* by Anne Hooper is another classic. Covers everything from beginner to advanced!

I blame my mother for my poor sex life. All she told me was, "the man goes on top and the woman underneath." For three years my husband and I slept on bunk beds.

—Joan Rivers

If sex is such a natural phenomenon, how come there are so many books on how to?

—Bette Midler

7. Bring out the animal in him with *Drive Him Wild: A Hands-on Guide to Pleasing Your Man in Bed* by Graham Masterson.

8. Entertaining and educational, *The Guide to Getting It On!: The Universe's Coolest and Most Informative Book About Sex for Adults of All Ages* by Paul Joannides will teach you something new and put a smile on your face.

9. We've all heard the rumors of Sting. See why, in *Tantric Love: A Nine Step Guide to Transforming Lovers into Soul Mates* by Ma Awanda Sarita and Swami Anand Geho.

10. *Sex for Dummies* by Dr. Ruth Westheimer is a great guide for everything sexual. From advice to techniques, from toys to health, Dr. Ruth always seems to have the answers.

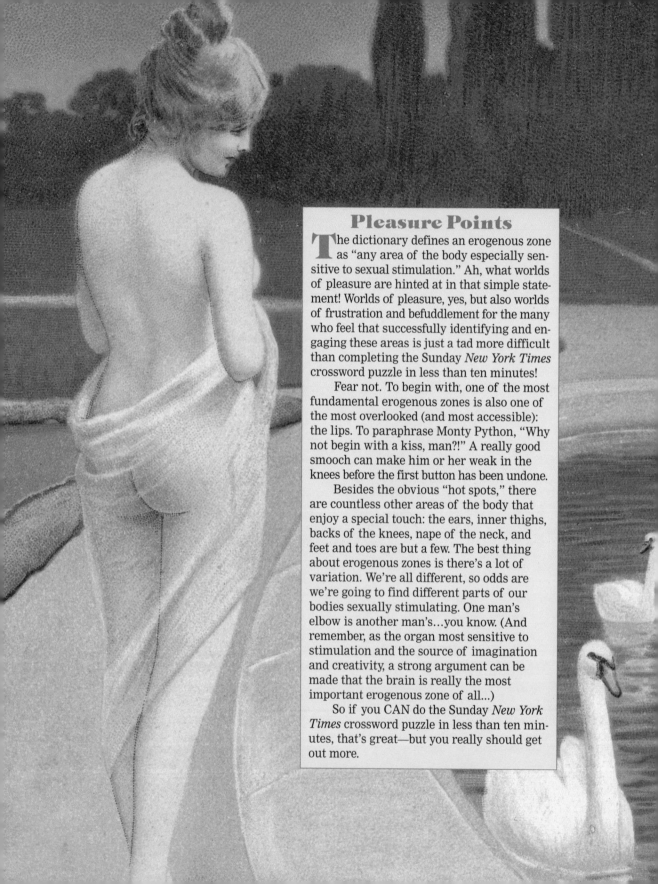

Pleasure Points

The dictionary defines an erogenous zone as "any area of the body especially sensitive to sexual stimulation." Ah, what worlds of pleasure are hinted at in that simple statement! Worlds of pleasure, yes, but also worlds of frustration and befuddlement for the many who feel that successfully identifying and engaging these areas is just a tad more difficult than completing the Sunday *New York Times* crossword puzzle in less than ten minutes!

Fear not. To begin with, one of the most fundamental erogenous zones is also one of the most overlooked (and most accessible): the lips. To paraphrase Monty Python, "Why not begin with a kiss, man?!" A really good smooch can make him or her weak in the knees before the first button has been undone.

Besides the obvious "hot spots," there are countless other areas of the body that enjoy a special touch: the ears, inner thighs, backs of the knees, nape of the neck, and feet and toes are but a few. The best thing about erogenous zones is there's a lot of variation. We're all different, so odds are we're going to find different parts of our bodies sexually stimulating. One man's elbow is another man's...you know. (And remember, as the organ most sensitive to stimulation and the source of imagination and creativity, a strong argument can be made that the brain is really the most important erogenous zone of all...)

So if you CAN do the Sunday *New York Times* crossword puzzle in less than ten minutes, that's great—but you really should get out more.

Letters of Love

D. H. Lawrence to Frieda Lawrence

Acclaimed English novelist D. H. Lawrence and his wife, Frieda von Richthofen Weekley, were married in 1914. The marriage lasted until Lawrence's death in 1930.

Waldbröl-Mittwoch, 1902

...You have got all myself—I don't even flirt—it would bore me very much—unless I got tipsy. It's a funny thing, to feel one's passion—sex desire—no longer a sort of wandering thing, but steady, and calm. I think, when one loves, one's very sex passion becomes calm, a steady sort of force, instead of a storm. Passion, that nearly drives one mad, is far away from real love. I am realizing things that I never thought to realize. Look at that poem I sent you—I would never write that to you. I shall love you all my life. That also is a new idea to me. But I believe it.

Auf Wiedersehen,
D. H. Lawrence

Excerpt from Frieda Lawrence: Memoirs and Correspondence:

...can I describe what it was like when we were first together? It just had to be. What others find in other ways, the oneness with all that lives and breathes, the peace of all peace, it does pass all understanding, that was between us, never to be lost completely. Love can be such a little thing with little meaning, then it can be a big one.

Everything seemed worth while, even trivial happenings; living with him was important and took on an air of magnificence.

After the first shock and surprise of this being together, as if a big wave had lifted us high on its crest to look at new horizons, it dawned on me: maybe this is a great man I am living with. I wish I knew what greatness consists of; if it were so obvious right away, it would not be great, because it's a man's uniqueness that makes him great.

We weren't soulful, Tristram and Isolde-ish. There wasn't time for tragedy. This new world of freedom and love kept us in its hold. His thoughts and impulses came up from such deep roots always more and more. I was on the alert all the time. The experience put us apart from other people that had not experienced it the same as we had. It made a barrier.

We quarreled so fiercely. But it was never mean or sneaky. We had come so close to each other, so we met each other without holding back, naked and direct.

Love is a fire. But whether it is going to warm your hearth or burn down your house, you can never tell.

—JOAN CRAWFORD

A Safe and Sexy History of the Condom

Condoms have been in use since ancient Egyptian men adorned their privates with decorative sheaths back in 3000 B.C. Even French cavemen in the second and third centuries knew that if you wanted to spread love and not disease, you had to protect yourself with a condom. In fifteenth-century Italy, linen sheaths doused in a chemical solution went on record as the first condoms with spermicide. Animal gut condoms, made of fish or sheep intestine with a ribbon tie at the base, predate their linen counterparts and can still be found today (minus the tie). Until the 1950s, animal condoms would be used, washed, rubbed with petroleum jelly, and stored in a box awaiting reuse (yuck!).

In 1844, five years after vulcanized rubber's advent, "rubber johnnies" burst onto the scene. Eventually, the invention of latex made rubber condoms cheaper, thinner, and, thankfully, disposable! Today, with condom production exceeding nine billion a year, it is the most popular and commonly used type of birth control. After all, what bachelorette party would be complete without its quota of edible and Day-Glo novelty condoms?

Did You Know...

Rumor has it that the word condom comes from the mysterious Dr. Condom, who supposedly provided King Charles II of England with prophylactics to prevent him from siring children and catching syphilis while consorting with prostitutes. More probable, however, is the explanation that it comes from the Latin *condon*, which means "receptacle." ♥ *The New York Times ran the first print advertisement for condoms: "Dr. Powers French Preservatives."* ♥ Condoms also are known as rubbers, *capotes d'anglais* (English raincoats), English riding coats, rubber johnnies, and French letters. ♥ *American GIs in World War I were the only soldiers not issued condoms. As a result, the American forces suffered from the highest rates of sexually transmitted diseases of all combatant armies. By World War II attitudes had changed, and GIs were encouraged to use condoms with the slogan: "Don't forget—put it on before you put it in!"*

Crimes of Passion

In **Harrisburg, Pennsylvania,** it is against the law to have sex with a truck driver in a toll booth. 💋 In **Nevada,** you could go to jail for having sex without a condom. 💋 In **Willowdale, Oregon,** it is against the law for a husband to talk dirty in his wife's ear during sex. 💋 In **Clinton, Oklahoma,** it is a crime to masturbate while watching two people have sex in a car. 💋 In the state of **Washington,** there is a law against having sex with a virgin under any circumstances (including the wedding night). 💋 In **Tremonton, Utah,** it is a crime to have sex in an ambulance. 💋 In **Newcastle, Wyoming,** having sex in a butcher shop's meat freezer ia a crime. 💋 In **Alexandria, Minnesota,** there is a law against a man having sex with his wife with the stink of onions, sardines, or garlic on his breath. 💋 In every state in the union, there is a law against having sex with a corpse. 💋 In **Ames, Iowa,** it is against the law to drink more than three slugs of beer while lying in bed with a woman. 💋 In **Fairbanks, Alaska,** there is a law that states that two moose can not have sex on city sidewalks. 💋 In **Kingsville, Texas,** there is a law against two pigs having sex on Kingsville airport property. 💋 In **Ventura County, California,** there is a law against cats and dogs having sex without a permit. 💋 In **Washington, D.C.,** there is a law against having sex in any position other than face-to-face.

Sex On Display

Not much a museum person, you say? What if it was a SEX museum? Here are a handful of the most famous ones from around the world:

💜 **The Beate Uhse Erotic Museum** in Berlin is one of the city's top ten most-visited tourist attractions. With a vast collection of erotic and sexual art and artifacts, this museum will not disappoint. Don't forget to visit the "gift" shop!

💜 **The Erotic Art Museum** in Hamburg, Germany houses a wide-ranging collection of ancient and modern erotic art.

💜 **Musee de l'Erotisme** in Paris takes a tamer approach to sex, with exhibits of multicultural erotic and sexual artifacts.

💜 **Museo de la Erotica** in Barcelona, Spain, houses a collection of multicultural erotic art through the ages. Of particular interest are its small collections of Picasso and Miró illustrations, which are on display.

💜 **The Museum Erotica** in Copenhagen, Denmark, exhibits the history of contraception, Danish pornography laws and prostitution, sex lives of famous people, and sex toys. Also of interest are the Playboy and Marilyn Monroe exhibits.

💜 **The Museum of Ancient Sex Culture** in Shanghai, China, is a historical collection of sexual art and artifacts compiled by Liu Dalin, a sex researcher at Shanghai University.

💜 **The Museum of Sex**, or **Mosex**, in New York City, strives to take a more academic view of sex. Using a multidisciplinary approach, Mosex explores the development of sexual attitudes and practices.

💜 **The National Museum of Erotica** in Canberra, Australia, is a vibrant mix of ancient and modern sexual art and artifacts.

💜 **The Venus Temple** in Amsterdam, Holland, was the first sex museum. Founded in 1985, it contains paintings, sculptures, engravings and other erotic art from antiquity through today.

Sexual Healing

Making love encourages the production of estrogen, good for the hair and skin. Sex is also a good aerobic workout: The average session of lovemaking burns from 100 to 150 calories! Having sex also produces endorphins, which may help alleviate mild depression.

To Have and To Hold

Married women engage in sexual activity approximately 111 times a year, as opposed to single gals—only 72 times. So there!

Don't Look Now, But

On any given day, approximately 200 million couples will have sex.

Ahh, Youth

The average teenager thinks about sex once every five minutes.

Beep-Beep!

The tradition of honking your car horn at a just-married couple was meant to guarantee the newlyweds great sex on their honeymoon.

Yaawwwn

Forty-six percent of American women would rather have a good night's sleep than have sex.

Top Ten Sexy Gifts

1. **A copy of the Kama Sutra** will spice things up in the bedroom.

2. **Erotic coupons** to make your lover's fantasies come true.

3. **Silk boxers or a negligée** to encourage cuddling.

4. **Chocolate body paints**—discover the artist within!

5. **Scented aromatherapy oils** accompanied by a sensual full body massage.

6. An artful and **sexy nude photograph or sketch** of yourself.

7. **A romantic music mix** with your favorite songs to put and keep you in the mood.

8. **A bottle of bubble bath and box of votive candles** with an invitation to take a tub for two.

9. A gift certificate to have **a couple's massage** at a nearby day spa.

10. **A hotel key** with a note that includes just the "Place" and "Time."

Touch
Octavio Paz

My hands
Open the curtains of your being
Clothe you in a further nudity
Uncover the bodies of your body
My hands
Invent another body for your body

Speak low if you speak of love.

—DON PEDRO

Letters of Love

Frida Kahlo to Diego Rivera

Celebrated Mexican painters, Frida Kahlo and Diego Rivera shared a lifelong love both for each other and their art. Married in 1929, they were together nearly twenty-five years when Frida died at the young age of forty-seven, in 1954.

Diego:
Nothing compares to your hands, nothing like the green gold of your eyes. My body is filled with you for days and days. You are the mirror of the night. The violent flash of lightning. The dampness of the earth. The hollow of your armpits is my shelter. My fingertips touch your blood. All my joy is to feel life spring from your flower-fountain that mine keeps to fill all the paths of my nerves which are yours.

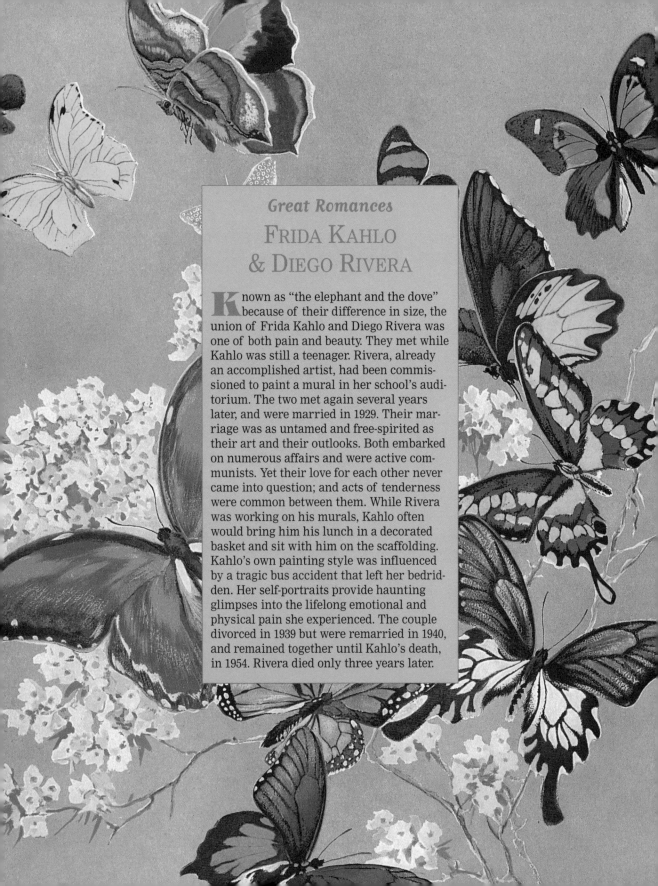

Great Romances
FRIDA KAHLO
& DIEGO RIVERA

Known as "the elephant and the dove" because of their difference in size, the union of Frida Kahlo and Diego Rivera was one of both pain and beauty. They met while Kahlo was still a teenager. Rivera, already an accomplished artist, had been commissioned to paint a mural in her school's auditorium. The two met again several years later, and were married in 1929. Their marriage was as untamed and free-spirited as their art and their outlooks. Both embarked on numerous affairs and were active communists. Yet their love for each other never came into question; and acts of tenderness were common between them. While Rivera was working on his murals, Kahlo often would bring him his lunch in a decorated basket and sit with him on the scaffolding. Kahlo's own painting style was influenced by a tragic bus accident that left her bedridden. Her self-portraits provide haunting glimpses into the lifelong emotional and physical pain she experienced. The couple divorced in 1939 but were remarried in 1940, and remained together until Kahlo's death, in 1954. Rivera died only three years later.

If love is blind, why is lingerie so popular?

—UNKNOWN

Naked at Night

Only 20 percent of men prefer to sleep "au naturel."

The Best Lingerie

Perhaps it's because you feel as if you're walking around with a sexy little secret. Perhaps it's the way silk and satin feels against the skin. Perhaps it's the promise of taking it off later, but wearing lovely lingerie never fails to make a woman feel beautiful. From raunchy to refined, ladies' undergarments are more popular and varied than ever before. So throw away those granny panties and indulge in a little ooh la la!

Bare Necessities An on-line lingerie store offering a great variety of brands from luxurious La Perla to trendy CosaBella to reliable Wacoal: *barenecessities.com* or (877) 728-9272.

Patricia Fieldwalker If you're looking for something a little more "tasteful," try a Patricia Fieldwalker design. Her luxurious lingerie has been featured in films and magazines, worn by such glamorous women as Kathleen Turner, Julia Roberts, Michelle Pfeiffer, Claudia Schiffer, Demi Moore, and Christy Turlington: *pfieldwalker.com*.

Fredrick's of Hollywood This classic lingerie chain is bit more risqué than its mainstream competitor. If you can't find a retail store nearby, don't hesitate to order their catalogue: *fredericks.com* or (800) 323-9525.

Spicy Lingerie It's so hard to find a chain-mail chemise these days, but don't worry: If you can imagine it, Spicy Lingerie probably has it. Besides the usual cornucopia of bustiers, teddies, and baby-dolls, Spicy has costumes and accessories to help you act out your fantasies: *spicylingerie.com* or (866) 893-1682.

Trashy Lingerie Trashy has been on the scene for twenty-five years, making playful and sexy lingerie for such famous clients as Cher, Drew Barrymore, and Madonna. Choose styles from their new Dude Ranch collection, the polar fleece collection, or the schoolgirl collection (there's even a bargain section): *trashy.com* or (310) 659-4550.

Passion Fruit Crepes with Strawberries

These are so insanely good that they'll satisfy both your passionate and cozy sides. There is a whisper of the memory of pancakes, but make no mistake, these are far more sophisticated. Serve as a dessert.

> *2¼ cups flour*
> *2 tablespoons sugar*
> *pinch salt*
> *4 eggs*
> *2¼ cups milk, boiled and cooled*
> *1¾ cups heavy cream*
> *¼ teaspoon vanilla-bean seeds*
> *4 fresh passion fruits, juice and pulp*
> *2 tablespoons clarified butter*
> *zest of 1 lemon*
> *1 pint fresh strawberries, quartered*
> *   (or raspberries)*
> *mint for garnish*

1. Combine the flour, sugar, and salt in a bowl and add the eggs, one at a time, mixing well. Stir in ⅔ cup milk, until batter is smooth. Pour in ⅞ cup cream and the rest of the milk. Leave batter to rest for an hour in a cool place.
2. To cook, stir the batter and add the seeds from the vanilla bean, passion fruit pulp, and juice.
3. Brush the skillet or crepe pan with clarified butter and heat. Ladle a little batter into the pan and cook for 1–2 minutes on each side, turning the crepe with a spatula.
4. Whip the rest of the heavy cream until stiff peaks form. Adjust sugar to taste and add lemon zest.
5. To serve, layer crepes with whipped cream, and top with lightly tossed sugared strawberries. Garnish with mint.

Serves 4–6

Top Ten Greatest Lovers

While most people love to be loved, some men and women over the course of history have made the very pursuit of love (or lovemaking) their reason for living. Here are ten of the busiest lovers of all time.

1. **Don Juan** Immortalized in Mozart's opera *Don Giovanni*, this legendary character was based on a fourteenth-century Spanish nobleman—Don Juan Teno'rio of Seville. Don Juan was famous for his romantic conquests and for his indifference to the suffering he caused. In one canto of Byron's poem, *Don Juan*, the famous lover, hides out in a harem, igniting fierce competition among the residents to be the one to share his bed.

2. **Casanova** Born in Venice, Casanova de Seingalt, Giovanni Giacomo (1725–98), studied for the priesthood in his youth. When a seminary expelled him because of his drinking and love affairs, his adventures began. He trav-

eled throughout Europe, gambling and seducing more than one hundred women, while also contracting several sexually transmitted diseases. His autobiography made famous his tales of the erotic life, and his name has become synonymous with the notion of libertinism.

3. **Rudolph Valentino** This Italian-born actor was a Hollywood heartthrob in movies such as *The Sheik* and *The Four Horsemen of the Apocalypse*. He was once fined $10,000 for bigamy. His funeral, in 1926, attracted eighty thousand mourners. For many years a mysterious lady in black marked the anniversary of his death by leaving a red rose on his grave.

4. **Catherine the Great** When her husband, Peter, emperor of Russia, was unable to consummate their marriage, Empress Catherine took up with a handsome officer in the Russian army. The son she bore was accepted as heir to the throne. In a bold coup, she had another of her many lovers kill her husband, and she ascended to the throne as Catherine the Great. It is rumored that her enormous sexual appetite sometimes led her into alliances with animals, particularly a favorite horse.

5. **Cleopatra** Born in 69 B.C., Cleopatra was the last pharaoh of Egypt. From an early age, the "Queen of the Nile" was known as a great beauty with many lovers. She even invented her own version of the diaphragm to make her alliances more convenient. Cleopatra seduced Julius Caesar, emperor of Rome, in order to increase her political power, and then caused Marc Antony, another Roman leader, to leave his wife and family. She pushed him into war against his former allies.

6. **Mae West** By the age of fourteen, Mae West was already known as the "Baby Vamp." The buxom blonde went on to become one of Hollywood's most famous sex symbols. She had an active love life into her eighties, and once said, "It's not the men in my life, but the life in my men."

7. **George Sand** French author Amandine Aurore-Lucie Dupin (1804–78), who wrote under the name George Sand, was famous for her eccentric behavior and many lovers. She

was an independent spirit who wore men's clothing, supported her children by writing novels, and demanded for women the same freedoms that men enjoyed. Among her lovers were some of the most important men of the century, including the poet Alfred de Musset and the composer Frederic Chopin.

8. Marquis de Sade Infamous libertine and philosopher of the erotic, the Marquis de Sade (1740–1814), whose real name was Comte Donatien-Alphonse-François, once wrote, "Lust is to the other passions what the nervous fluid is to life; it supports them all." He served twenty-seven years in prison for "scandalous conduct" and sexual offenses. His writings, which argued a connection between pleasure and pain, were condemned as obscene but nonetheless remain in print.

9. King Solomon Revered king of the Ancient Hebrews, (930 B.C.) Solomon had three hundred wives and six hundred concubines. When his half brother asked for just one of these concubines, Solomon had him executed. The *Song of Solomon*, traditionally attributed to him, uses erotic imagery to express religious devotion. Verses such as "Thy two breasts are like two young roes that are twins, which feed among the lilies" have secured Solomon's reputation as a lover throughout the ages.

10. Henry VIII Born in 1491, this king of England was notoriously hard to please when it came to women. Beginning his nuptial career by marrying his brother's widow, he went on to wed five more times in search of the perfect mate. When relationships turned sour, he simply divorced or beheaded yesterday's girl and moved on to the next one.

Mae West says...

I've been in more laps than a napkin.

It's better to be looked over than overlooked.

I used to be snow white, but I drifted.

Ten men waiting for me at the door? Send one of them home, I'm tired.

Love's Philosophy
Percy Bysshe Shelley

*The fountains mingle with the river
   And the rivers with the Ocean,
The winds of Heaven mix for ever
   With a sweet emotion;
Nothing in the world is single;
   All things by a law divine
In one spirit meet and mingle,
   Why not I with thine?—*

*See the mountains kiss high Heaven
   And the waves clasp one another;
No sister-flower would be forgiven
   If it disdained its brother;
And the sunlight clasps the earth
   And the moonbeams kiss the sea:
What is all this sweet work worth
   If thou kiss not me?*

The Mile High Club
Bats have sexual intercourse while in flight.

All Night Long
The average duration of intercourse between minks is eight hours!

The Best of Both Worlds
Did you know that oysters are ambisexual? During their lifetimes they change from male to female and back again several times.

Sex is like bridge: If you don't have a good partner, you better have a good hand.

—CHARLES PIERCE

Chapter Five
Enduring Love

The Elephant
and
the Butterfly

E. E. CUMMINGS

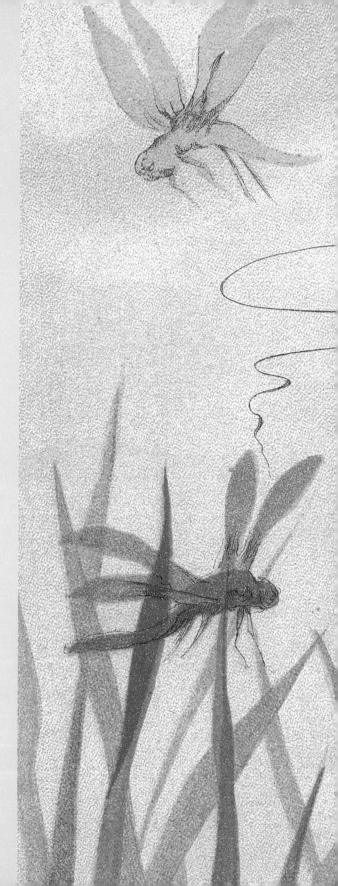

Once upon a time there was an elephant who did nothing all day.

He lived by himself in a little house away at the very top of a curling road.

From the elephant's house, this curling road went twisting away down and down until it found itself in a green valley where there was another little house, in which a butterfly lived.

One day the elephant was sitting in his little house and looking out of his window doing nothing (and feeling very happy because that was what he liked most to do) when along this curling road he saw somebody coming up and up toward his little house; and he opened his eyes wide, and felt very much surprised.

"Whoever is that person who's coming up along and along the curling road toward my little house?" the elephant said to himself.

And pretty soon he saw that it was a butterfly who was fluttering along the curling road ever so happily; and the elephant said: "My goodness, I wonder if he's coming to call on me?" As the butterfly came nearer and nearer, the elephant felt more and more excited inside of himself. Up the steps of the little house came the butterfly and he knocked very gently on the door with his wing. "Is anyone inside?" he asked.

The elephant was ever so pleased, but he waited.

Then the butterfly knocked again with his wing, a little louder but still very gently, and said: "Does anyone live here, please?"

212

Still the elephant never said anything because he was too happy to speak.

A third time the butterfly knocked, this time quite loudly, and asked: "Is anyone at home?" And this time the elephant said in a trembling voice: "I am." The butterfly peeped in at the door and said: "Who are you, that live in this little house?" And the elephant peeped out at him and answered: "I'm the elephant who does nothing all day." "Oh," said the butterfly, "and may I come in?" "Please do," the elephant said with a smile, because he was very happy. So the butterfly just pushed the little door open with his wing and came in.

Once upon a time there were seven trees which lived beside the curling road. And when the butterfly pushed the door with his wing and came into the elephant's little house, one of the trees said to one of the trees: "I think it's going to rain soon."

"The curling road will be all wet and will smell beautifully," said another tree to another tree.

Then a different tree said to a different tree: "How lucky for the butterfly that he's safely inside the elephant's little house, because he won't mind the rain."

But the littlest tree said: "I feel the rain already," and sure enough, while the butterfly and the elephant were talking in the elephant's little house away at the top of the curling road, the rain simply began falling gently everywhere; and the butterfly and the elephant looked out of the window together and they felt ever so safe and glad, while the curling road became all wet and began to smell beautifully just as the third tree had said.

Pretty soon it stopped raining and the elephant put his arm very gently around the little butterfly and said: "Do you love me a little?"

And the butterfly smiled and said: "No, I love you very much."

Then the elephant said: "I'm so happy, I think we ought to go for a walk together you and I; for now the rain has stopped and the curling road smells beautifully."

The butterfly sail: "Yes, but where shall you and I go?"

"Let's go away down and down the curling road where I've never been," the elephant said to the little butterfly. And the butterfly smiled and said: "I'd love to go with you away and away down the curling road—let's go out the little door of your house and down the steps together—shall we?"

So they came out together and the elephant's arm was very gently around the butterfly. Then the littlest tree said to his six friends: "I believe the butterfly loves the elephant as much as the elephant loves the butterfly, and that makes me very happy, for they'll love each other always."

Down and down the curling road walked the elephant and the butterfly.

The sun was shining beautifully after the rain.

The curling road smelled beautifully of flowers.

A bird began to sing in a bush, and all the clouds went away out of the sky and it was Spring everywhere.

When they came to the butterfly's house, which was down in the green valley which had never been so green, the elephant said: "Is this where you live?"

And the butterfly said: "Yes, this is where I live."

"May I come into your house?" said the elephant.

"Yes," said the butterfly. So the elephant just pushed the door gently with his trunk and they came into the butterfly's house. And then the elephant kissed the butterfly very gently and the butterfly said: "Why didn't you ever before come down into the valley where I live?" And the elephant answered, "Because I did nothing all day. But now that I know where you live, I'm coming down the curling road to see you every day, if I may—and may I come?" Then the butterfly kissed the elephant and said: "I love you, so please do."

And every day after this the elephant would come down the curling road which smelled so beautifully (past the seven trees and the bird singing in the bush) to visit his little friend the butterfly.

And they loved each other always. ♥

"Warm Your Heart" Hot Chocolate

Nothing warms the heart—or the stomach—more than a great cup of hot chocolate. This one is suited for adult tastes, with a shot of peppermint schnapps guaranteed to leave you feeling cozy and relaxed. Perfect for a fireside cuddle.

> *3 cups milk*
> *2 tablespoons unsweetened cocoa*
> *4 tablespoons sugar*
> *2 tablespoons peppermint schnapps*
> *peppermint whipped cream*

1. Combine milk, cocoa, and sugar in a saucepan and heat on low flame, stirring constantly with an eggbeater.
2. When mixture is smooth and just starting to bubble, remove from stove and pour into two mugs. Add one tablespoon of peppermint schnapps to each mug. Top with peppermint whipped cream!

Peppermint Whipped Cream

> *1 small container whipping cream*
> *1 tablespoon sugar*
> *1 teaspoon peppermint extract*

1. Combine ingredients in a nonslip bowl and beat with electric mixer on high until cream has thickened and peaks form. Whipped cream can be made several hours ahead of time and stored in the refrigerator.

Serves 2

The longest marriage was between Sir Temuji Bhicaji Nnman and Lady Nariman. It lasted for 87 years.

Great Romances
WINSTON & CLEMENTINE CHURCHILL

In the world of politics, a spouse is very often the most important supporter of all. For Winston and Clementine Churchill, this was especially true. They were wed in 1908 and had five children together. Their marriage withstood two wars, the death of a child, and Winston's failure to win reelection as prime minister of England in 1945. Their private life and devotion to each other is evident in the extensive collection of letters they exchanged over the years. Early in their marriage they signed their correspondence with drawings of their respective nicknames. He was "pug" or "pig" and she was "cat." Their marriage lasted fifty-seven years, until Winston's death, in 1965.

Although I Conquer All the Earth
from the Sanskrit

Although I conquer all the earth,
Yet for me there is only one city.
In that city there is for me only one house;
And in that house, one room only;
And in that room, a bed.
And one woman sleeps there,
The shining joy and jewel of all my kingdom.

> *Age does not protect you from love. But love, to some extent, protects you from age.*
>
> —JEANNE MOREAU

Letters of Love

Winston Churchill and his wife, Clementine

Winston Churchill, British prime minister and author, wed Clementine Hozier in 1908. They were happily married for fifty-seven years.

To Winston   November 28, 1915

. . . But when I think of you my Dearest Darling, I forget all disappointment, bitterness or ambition & long to have you safe & warm & alive in my arms. Since you have re-become a soldier I look upon civilians of high or low degree with pity & indulgence—The wives of men over military age may be lucky but I am sorry for them being married to feeble & incompetent old men. I think you will get this letter on your birthday & it brings you all my love & many passionate kisses—My Darling Darling Winston—I find my morning breakfast lonely without you, so Sarah fills your place & does her best to look almost exactly like you. I'm keeping the flag flying till you return by getting up early & having breakfast down-stairs.

To Clementine   December 1, 1915

I reopen my envelope to tell you I have recd your dear letter of the 28th. I reciprocate intensely the feelings of love & devotion you show to me. My greatest good fortune in a life of brilliant experience has been to find you, & to lead my life with you. I don't feel far away from you out here at all. I feel vy near in my heart; & also I feel that the nearer I get to honour, the nearer I am to you.

> *Immature love says, 'I love you because I need you.'*
> *Mature love says, 'I need you because I love you.'*
>
> —ERICH FROMM

Still Life with Woodpecker

TOM ROBBINS

When the mystery of the connection goes, love goes. It's that simple. This suggests that it isn't love that is so important to us but the mystery itself. The love connection may be merely a device to put us in contact with the mystery, and we long for love to last so that the ecstasy of being near the mystery will last. It is contrary to the nature of the mystery to stand still. Yet it's always there, somewhere, a world on the other side of the mirror (or the Camel pack), a promise in the next pair of eyes that smile at us. We glimpse it when we stand still.

The romance of new love, the romance of solitude, the romance of objecthood, the romance of ancient pyramids and distant stars are means of making contact with the mystery. When it comes to perpetuating it, however, I got no advice. But I can and will remind you of two of the most important facts I know:

(1) Everything is part of it.
(2) It's never too late to have a happy childhood.

♥

Top Ten Terms of Endearment

Sure, your "significant other" has a real name, but so does everyone else! If you really love someone, you call them by a name that is often so foolish and full of affection that you would be embarrassed to see it in print. Here are just a few of the silly and endearing ways we refer to our little "love bunnies."

From the Food Group

1. Cupcake
2. Cookie
3. Sweetie pie
4. Pumpkin
5. Sugar
6. Honeybun
7. Muffin
8. Peanut
9. Pork Chop
10. Jellybean

From the Animal Kingdom

1. Pussycat
2. Puppydog
3. Bunny
4. Kitten
5. Honeybear
6. Little Lamb
7. Munchkin
8. Pooh Bear
9. Tiger
10. Foxy

Other Favorites

1. Hotstuff
2. Cherie
3. Snookums
4. Sexy
5. Cara Mia
6. My one and only
7. Dear Heart
8. Lovey
9. Darlin'
10. Babe

When You Are Old
William Butler Yeats

When you are old and grey and full of sleep,
And nodding by the fire, take down this book,
And slowly read, and dream of the soft look
Your eyes had once, and of their shadows deep;

How many loved your moments of glad grace,
And loved your beauty with love false or true,
But one man loved the pilgrim soul in you,
And loved the sorrows of your changing face;

And bending down beside the glowing bars,
Murmur, a little sadly, how Love fled
And paced upon the mountains overhead
And hid his face amid a crowd of stars.

A Monument to Love
The Taj Mahal

Located on the banks of the Yamuna River in Agra, India, the Taj Mahal is one of the seven wonders of the world and the ultimate monument to undying love. Built by Shah Jahan in the seventeenth century, the Taj Mahal fulfilled the dying request of his wife, Arjumand Banu, to build a memorial to their love. The couple met at a bazaar when the prince was fourteen and Arjumand was fifteen, and they were married five years later. Though Shah Jahan had other wives, he was deeply smitten with Arjumand, whom he lovingly referred to as Mumtaz Mahal, or "Jewel of the Palace." Mumtaz Mahal became Shah Jahan's dearest, most trusted wife, traveling with him on military expeditions and even advising the emperor on matters of state.

Mumtaz Mahal died in 1631 while giving birth to her and the Shah's fourteenth child. The Taj Mahal, with its white-domed tomb and its sprawling 42 acres of gardens, mosques, and minarets, was completed over the next two decades at considerable expense to the royal treasury. Supposedly the chief architect of the Taj was beheaded and the fingers of the workmen who worked on the monument were cut off to prevent them from building a similar monument. Legend has it that the Shah, imprisoned by his ambitious son, died with a mirror in his hand, gazing upon the  reflection of the Taj Mahal and the memory of his beloved wife and their immortal love.

On Golden Pond

*Starring Katharine Hepburn
and Henry Fonda, 1981*

NORMAN
Hello, there.

ETHEL
Hi.

NORMAN
Wanna dance or do you just want to suck face?

Even clothed in wrinkles, dear Philinna,
you are more beautiful than the young.

I'd sooner taste the apples
hanging heavy from your boughs

than pinch the firm breasts of girls.
I've no taste for the young.

Your autumn outshines a mortal spring,
your winter warmer than a summer sun.

—Paulus Silentiarius

Top Ten Classic Romantic Movies

Filmmakers have expressed every point of view imaginable on the subject of love—from the hilarious to the unbearably tragic. What do all of our picks have in common? Pure magic. They are considered classics in their genre and are sure to withstand the test of time.

1. **Breakfast at Tiffany's** Like Audrey Hepburn's Holly Golightly, you dream of reinventing yourself in a big city, living the glamorous life. But when life's curve ball comes in the form of a penniless yet handsome neighbor destined to be your soul mate, do you surrender to his charms? True love and character are the real underdogs in this story.

2. **The Way We Were** It's young Robert Redford, irresistible in that creamy cable-knit sweater. It's Barbara Streisand at her 1970s diva, smoky cat-eyed best. It's romance, politics, communism, capitalism, New York grit, LA glitz, and one of the most heartwrenching endings in history—all done to epic perfection.

3. **Manhattan** Charming, funny, chatty. The quirky genius of Woody Allen makes you believe there is nothing more romantic than falling in love in his beautiful black-and-white celluloid New York.

4. **When Harry Met Sally** Meg Ryan at the height of adorableness. Billy Crystal at his cutest but, let's face it, dorkiest. You want to hang out with them. Drive cross-country with them. Eat Reubens with them—you want to BE them. Nora Ephron creates a world in which love is possible for everyone. Even best friends.

5. **Singin' in the Rain** From the charming Debbie Reynolds, to the umbrella-swinging Gene Kelly, this delightful love story will leave you with the irresistible urge to jump in the next puddle you come across.

6. **Love Story** It's an age-old story—Ryan O'Neal plays a privileged young man who goes off to law school where he meets a poor, smart-talking music student (Ali McGraw). Surmounting all the obstacles, they fall passionately in love, only to be hit with tragedy. This cinematic classic coined the phrase: "Love means never having to say you're sorry."

7. **Romeo and Juliet** Zeffirelli's version, of course. First of all, the music. Secondly the beauty of both tragic heroes—Olivia Hussey and Leonard Whiting so ripe with youth and intoxicated with love, by the time Romeo falls on Juliet's chest you want to say to the friar, "I'll have what Juliet had." Oh happy dagger, indeed. Just make sure all sharp objects are out of reach.

8. **On Golden Pond** Every year, the Thayers, played to perfection by Henry Fonda and Katharine Hepburn, head out to their summer cottage to enjoy their twilight years in peaceful solitude. But this time, a surprise visit from his daughter (Jane Fonda), her fiancé, and their son complicates matters in this heartfelt story about forgiveness and family love.

9. **The Philadelphia Story** For the nuptially challenged. A witty verbal romp that makes you wish you could time warp back to 1940 and those grand Main Line rooms—chatting it up with Katharine Hepburn, Cary Grant, and Jimmy Stewart. Smart and sassy. Class meets pretense. Wouldn't your heart go pitter-pat if your ex-husband showed up before your wedding, and perhaps the most dreadful mistake of your life? C'mon, it's Cary Grant.

10. **Splendor in the Grass** A coming of age story in 1920s Kansas, Warren Beatty and Natalie Wood play two smoldering high school lovers with big plans after graduation. But when their desires are repressed by societal standards, their shared path is painfully rent apart. A devastating love story.

I love Mickey Mouse more than any woman I have ever known.

—WALT DISNEY

When They Dance
Judith Sornberger

Nothing's ever been as sexy
as your dad handing your mom's purse
to her sister as they turned,
as in one body, into music
on the dance floor.

No one has ever touched us like that.
The boys we learned our bodies with
we never touched while dancing,
not that way. In "Purple Haze"
we kissed the sky, strobe lights chopping
your arms flailing into a million stills.

Not like our parents getting misty
holding hands, the outlines
of their fingers blurring, bodies
belonging more and more
to music and that union.

Sure, we had the slow songs:
his hands around our waist,
ours clasped behind his neck.
We hugged and pressed ourselves
into each other, thought sex
meant the body.

We ignored our mothers'
save yourself for marriage,
and when we tried on bikinis,
their advice: leave something
to the imagination. We saved
our imaginations for self-expression,
saved ritual for separation.

Sometimes we envy them,
still dancing with their first loves
while we keep changing partners,
as if changing teaches how
to let the music change us.

But we sense they've missed some things.
As we whispered once about our bodies
and their secrets, we whisper now
about our mothers: Do you think
they have oral sex, orgasms?

We know how to dance alone,
a useful art they never taught us.
But when we watch the alchemy
their bodies work with music
and the ordinary bodies of our fathers
we know there's something they have
yet to tell us.

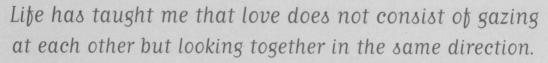

*Life has taught me that love does not consist of gazing
at each other but looking together in the same direction.*

—ANTOINE DE SAINT EXUPÉRY

These Things Remain . . .

If I speak in the tongues of men and of angels, but have not love, I am only a resounding gong or a clanging cymbal. If I have the gift of prophecy and can fathom all mysteries and all knowledge, and if I have a faith that can move mountains, but have not love, I am nothing. If I give all I possess to the poor and surrender my body to the flames, but have not love I gain nothing. Love is patient, love is kind. It does not envy, it does not boast, it is not proud. It is not rude, it is not self-seeking, it is not easily angered, it keeps no record of wrongs. Love does not delight in evil but rejoices with the truth. It always protects, always trusts, always perseveres. Love never fails. But where there are prophecies, they will cease; where there are tongues, they will be stilled; where there is knowledge, it will pass away.... And now these things remain: faith, hope and love. But the greatest of these is love.

—1 CORINTHIANS 13:1-8, 13

Grow old along with me, the best is yet to be.

—WILLIAM BLAKE

Anniversary Gift Ideas

Here are some unique suggestions based on the traditional wedding anniversary gifts for every major year of marriage:

Year 1 (paper): Sports tickets for him; ballet or concert tickets for her

Year 2 (cotton): His & Her monogrammed beach towels

Year 3 (leather): Sexy boots for her; a leather jacket for him

Year 4 (linen): New sheets for the bed

Year 5 (wood): A tree to plant in your garden

Year 6 (iron): Doorstop or old-fashioned bubble-gum machine

Year 7 (copper, brass): Crepe pan complete with recipe book, mix, and jams, OR an antique bed frame

Year 8 (bronze): Donate a bench to your favorite park, with a dedication plaque bearing your names

Year 9 (pottery): Dog or cat bowls, complete with a cuddly puppy or kitten

Year 10 (tin): Soldiers for him; jewelry wrapped in tin box for her

Year 11 (steel): A new stove, dishwasher, refrigerator, or washer/dryer

Year 12 (silk): lingerie for her; pj's for him

Year 13 (lace): Curtains for the bedroom or a sexy pinoir (to be enjoyed by both of you!)

Year 14 (ivory): A piano—and lessons, if necessary, or a donation to help protect African elephants, made in your names

Year 15 (crystal): Decanters for him; a chandelier for her

Year 20 (china): Replenish your by now incomplete set of wedding dishes

Year 25 (silver): Silver-plated golf clubs for him & her and a romantic golf trip

Year 30 (pearls): A mother-of-pearl letter opener for him along with a love letter; opera glasses for her and a pair of opera tickets

Year 35 (coral): A pillbox for him; a cameo brooch for her

Year 40 (rubies): Cuff links for him; a heart-shaped ruby necklace for her

Year 45 (sapphires): An antique tie clip and cufflinks for him; drop earrings for her

Year 50 (gold): New wedding bands

Great Romances
JOHN ADAMS & ABIGAIL SMITH

John Adams and Abigail Smith began their lifelong marriage in 1764. Adams was a Harvard graduate, and though Abigail had no formal education, she was a voracious reader. Bright and articulate, she was the perfect companion to her erudite husband.

With the outbreak of the American Revolution ten years later, John spent the majority of his time abroad on political business. Abigail remained at home to raise their children, manage their farm, and tend to her husband's affairs. Their extensive correspondence throughout their marriage provides a unique and touching view into the life of a patriotic and devoted couple. John often turned to his wife for political guidance, and Abigail wrote of her longing for her "dearest friend." Years ahead of her time, Abigail shared the convictions of her husband and was well versed in the political rhetoric that surrounded her. After being elected the second president of the United States, John wrote Abigail, " I never wanted your advice and assistance more in my life."

The relationship of John and Abigail Adams was one of unwavering support and adoration. Abigail Adams died in 1818. John Adams passed away in 1826.

Such Different Wants

By Robert Bly

The board floats on the river.
The board wants nothing
but is pulled from beneath
on into deeper waters.

And the elephant dwelling
on the mountain wants
a trumpet so its dying cry
can be heard by the stars.

The wakeful heron striding
through reeds at dawn wants
the god of sun and moon
to see his long skinny neck.

You must say what you want.
I want to be the man
and I am who will love you
when your hair is white.

Contemporary Anniversary Gifts

Year 1	clocks	Year 12	pearls
Year 2	china	Year 13	textiles, fur
Year 3	crystal, glass	Year 14	gold jewelry
Year 4	appliances	Year 15	watches
Year 5	silverware	Year 20	platinum
Year 6	wood	Year 25	sterling silver
Year 7	desk sets	Year 30	diamonds
Year 8	linen, lace	Year 35	jade
Year 9	leather	Year 40	garnets
Year 10	diamond jewelry	Year 45	tourmalines
Year 11	fashion jewelry	Year 50	gold

I married the first man
I ever kissed. When I tell
this to my children they
just about throw up.

—Barbara Bush

Letters of Love

Abigail to John Adams

John Adams, second president of the United States, married Abigail Smith in October 1764 after a brief courtship. They were happily married for 54 years.

My Dearest Friend,   23 December 1792

. . . Should I draw you the picture of my heart it would be what I hope you would still love though it contained nothing new. The early possession you obtained there, and the absolute power you have obtained over it, leaves not the smallest space unoccupied. I look back to the early days of our acquaintance and friendship as to the days of love and innocence, and, with an indescribable pleasure, I have seen near a score of years roll over our heads with an affection heightened and improved by time, nor have the dreary years of absence in the smallest degree effaced from my mind the image of the dear untitled man to whom I gave my heart.

The Love Box

A single photograph, ticket stub, or matchbook is sometimes all it takes to relive a first kiss, a romantic date, your wedding day, or a special anniversary or vacation. Savor those tender moments by storing keepsakes from your times together in a Love Box. Then, whenever you want to experience your tender memories anew, simply open the box, smile, and dream. Or present it to your partner as a gift on Valentine's Day or a meaningful anniversary.

Materials: Boxes and tins in various shapes, decorative paper (such as marbled paper, papyrus, or flower petal paper), scissors, fast-drying glue or glue gun, paints (tempera, fabric paint, metallic paint), metallic ink pens, trimmings & notions (ribbon, lace, braiding, piping), photographs, fabric scraps

1. Choose a favorite size and shape box to decorate to your liking. If the box is made of wood or cardboard, you may wish to paint it or cut decorative paper to glue around the outside. Decorate a tin box with metallic paint or script a love poem around the sides with a metallic pen.
2. You can add a bit of romantic flair on the lid with a satin ribbon or lace trim. Glue the trim in place and allow it to dry. Top the lid with a photograph that you frame with old-fashioned picture corners or additional ribbon.
3. For wood or cardboard boxes, use glue to line the box with sensual fabric, such as velvet or silk. For a tin box, use your metallic paints to decorate the interior in any way you like.
4. Fill your Love Box to your heart's content with tickets from movies, museums, concerts, and sporting events. Save wine labels, corks, and menus from memorable dinners. You can also store travel souvenirs, wedding favors, and romantic trinkets inside. If you plan to give the box as a gift, add love poems and candy kisses for an extra bit of sweetness.

Tea for Two

Enjoying teatime with your loved one is a great excuse to spend a peaceful hour together. Scones are a traditional accompaniment, and this recipe couldn't be easier to make. Serve them warm or at room temperature: They need only butter or clotted cream, your favorite preserves, and a pot of freshly brewed tea. Add a tray of Love Bites (recipe on page 66) to make this a more satisfying meal.

> 3$\frac{1}{2}$ cups flour
> 1$\frac{1}{2}$ tablespoons baking powder
> $\frac{1}{4}$ tablespoon salt
> $\frac{1}{2}$ cup granulated sugar
> 7 tablespoons butter, softened
> 3 large eggs
> $\frac{1}{2}$ cup half-and-half
> egg wash (1 egg beaten with 1 tablespoon
>   water and a pinch of salt)

1. Sift flour, baking powder, salt, and sugar together in a large bowl. Cut in butter until the mixture looks like coarse breadcrumbs.
2. In a separate bowl, combine eggs and half-and-half. Then add to dry mix.
3. Turn dough out onto well-floured surface and cover with plastic wrap. Allow to rest for 15 minutes.
4. Preheat oven to 375° F. Prepare egg wash. Set aside.
5. After 15 minutes, knead dough gently, adding flour from the board until dough does not stick to your hands.
6. Pat out dough until $\frac{3}{4}$ inch thick. Use biscuit cutter or sharp-edged object (a clean soup can works well) to cut out scones. Place on ungreased cookie sheet. Brush with egg wash.
7. Bake for approximately 20 minutes or until light golden brown.

*Makes 12 to 15 scones
depending on size*

Thirty-five Tanka
Ki no Tsurayuki

*Along the Yodo
where they cut wild rice,
when it rains the marsh waters overflow,
like my love,
growing deeper than ever*

229

Top 10 Classic Romantic Novels

When you just want to curl up and get lost in a great romance, the books on this list of classics have endured the test of time and won't disappoint.

Wuthering Heights by Emily Brontë
Dr. Zhivago by Boris Pasternak
Pride and Prejudice by Jane Austen
Anna Karenina by Leo Tolstoy
Rebecca by Daphne du Maurier
Gone With the Wind by Margaret Mitchell
The Thorn Birds by Colleen McCullough
Great Expectations by Charles Dickens
The Great Gatsby by F. Scott Fitzgerald
Jane Eyre by Charlotte Brontë

Lazy Sunday French Toast

This delicious French Toast Casserole is perfect for those lazy Sundays when you want to stay in bed with your honey reading the paper and cuddling until noon. The prep work is done the night before, so all you have to do is roll out of bed and pop it in the oven. You can even go back to snuggling under the covers for the 45 minutes it bakes and rise to the sweet smell of cinnamon wafting through the house.

French Toast Casserole

¼ cup brown sugar
2 tablespoons melted butter
1 teaspoon ground cinnamon
1 apple, peeled, cored and sliced
2 tablespoons raisins
⅓ of a 1-lb. loaf of French bread, sliced
2 eggs, beaten
½ cup milk
1 teaspoon vanilla extract
¼ cup chopped pecans

1. Mix together brown sugar, melted butter, and ¼ teaspoon of the cinnamon. Add apple slices and raisins; stir to coat. Pour into greased baking dish. Arrange bread slices in an even layer over apple-raisin mixture.
2. Whisk together eggs, milk, vanilla, and remaining ¾ teaspoon cinnamon. Pour over bread, covering it evenly so that all slices are soaking in the mixture. Top with chopped pecans. Cover (with aluminum foil) and refrigerate overnight.
3. Preheat oven to 375º F. Remove dish from refrigerator while oven heats. Bake, covered, for 40 minutes. Remove cover and bake an additional 5 minutes. Let stand 5 minutes before serving.
   2–4 servings

Looking back, I have this to regret, that too often when I loved, I did not say so.

—DAVID GRAYSON

Looking for a romantic, yet classy gift for your sweetheart (read: no lingerie)? Try *Love: A Celebration in Art and Literature*. The beautifully printed coffee table book has become a proven winner in the romantic gift department, recently celebrating 20 years in print. It matches great literary excerpts from the likes of Vladimir Nabokov, James Joyce, and Carl Sandberg with stunning works of art by Gustav Klimt, Marc Chagall, Paul Klee, and John Singer Sargent, just to name a few. ($50.00; available at bookstores, *amazon.com* or *bn.com*)

THE BEST JEWELERS

Try out any one of these fine jewelers next time you're looking for that extra-special way to say "I love you."

Bulgari Originally known for their watches, Bulgari has expanded to become the premier contemporary Italian jeweler. Besides watches, Bulgari makes jewelry, silks, leather goods, home designs, and eyewear. They have a comprehensive on-line catalogue as well as boutiques worldwide: *bulgari.com*.

Cartier It was Cartier that offered Richard Burton the 69-carat diamond for his paramour, Elizabeth Taylor. The Taylor-Burton diamond and their other custom-designed pieces have made Cartier one of the most famous jewelers in the world. Cartier's catalogue includes watches, brooches, and vintage pieces: *cartier.com* or (800) CARTIER.

DeBeers Not only have we all heard their slogan, "A diamond is forever," but DeBeers also is famous for the whopping 777-carat "Millennium Star" diamond. DeBeers invented the "Four C's" of diamond evaluation: cut, color, clarity, and carat: *debeers.com*.

The House of Harry Winston Harry Winston has made his name as the jeweler to the stars by lending his designs to the necks, ears, and wrists of such famous women as Jennifer Lopez, Gwyneth Paltrow, Halle Berry, and Renée Zellweger. Harry Winston has exclusive boutiques in New York, Paris, Geneva, Beverly Hills, and Tokyo: *harry-winston.com*.

Tiffany & Co. The 1961 film version of Truman Capote's novel *Breakfast at Tiffany's* put the name "Tiffany and Company" on everybody's lips. For more than 150 years, Tiffany's has been supplying lovers with gifts of jewelry and wedding rings. Tiffany designs are available everywhere, but the most famous store is located in New York City on 5th Avenue: *tiffany.com*, (800) 843-3269.

How Do I Love Thee?
Elizabeth Barrett Browning

How do I love thee? Let me count the ways.
I love thee to the depth and breadth and height
My soul can reach, when feeling out of sight
For the ends of Being and ideal Grace.
I love thee to the level of everyday's
Most quiet need, by sun and candle-light.
I love thee freely, as men strive for Right;
I love thee purely, as they turn from Praise.
I love thee with the passion put to use
In my old griefs, and with my childhood's faith.
I love thee with a love I seemed to lose
With my lost saints!—I love thee with the breath,
Smiles, tears, of all my life!—and, if God choose,
I shall but love thee better after death.

The Meaning of Gemstones

The next time you give the gift of jewelry consider sending your sweetheart a message with your choice of gemstones. Many precious and semi-precious stones are imbued with specific meanings, some of which are listed below.

Amethyst—sincerity
Aquamarine—courage
Diamond—innocence, purity
Emerald—happiness, success in love
Garnet—constancy, fidelity
Jade—peace, tranquility
Opal—consistency, fearlessness
Rose Quartz—love
Pearl—beauty
Peridot—joy
Ruby—love, clarity of heart
Sapphire—wisdom, faithfulness
Topaz—fidelity
Turquoise—friendship

"I Love You"
in Many Languages

Eu te amo! Brazilian

Wo ai ni! Chinese

Jeg elsker dig! Danish

Ik hou van je! Dutch

I love you! English

Tora dost daram! Farsi

(Mä) rakastan sua! Finnish

Je t'aime! French

Ich liebe dich! German

Se agapo! Greek

Aloha wau ia 'oe! Hawaiian

Ti amo! Italian

Kimi o aishiteiru! Japanese

Te iubesc! Romanian

Ya tyebya lyublyu! Russian

Te amo! Spanish

Jag älskar dig! Swedish

Rwy'n dy garu di! Welsh

Ngiyakuthanda! Zulu